EFFECTIVE LEGAL WRITING

FOR LAW STUDENTS AND LAWYERS

THIRD EDITION

By

GERTRUDE BLOCK

Lecturer and Writing Specialist
University of Florida College of Law

Mineola, New York
THE FOUNDATION PRESS, INC.
1986

Library of Congress Cataloging in Publication Data

Block, Gertrude.
  Effective legal writing.

  Includes index.
  1. Legal composition. I. Title.
KF250.B56 1986   808'.06634   86–7534
ISBN 0–88277–283–X

Block Legal Writing 3rd Ed. FP
3rd Reprint—1988

∞

TABLE OF CONTENTS

TABLE OF CONTENTS

GETTING STARTED
(A Short Introduction)

The writing of lawyers has long been the butt of ridicule and sarcasm. Thomas More, in the sixteenth century, called lawyers "the sort of people whose profession it is to disguise matters." Benjamin Franklin called lawyers men who "say little in much." More recently, Groucho and Chico Marx satirized lawyers in the following dialogue:

Groucho: Pay particular attention to this first clause because it's most important. Says the . . . uh . . . party of the first part shall be known in this indenture as the party of the first part. How do you like that? That's pretty neat, huh?

Chico: I don't know. I don't even have dentures. Let's hear it again.

Groucho: The party of the first part should be known in this contract as the party of the first part.

Chico: That sounds a little better this time.

Groucho: Well, it grows on you. Would you like to hear it again?

Chico: Just the first part.

Groucho: The party of the first part?

Chico: No, the first part of the party of the first part.

More serious critics of legal writing include members of the legal profession itself, like Professor Fred Rodell, who once said that there were only two things wrong with legal writing, its style and its content; and a lawyer/author [1] who re-wrote Genesis as a lawyer might have written it:

In, at, around and/or in close proximity to the beginning, God, in conjunction with his agents, assignees and successors in interest created, devised, caused to be made, made, fashioned, formed, brought into being, conceived, invented and occasioned the Heaven and the Earth. And said Earth was voidable. . . .

This third edition of *Effective Legal Writing,* like its predecessors, seeks to prevent that kind of writing. The contents will, I hope, help legal professionals (lawyers and paralegals) and persons learning to be legal professionals (law students, pre-law students, and paralegal students) to write effectively. For legal professionals have an obligation to write better—more precisely, more succinctly, more clearly—than other people. Even when—especially when—

---

1. Douglas Lavine, in "At Issue," *American Bar Association Journal,* Volume 69, September 1983, p. 1192.

they deal with complex and abstract subjects, they should write about them so that others can understand them. As E.B. White said, "Be obscure clearly!"

But good legal writing skills are hard to acquire for at least two reasons: The first is that some undergraduate disciplines de-emphasize writing, and even when undergraduate disciplines teach writing, the writing style students learn is not *legal* writing style. So when college graduates come to law school or begin paralegal studies, they must shift gears in order to write "legally."

The second reason writing skills are hard to learn is that there are numerous bad examples of writing in the assigned materials law students read. Case law and statutory law contain bad as well as good writing. Students who do not write well are just as apt to use as models the bad writing as the good. For, in law school, there is little writing instruction; law students are largely left to their own resources to improve their writing skills.

This book tells you what writing skills you need and how to gain them. It can be used as a text or as a supplement to your legal writing course. It can help you to carry out your law professors' writing assignments. If you are planning to attend law school, this book will prepare you for the writing you will need to do there. (The writing assignments in this book are accompanied by legal rules, so that you do not need to know what the law is in order to write your essay answers.) The list of legal terms that begins the book defines words you will need to know during your first year in law school; become familiar with them now, so they will not seem foreign to you when you hear them used.

Paralegal students and paralegals can use *Effective Legal Writing* in your legal studies and in your legal duties. Paralegals need to know how to brief and synthesize cases. As paralegals, you will need to analyze court opinions and to write about them clearly and succinctly. Chapter Six contains legal problems that require essay answers, and a sample answer follows each problem so that you can compare your answer to one written by a person like yourself.

You need not read the chapters of *Effective Legal Writing* in order. Senior law students may want to read Chapter Three first, which deals with organiz- ing and writing a senior thesis. Law students, pre-law students and lawyers who have the habit of redundancy, verbosity, and discursiveness should turn first to Chapter Two, which teaches the do's and don'ts of legal style.

I have, of course, put the chapters into their particular order for a reason. The first chapter, on grammar, is also the most fundamental. Nothing can overcome the damage you do yourself by using substandard grammar; the blemish it gives your writing may prevent your professors from noticing your excellent legal reasoning and analysis. Bad grammar may even cost you a job after law school.

Standard English grammar is a must for legal writers for an even more important reason than good grades in law school and a good job afterwards. Grammatical errors may cause costly litigation. Consider the legal "Doctrine of the Last Antecedent." If you turn to the legal encyclopedia, 82 *Corpus Juris Secundum*, § 334, you will find it described, along with a long list of court opinions construing the doctrine. Courts have construed statutory meaning solely under the last antecedent doctrine, dismissing evidence of legislative intent as irrelevant.[2] The last antecedent doctrine is nothing more than a legal statement of the grammatical principle that modifiers must be placed next to words they modify. This grammatical principle is discussed in Chapter Two, § 7 of this book.

In previous editions of this book, I have told students who have had a good grounding in grammar to skip Chapter One. I am less sure now than I was then that that advice was justified. Take commas, for example. In legal writing, you will need more than just a vague idea of where to place them. Courts have construed the meaning of statutes merely on the basis of one comma.[3] Chapter One of this book will take the guesswork out of comma use.

A caveat: This book does not purport to teach the substance or the doctrines of any field of law. Although the hypothetical legal rules that precede the writing problems are sound, they should not be relied upon as legally sufficient. This book is intended only to fill an important need, the teaching of writing skills essential to members of the legal profession.

A word about gender: my linguistic background causes me to view the masculine pronoun as a grammatical, not a sexual (or "sexist") designation. Nevertheless, I am aware that its invariable use in books and other writing offends a fairly large group of persons, and one should try to avoid that. In this edition, therefore, I have used the feminine pronoun (she, her) instead of the masculine pronoun (he, his, him) at least half of the time. For other devices that you too can use to avoid "sexist" language, see Chapter One, § 13.

Thanks are due to colleagues at this law college for their interest and helpful criticism in the preparation of this third edition, to my students who have made valuable suggestions, and to my husband Seymour Block, for his constant support and constructive criticism. Whatever shortcomings this book has are my responsibility alone.

GERTRUDE BLOCK

Gainesville, Florida
March, 1986

---

2. For example, see *Commonwealth v. Alcoa Properties, Inc.*, 440 Pa. 42, 269 A.2d 708, 750 (1970).

3. See, for example, Judge Boyd's opinion in *State v. Creighton*, 469 So.2d 735 (Fla.1985).

*

SOME LEGAL DEFINITIONS

Below are definitions of a few of the legal terms you are likely to encounter during your first year at law school. They are not necessarily comprehensive; for more exhaustive definitions, consult your law dictionary. The legal terms in this list are terms not usually found in lay usage, or terms whose legal meanings differ from their lay meanings, or "law Latin" terms, used almost exclusively by legal professionals. Words defined elsewhere in this book and Latin terms in general non-legal use are omitted from the list.

action: Shorthand for "cause of action"; for example, a court action to obtain relief, a judicial remedy to enforce or protect a right, or a proceeding by a plaintiff against a defendant to enforce an obligation of the defendant to the plaintiff.

Actus non facit reum, nisi mens sit rea: *An act does not make one guilty, unless he has a guilty mind.* (For crime, there must be both act and evil intent.)

adhesion contract: A contract drafted by the stronger party, then presented for acceptance to the weaker party, who has no power to modify its terms.

ad litem: (Latin: *For the suit.*) A "guardian ad litem" is a guardian appointed to represent a person who is incapable of acting on his own behalf.

affirmative defense: A defense which does more than deny the plaintiff's allegations; it also brings forth new allegations.

allegation: A statement that a party to a lawsuit intends to prove.

aforethought: Arrived at beforehand; a premeditated.

amicus curiae: (Latin: *A friend of the court.*) One who interposes in a legal action.

appellant: The party who appeals to a higher court from the judgment against himself in a lower court, sometimes called "petitioner."

appellee: The party against whom a case is appealed from a lower court to a higher court, sometimes called "respondent."

assumpsit: A common law action to recover damages for the nonperformance of a contract.

attractive nuisance: A condition on one's premises that is dangerous to children and yet so alluring to them that they may enter.

bad faith: The opposite of "bona fide" (in good faith): motivated by ulterior motives or by furtive intent.

beyond a reasonable doubt: The proof required of the prosecutor in criminal proceedings.

breach: Violation of a duty; the breaking of an obligation.

burden of evidence: The duty of one party to produce evidence to meet or present a prima facie case.

burden of proof: The duty to establish in the trial the truth of a proposition or issue by the amount of evidence required.

case: a controversy to be decided in a court of justice.

case in point: a previously decided case that is similar in important respects to the one now being decided.

case system: Analysis of actual cases that have been decided, the method used in many law school courses to teach law students.

causa sine qua non: (Latin: *cause without which nothing.*) The determining cause, without which a result would not have occurred.

cause: An action or suit; sometimes used synonymously with "case."

caveat: (Latin: *Let him beware.*) Used in phrases like "caveat emptor," (let the buyer beware).

certiorari: Literally, *to be made certain,* a writ of review or inquiry by an appellate court re-examining an action of an inferior tribunal or to enable the appellate court to obtain further information in a pending cause.

change of venue: The removal of a suit for trial from one county to another.

charged with crime: Accused of a crime, either formally or informally.

chattels: Movable property, in contrast to real estate.

chose: From Old French: a *thing.* An item of personal property, a chattel.

civil action: An action to enforce a civil right, as distinguished from a criminal action.

class action: An action brought on behalf of a class of persons by one or more nominal plaintiffs.

clean hands doctrine: The principle by which the court of equity requires that one who comes to it for relief must not be guilty of wrongful conduct.

clear and convincing evidence: A degree of proof higher than that of preponderance of the evidence and lower than that of evidence beyond a reasonable doubt.

color: Mere semblance of a legal right.

common law: Legal rules, principles, and usage that rest upon court decisions rather than upon statutes or other written declarations.

condition precedent: A condition that must occur before something else comes into effect.

contract: (Williston) An agreement upon sufficient consideration to do or refrain from doing a particular lawful thing.

conversion: A wrongful act of dominion over another's property.

convict: (verb) To find a person guilty of the crime charged.

court of last resort: The highest court to which a case may be taken, from which no appeal can be made.

criterion: The test on which a judgment or a decision is based.

damage: Harm resulting from illegal invasion of a legal right.

damages: Compensation imposed by the law to one who has suffered harm due to another's wrong doing.

decision: The conclusion reached by a court in adjudication of a case, or the decision reached by arbitration; sometimes synonymous with judgment.

declaratory judgment: A decision stating the rights and duties of the parties, but involving no relief as a result.

de facto: (Latin: *from the fact.*) In fact or reality, as contrasted with de jure, *by right or by law.*

defamation: Libel or slander.

degree of care: A standard, testing conduct to decide whether the conduct is negligent.

degree of proof: The amount of evidence required in action to establish the truth of an allegation.

de minimis non curat lex: (Latin, *The law is not concerned with trifles.*)

demurrer: A statement that even if the facts as stated are true, their legal consequences do not require that the action proceed further.

detriment: (In contract law.) Some forbearance on the part of one party, as consideration for the contract.

devise: A testamentary gift of real estate.

doctrine: A rule or principle of law developed by court decisions.

due care: The care that a person of ordinary prudence would take in similar circumstances.

due process of law: A course of legal proceedings according to the rule of justice established to enforce and protect private rights.

earnest money: A payment of part of the purchase price to bind the contract.

ejusdem generis: (Latin: *of the same kind.*)

embezzlement: The fraudulent appropriation of property or money entrusted to one person by another.

encumbrance: A hindrance or impediment that burdens or obstructs the use of land.

entirety: The whole as distinguished from a part, as used to refer to the joint estate of spouses.

equal protection: Generally refers to the guaranty under the Fourteenth Amendment to the Constitution that all persons should enjoy the same protection of the law.

equity: A principle which provides justice when ordinary law may be inadequate.

escheat: The reversion or forfeiture of property to the government because persons who have a legal claim to it are absent.

establish: In evidence, to settle a disputed or doubtful fact.

estop: (From Old French: *to stop up.*) To bar, preclude, prohibit.

except: (Verb) To object; to take exception to a court order or ruling.

facial: Pertaining to the language on the face of a document, pleading, statute, or writ.

for cause: For legal cause, as in the challenge of a juror.

four corners: The entire face of a document; thus, the construction of a document itself, as a whole.

frivolous: So unmeritorious as to require no argument to convince the court of this fact.

fungible goods: Goods of a kind in which all units are identical.

fundamental error: In appellate practice, an error so material as to render a judgment void.

garnish: To warn, summon, or notify.

good cause: Substantial legal reason.

good faith: Sincere motivation or behavior lacking fraud or deceit.

guardian: One entrusted by law with the control and custody of another person or estate.

guilty mind: Criminal intent (Latin: *mens rea.*)

harmless error: In appellate practice, error committed during the trial below, but not prejudicial to the rights of the party assigning it, and because of which, therefore, the court will not reverse the judgment below.

hostile possession: Possession of land under a claim of exclusive right.

hypothetical fact situation: A fictional legal problem, postulated by law professors, in order to sharpen their students' analytical skills.

Id.: Abbreviation of "idem," Latin: *the same.*

i.e.: Abbreviation of "id est," (Latin: *that is.*)

in absentia: (Latin: *In [someone's] absence.*)

in banco: (Latin: *On the bench*); that is, when all judges are sitting.

inferior: With less legal power, subordinate.

in jure: (Latin: *in law.*)

injuria: (Latin: *a wrong*); a violation of a legal right.

in personam: (Latin: *involving the person.*)

in rem: (Latin: *involving the matter or thing.*)

inter alia: (Latin: *among others.*)

in toto: (Latin: *in total*); altogether, wholly.

ipso facto: (Latin: *by that fact.*)

lessee: One who has leased property from another; tenant.

lessor: One who has leased property to another; landlord.

lex talionis: The law of retaliation.

malfeasance: Legal misconduct; an act that is legally wrong.

material (adjective): Important, of the essence.

matter: Those facts that constitute the entire ground or a part of the ground for an action or a defense.

misfeasance: The doing of a lawful act in an unlawful manner.

moiety: A part of something. (From Old French: moiete; *half.*)

moot question: (1) an academic question; (2) a question which has lost significance because it has already been decided, or for other reasons.

mortgagee: One to whom a mortgage is made.

mortgagor: One who takes out a mortgage on his property.

natural person: A real person, in contrast to a corporation.

negligence per se: (Latin: *negligence in itself*); negligence as defined by the law.

nolo contendere: Latin: *I do not wish to contend.*

nonfeasance: The failure to act, when action is legally required.

n.o.v.: Abbreviation of Latin: "non obstante veredicto", *notwithstanding the verdict.*

notorious possession: Possession of real property openly.

nudum pactum: (Latin) Literally, *a bare pact,* thus a promise lacking consideration.

nullity: Something that has no legal effect.

parol: Oral, as contrasted to "in writing."

patent ambiguity: Obvious upon ordinary inspection; contrasts with "latent ambiguity."

per curiam: (Latin: *by the court,* as a whole).

person: Either an individual or an organization, e.g. a corporation.

per stirpes: (Latin: *by class*); distribution according to the share a deceased ancestor would have taken.

plaintiff: The party bringing an action.

precatory words: Words expressing desire rather than command.

prejudicial: Detrimental to one party in a dispute.

preponderance of evidence: The greater weight and value of the evidence adduced.

presumption: An assumption about the existence of a fact; a presumption may be either rebuttable or irrebuttable (conclusive).

prima facie case: A cause of action sufficiently established to justify a favorable verdict if the other party to the action does not rebut the evidence.

probable cause: Reasonable cause.

proximate cause: That event or occurrence which produces the injury, and without which the injury would not have occurred.

punitive damages: Damages beyond compensatory damages, imposed to punish the defendant for his act.

quantum meruit: (Latin: *As much as it is worth*); the amount deserved.

question of fact: A question for the jury to decide, upon conflicting evidence.

question of law: A question about the law affecting the case, for the court to decide.

recovery: The amount a claimant receives as a result of a judgment.

remedy: The means of enforcing a legal right or redressing a legal injury.

res: (Latin: *thing*); matter.

res ipsa loquitur: (Latin: *The thing speaks for itself.*)

res judicata: (Latin: *The thing having been adjudicated.*) The earlier judgment thus bars a second action.

respondeat superior: (Latin: *The superior is responsible.*) The doctrine that imposes liability upon an employer for the acts of his employees in the course of their employment.

rule: A statement of law that will henceforth act as precedent; a principle established by authority.

satisfaction: Performance of the terms of an agreement; discharge of an obligation.

scienter: (Latin: *knowingly.*) Often means defendant's "guilty knowledge."

seasonable: Within the agreed time or at the agreed time. If no time is stipulated, a "reasonable" time.

seisin: Possession coupled with the right of possession.

strict construction: Narrow or literal construction of language.

sui generis: (Latin: *of its own kind*); thus the only one of its kind.

tort: A wrong, for which a civil action is a remedy, outside of contract law.

tortfeasor: One who commits a tort; a wrongdoer.

vicarious liability: The imposition of liability upon one person for the acts of another.

*

EFFECTIVE LEGAL WRITING

FOR LAW STUDENTS AND LAWYERS

*

CHAPTER ONE

Grammar and Meaning

"The student ought to carefully reperuse what he has written [and to] correct . . . every error of orthography and grammar. A mistake in either is unpardonable." (From John Marshall's letter to his grandson, December 7, 1834. The Nation, LXXII, Feb. 7, 1901.)

You may choose to skip this chapter. That is, you may if you are one of the fortunate persons who have had a thorough grounding in grammar, and if you are confident that you remember what you were taught. But most law students are not that lucky. In fact, the first edition of this book (1981) came about partly as a response to the requests of my students to put into a book the information they needed to enable them to write with grammatical competence. This third edition has other aims as well, but, like its predecessors, it deals with grammatical problems. But it does not attempt to answer *all* grammatical questions; it deals only with the grammatical skills that legal writers need and sometimes lack.

How important are basic grammatical skills to legal writing? Surely no one would want to spend time learning them if they were not important, but they are important in legal practice. Grammatical construction is one method by which courts interpret contracts and statutes. Thus grammatical errors can lead to misconstruction of contracts and statutes. One court held that the absence of a single comma permitted a plaintiff trucking company to ship beyond a 100-mile limit, although both plaintiff and defendant knew that the contract intended to so limit shipping.[a]

Grammar is all-important for another, more subtle, reason. Readers make the often-unconscious assumption that grammatical (and even orthographical) errors indicate general incompetence. I call this the "can't even" theory. It goes something like this: "This poor guy can't even couch his ideas in standard English. How, then, can he ever understand and master complex legal problems?" The writer of a final examination that contains spelling or grammar errors is thus handicapped even before the professor assesses the content of the examination. A final examination that is worth no more than a "D" in writing ability almost never earns a "B" for its legal insights, be they ever so profound.

Since good grammar is so disproportionately important, it is fortunate that it is also easy to learn. Chapter One contains all that most law students need to know. Skim through the chapter to discover how much of it you need to review. Then begin to read. If you want to practice your skills, turn to the

a. T.I. McCormack Trucking Company v. United States, 298 F.Supp. 39 (1969).

1

Appendix, which contains exercises (largely drawn from law student writing) and answers. If you don't need the practice, move on to Chapter Two!

The best reason for using correct grammar is so that your readers can focus on what you are saying, and not how badly you are saying it.

1. Short Grammar Review

Defined below are some of the terms that appear in this book. Grammatical definitions are risky, however because grammarians disagree about them. For example, the traditional definition of a sentence is that it is a group of words conveying a complete thought, but this definition leaves out more sentences than it includes, and it has been rejected by modern grammarians. Even among modern grammarians, there is no consensus regarding the definition of a sentence; I have read at least 10 definitions, the simplest (and least helpful) being that it is a group of words between a capital letter and a period! So take the definitions offered below with a grain of salt. Do not memorize them; just use them to aid you in understanding the discussions in this book.

Verbs: Verbs are sometimes called the action words of a sentence. An important function of verbs is that they indicate what the subject of the sentence is doing. Finite verbs contain tense, mood, and voice. Sentences must contain finite verbs. (For a more complete description of the functions of verbs, consult a grammar.)

Tense:

When you think of **tense**, think of **time**. **Verbs** can express three main time divisions (past, present, and future). In English only two tenses, present and past, are indicated in the verb itself. Other time indications are added with helping words. For example,

- Present Tense: walk, throw, is thrown
- Past Tense: walked; threw, was thrown
- Future Tense: will walk, shall walk; will throw, shall throw, will be thrown, shall be thrown
- Present Perfect Tense: have (has) walked; have (has) thrown, have (has) been thrown
- Past Perfect Tense: had walked; had thrown, had been thrown
- Future Perfect Tense: will have walked; shall have walked; will have thrown, shall have thrown, will have been thrown, shall have been thrown

Mood: English verbs can indicate three moods, indicative, imperative, and subjunctive.

- **Indicative:** used in statements and questions.
  - He has left. Are you going?

- **Imperative:** used in commands, directions, requests.
  - Stop doing that!
  - Go four blocks east.
  - Get me an eraser.
- **Subjunctive:** used to express conditions contrary to fact, following words of command or desire, and in a few idiomatic sayings.
  - (Condition contrary to fact) If the plaintiff **were** present, we could proceed.
  - (Following command) He requires that dress code **be** observed.
  - (Following desire) She is eager that the facts **be** known.
  - (Idioms) Heaven **forbid**! Far **be** it from me to object! Come what **may** . . .

Voice: Verbs may be either active or passive in voice.

- **Active voice:** John **threw** the ball to Jean.

Note that the active voice verb has a **subject** (John) and an **object** (ball).

- **Passive voice:** The ball **was thrown** to Jean by John.

When you change the verb to passive voice, you move the former *object* to the *subject* slot, and the former subject becomes the *object* of a preposition (or is often deleted).

Nouns: Nouns usually denote persons, places, things, actions, or qualities. They can be **count** (apples, chairs) or **non-count** (happiness, information). Then can be **common** (man, idea) or **proper** (Buffalo, John Jones). They can be **concrete** (trees, table) or **abstract** (irony, love). Nouns function in sentences as subjects (the *sun* is shining), objects (visit *Russia*), indirect objects (Give *John* the book) and objects of prepositions (Listen to the *music*). (For other functions of nouns, check a grammar.)

Pronouns: These substitute for nouns and function like nouns. The most common kinds are **personal pronouns** (*I, you, he, she, it, we,* and *they*); **indefinite pronouns** (*anyone, anybody, anything, someone, somebody, something, everyone, everybody, everything*); and **relative pronouns** (*who/whom, which, that*).

Adjectives: These modify nouns and pronouns, and should be placed near the words they modify. Some examples of adjectives are:

- The *uncooperative* witness
- A *just* claim
- A *directed* verdict

Adverbs: They modify verbs or adjectives, other adverbs, and many other words. Adverbs often state *where, how, when,* or *how often.* Some examples are:

- An *extremely* old contract.
- He needs the answer *now*.

- She is *very* pleasant to work with.

- They *seldom* need help.

Sentence: A group of words that conveys an idea and contains a subject and a predicate. However, when such a group of words is preceded by a subordinator, it is not a sentence but a subordinate (dependent) clause.

Subjects: Nouns and pronouns can be subjects. Phrases and gerunds are sometimes subjects too.

- The defense *attorney* persuaded the jury. (Noun subject)

- *Someone* entered the house without permission. (Pronoun subject)

- *Almost unbelievable* is how he got in. (Phrase subject)

- *Seeing* is believing. (Gerund subject)

Predicate: The part of a sentence that expresses something about the subject. The predicate of a sentence always includes a finite verb and sometimes includes other components.

- The defendant *collapsed*. (Verb as predicate)

- The prosecuting attorney *questioned the witness*. (Verb plus object as predicate)

Finite verb: A verb that contains tense.

Clause: A group of words containing a subject and a predicate, and conveying an idea. If the clause can stand alone as a sentence, it is called an independent (main) clause; if it can not, it is called a dependent (subordinate) clause.

- The plaintiff applauded the decision; the defendant deplored it. (Each clause is **independent.**)

- Although the plaintiff applauded the decision, the defendant deplored it. (The first clause is **dependent**; the second clause is **independent.**)

Subordinators: Words that, when they introduce a clause, make it a dependent (subordinate) clause. Some subordinators are *when, if, after, whereas, although, while, because, since, that, which, whoever, whichever.*

Coordinators: Words that join **independent** (main) clauses. These include **coordinating conjunctions,** e.g., *and, but, for, nor, or, so;* **correlatives** (coordinating conjunctions in pairs), e.g., *both . . . and; either . . . or; not only . . . but also;* and **conjunctive adverbs,** e.g., *however, moreover, nevertheless, consequently, thus, furthermore, therefore.*

Phrase: A group of related words that lack either a subject or a predicate, or both. Some phrases are:

- John, the defendant's counsel, ... (no predicate)

- Lacking the proper evidence, ... (no subject)

- Without further ado, ... (no subject, no predicate).

1. a lawsuit is an action or proceeding in a civil court that takes the form of a judicial contest. (litigation-legal action)

2. litigants are parties to the suit.

3. plaintiff-injured party who initiates the suit.

4. defendant-the accused party

5. propria persona (pro per)- litigants represent themselves.

6. pendente lite- latin term used to indicate that there is litigation in process.

7. Complaint- a written declaration or petition setting forth the cause of action.

8. A legal action is commenced by the filing of the complaint.
   1. filing fee
   2. cover sheet
   3. summons
   4. complaint
   5. attachments/exhibits
   * must make at least three copies of complaint

8. Complaint (cont) - pleading paper

    1. Line 1 - Case #
    2. Line 2 - Dept #
    3. Line 6 - establish Jurisdiction
    4. Line 7 - establish Venue
    5. Line 9 - Full Name of plaintiff
    6. Line 10 - Plaintiff
    7. Line 12 - versus (vs.)
    8. Line 13 - Full name of Defendant
    9. Line 14 - + doe clause Defendants
    10. on Right side COMPLAINT FOR
           (cause of Action)
    11. Plaintiff alleges I II III etc
    12. Prayer
    13. Dated
    14. ~~Attorneys~~ Line for ATTY sign.
    15. Attorneys Name, address
    16 Attorney For Plaintiff

9. Summons - clerk issues summons when
    complaint is filed. Summons is a
    written legal order to the defendant
    to respond within a specified time
    (20 days) to the plaintiff's complaint.

10. Pleadings- plaintiff's complaint & defendant's reply; Pleadings reduce the issues to definite terms,

11. Judgment by Default- If the defendant fails to file an answer within the 20 days, the defendant is in default & the plaintiff is entitled to a judgment against the defendant. If either party fails to appear in Court on the day set for trial, the other party is entitled to a judgment by default.

Trial:

1. In a jury trial, the judge, (trier of ~~law~~ (law)) rules on points of law and the jury (trier of fact) decides on the basis of the facts.

   1. Jury selection- voir dire - each attorney can reject any prospective juror on legal grounds for cause, providing challenge is approved by Judge; and
   2. the attorney has the right to reject any juror for no reason called peremptory challenge - certain # of

2.

2. When to Use a Comma

If you don't know the rules, you probably rely on guesswork in using commas. Guessing will work some of the time, because your vocal intonation and pauses ('sentence contour') help you decide where commas belong. But guesswork is not infallible, and what usually happens is that if you don't know the rules you will omit commas where they belong and put them in where they don't belong. The following constructions require commas; if a construction does not appear here, it probably needs no comma. One good rule to follow: never separate the subject of a sentence from its predicate unless you have a good reason—like one of the ones listed below.

Use a comma:

(1) **Before coordinating conjunctions** (and, but, or, for, nor . . .) that join independent clauses:

- The defense was inadequate, and an appeal is probable.
- The landlord was not liable for the defect, for he was unaware of it.
- The Socratic method of teaching is pedagogically stimulating, but it has drawbacks.

(2) **After dependent clauses,** when they precede independent clauses:

- Although she has retired, [dependent clause] she is still active. [independent clause]
- Before the defendant is sentenced, [dependent clause] the court considers mitigating circumstances.

Note: When the dependent clause follows the independent clause, use a comma if the dependent clause is fairly long, but if the dependent clause is short, no comma is necessary:

- The landlord was not liable for the tenant's injury, since at common law he had no duty to repair the tenant's apartment.
- The jury retired to deliberate after the trial ended.

(3) **Following other introductory language:**

   a. **Introductory phrases:**

   - Although nearly 80, he still practiced law.

   b. **Transitional phrases:**

   - On the other hand, the victim suffered no damages.

   c. **Interjections:**

   - Amazingly, there were no injuries.
   - Consequently, the claim failed.
   - However, it is too late to consider another plan.

(4) **After items in a series:**

- Stolen during the armed robbery were credit cards, checks, and cash of an unknown amount.

Note: It is grammatically correct, but sometimes confusing, to delete the final comma in a series.

(5) **To separate non-restrictive relative clauses:**

- Professor Mary Smith, who is a member of this faculty, is on sabbatical at present.

(6) **To set off appositives:**

- John Jones, the lieutenant-governor, is a graduate of this law school.

(7) **To set off interrupters** (words, phrases, clauses):

- It is up to Congress, not the courts, to change the law.

(8) **To punctuate geographical names, dates, and addresses:**

- My address is 222 Fischer Street, Gainesville, Florida.
- Summer term begins on June 22, 1987.

3. When to Use a Semi-Colon

When you have two ideas that could be sentences, but you want to indicate a closer relationship between them than would be shown by two sentences, you might choose a semi-colon. Or to indicate less relationship between two independent clauses than shown by a comma, you might choose a semi-colon.

Use a semi-colon:

(1) **To join two independent clauses** (instead of a period):

- The elements of battery were all present; it was a prima facie case.

(2) **As a substitute for a comma** (to join two independent clauses separated by a coordinating conjuncton):

- The suggestion has been made before; but I am not going to follow it.

(3) **To join two independent clauses** (when you use a conjunctive adverb between them):

- The jury decision was inconsistent with the facts; therefore an appeal is probable.
- An important witness was out of the country; however, the trial took place without her.
- The recent typhoon was a tragedy; nevertheless, it taught an important lesson.

Note: Decide whether to place a comma *after* the conjunctive adverb by saying the sentence out loud and listening for a pause in your voice at that position.

(4) To separate components when a list already contains commas:

- In attendance at the meeting were the firms of Abel, Baker and Crony; Gargle, Koff and Sneaze; and Mountain, Hill and Valley.

(5) To separate items in a list introduced by a colon:

- The following elements of assault are present: (1) the act was intentional and unconsented to; (2) the gesture caused reasonable apprehension of an imminent and harmful touching; and (3) the actor was unprivileged to make the gesture.

(The numbering of three or more items in a list, as was done in (5), is not necessary grammatically, but helpful stylistically.)

Note: Use a comma instead of a semi-colon, if you like, to link short clauses, parallel in construction and closely related. For example, "That was his last speech, it was also his best."

4. When to Use a Colon

The colon is another handy mark of punctuation that is largely ignored by law students except as part of the salutation in business letters (Dear Attorney Smith:). As it does in the salutation, the colon signals to the reader that more on the subject is to come.

- Both the public and criminals suffer from overcrowded jails: the public because criminals are often released prematurely; the criminals because the quality of life suffers in overcrowded prisons.

- Upon examining the contents of the glove compartment, officers found: 30 quaaludes; 10 syringes; one rubber hose; 20 packages of marijuana.

Note: When the items in the list are short, numbering them is probably not necessary; if you prefer, you can also separate them with commas instead of semi-colons.

5. How to Avoid Sentence Fragments

A sentence fragment results when you place a capital letter at the beginning and a period at the end of a group of words that are not a grammatical sentence. Legal professionals do not make this error often, but when they do, their writing suffers a cosmetic blemish that is hard to overcome. The two main kinds of sentence fragments are

(1) Dependent clauses used as sentences:

* Whereas, the defense attorney asked for acquittal.

To avoid the sentence fragment, attach the dependent clause to the independent clause that it follows:

- The prosecutor asked that the accused be given a life sentence, whereas the defense attorney asked for acquittal.

Note: If you remember that a clause introduced by a subordinator is a dependent clause, and it cannot stand alone as a sentence, you will avoid this kind of sentence fragment.

(2) Groups of words lacking a finite verb:

* The defense attorney's motion for a directed verdict pending.

To avoid this sentence fragment, add a finite verb:

- The defense attorney's motion for a directed trial is pending.

  * The employee consenting to waive the defects.

---

* Indicates an incorrect construction.

To avoid this sentence fragment, attach it to a clause containing a finite verb:

- In consenting to waive the defects, the employee has assumed the risk.

6. How to Avoid Run–On Sentences

Run-on sentences are sentence fragments in reverse; instead of half a sentence, the run-on sentence is two sentences, incorrectly joined to make one:

- The victim of the attack was blind he could not see the threatening gestures of his attackers.

You can correct a run-on sentence in several ways:

(1) Divide it into two sentences.

- The victim of the attack was blind. He could not see the threatening gestures of his attackers.

(2) Divide it into two independent clauses. You may add either a coordinating conjunction or a conjunctive adverb—or neither.

- The victim of the attack was blind, *so* he could not see the threatening gestures of his attackers. (coordinating conjunction)
- The victim of the attack was blind; *therefore* he could not see the threatening gestures of his attackers. (conjunctive adverb)
- The victim of the attack was blind; he could not see the threatening gestures of his attackers. (no connecting word)

Note: You may, if you wish, use a coordinating conjunction preceded by a semi-colon.

(3) Divide it into independent clauses joined by a colon (indicating to your readers that the second clause will explain or amplify the first).

Note: These three choices are stylistic, not grammatical, and depend upon what relationship you wish to indicate between the clauses. Chapter Two will further discuss relationships between ideas.

7. How to Punctuate Restrictive and Non-Restrictive Relative Clauses

A **relative clause** is a group of words introduced by a relative pronoun (**which, that, who/whom**) that modifies a preceding noun or pronoun. In each of the following examples the relative clause follows the relative pronoun:

- The lecture *which* I forgot to attend . . .
- The book *that* was open to page 65 . . .
- The defense attorney, *who* had left the courtroom . . .
- The plaintiff, to *whom* she had sent the letter . . .

Relative clauses are the source of two problems. One problem is which form of the pronoun "who/whom" to use. This problem will be discussed in the next section. The other problem is whether to use commas to set off the relative clause from the rest of the sentence. The usual explanation is somewhat circular and not very helpful: when the relative clause restricts the noun it modifies (as in the first two examples above), do not use commas. When the relative clause is already restricted by the language in the sentence (as in the last two examples above), use commas.

A better way to explain the difference between restrictive and non-restrictive relative clauses is by example. Note the difference in meaning and in punctuation between the two following sentences:

(1) People who live in glass houses should not throw stones.

(2) The Glassmans, who live in a glass house, should not throw stones.

Sentence (1) contains a restrictive relative clause. The clause does not need commas to separate it from the rest of the sentence because it identifies which people should not throw stones. The relative clause is therefore necessary to the meaning of the sentence; only those people who live in glass houses should not throw stones.

Sentence (2) contains a non-restrictive clause. The Glassmans are identified by name, not by the relative clause. The clause is not necessary to the meaning of the sentence; it merely adds information, and thus must be separated by commas from the main clause.

If you are a native speaker of English, you observe this distinction orally whether you realize it or not, whenever you use relative clauses. Listen to the sound of your voice as you read each sentence. The sound (intonation contour) of a spoken sentence containing a restrictive relative is like this:

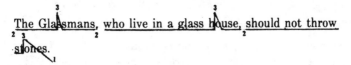

The voice of the speaker rises during the vowel sound of the word "stones," then falls, to indicate the period at the end of the sentence. Contrast the sound (intonation contour) of the second sentence:

In this sentence (because of its non-restrictive clause) the speaker's voice rises during the vowel sound in the first syllable of "Glassmans" and again during the vowel sound of "house," indicating the presence of a comma following those words. After the rise in pitch (indicated by the number 3) the voice falls to the normal pitch (indicated by the number 2) until the end of the sentence where the voice drops slightly (as indicated by the number 1). This intonation contour is represented by commas in writing. The commas indicate also a slight pause in the flow of words.

So one way to determine whether you are dealing with a restrictive clause (no commas) or a nonrestrictive clause (commas) is to "say" the sentence and listen to your voice. If your voice rises and then returns to normal pitch just before the relative pronoun, within the sentence, (2–3–2, 2–3–1), the sentence contains a non-restrictive relative clause. If your voice rises only at the end of the sentence, it contains a restrictive relative clause (2–3–1). Listen, also, for a slight pause at each comma. The test will be invariably accurate if you are a native American using standard English.

Now for the grammatical rule: if the relative clause identifies, restricts, or delimits the noun it modifies, the clause is restrictive and no commas are needed; if the relative clause is not necessary to identify, restrict, or delimit the noun it modifies, the clause is non-restrictive and commas are needed. Consider the following sentences. In sentence (3) there are two lakes near Joan's house; in sentence (4) there is only one lake near Joan's house.

(3) The lake which (or *that*) is in front of Joan's house overflowed.

(The relative clause explains *which* lake overflowed.)

(4) The lake, which is in front of Joan's house, overflowed.

(Since there is only one lake near Joan's house, the relative clause merely provides additional information.) If you read sentence (4) aloud, it will sound like this:

Note, too, the pause, indicated by a break in the contour line, that occurs in non-restrictive relative clauses where commas belong.

Now look back at the four examples of relative clauses at the beginning of this Section:

- The lecture which I forgot to attend . . .
- The book that was open to page 65 . . .
- The defense attorney, who had left the courtroom . . .
- The plaintiff, to whom she had sent the letter . . .

You can now explain why there are no commas in the first two examples and why commas are necessary in the third and fourth examples. The reason is that the relative clause in the first example is necessary to tell *which* lecture, and the relative clause in the second example is necessary to explain *which* book. But in the third example, the defense attorney is already defined by his title; and in the fourth example, the plaintiff is also defined by title. If, however, in the third example, more than one defense attorney had been present in the courtroom, and if, in example four, there had been more than one plaintiff, both of those clauses would be restrictive, and no commas would be used.

- **Easy test:** If the relative clause answers the question *which one* (or *which ones*), the clause is restrictive.

Whether or not to use commas in relative clauses may seem unimportant. But, especially in legal writing, the presence or absence of even one comma may be crucial. Note the opposite effect of the two news dispatches that follow:

- There is nothing being reported from the combat area which indicates the early cessation of hostilities.

- There is nothing being reported from the combat area, which indicates the early cessation of hostilities.

The first sentence is pessimistic; the second sentence is optimistic. The only difference is one comma.

In the following sentences, was the plaintiff deprived of five diamonds or only one? The presence or absence of one comma provides this crucial information:

According to the terms of the contract, plaintiff had reason to expect the delivery of five carefully selected diamonds, including one of rare color, of which he was deprived. (Plaintiff was deprived of five diamonds.)

According to the terms of the contract, plaintiff had reason to expect the delivery of five carefully selected diamonds, including one of rare color of which he was deprived. (Plaintiff was deprived of only one diamond.)

When do you use *that* instead of *who/whom* or *which* in relative clauses?

(1) Use *that* only in restrictive relative clauses.

- The dog *that* I bought for my son barks constantly.

- The books *that* I left on the table are missing.

- The commission *that* promulgated the ordinance has convened.

- The argument *that* the plaintiff advances is fallacious.

Note: In written English, do not use *that* to refer to human beings, although in spoken, informal usage, *that* is sometimes used.[1]

- Written English: Anyone *who* wishes to comment may do so.

- Informal English: Anyone *that* wishes to comment may do so.

(2) Use *which* instead of *that* in restrictive relative clauses, if you prefer. (*Which* is somewhat more formal than *that*.)

- The erroneous information *which* my client received . . .

- The erroneous information *that* my client received . . .

---

1. Since most legal writing requires the use of formal English (and indeed legal usage tends to be conservative and somewhat old-fashioned), the student is well-advised to avoid colloquial, casual usage in law school writing assignments.

(3) Use *which* and *who* (not *that*) in non-restrictive relative clauses:

- The "establishment of religion" clause, *which* is in the first amendment
  .　.　.

- Senator Blank, *who* is the keynote speaker .　.　.

Note: Groups of humans (corporations, courts, institutions, etc.) are usually referred to by *which* and a singular verb:

- Congress, *which is* in session .　.　.
- The committee, *which meets* in Room 10 .　.　.
- The Supreme Court, *which is* in session .　.　.

In **restrictive relative clauses,** you may delete the pronouns *who, which,* and *that* when those pronouns function as objects in their own clauses.

- The dog that I bought for my son barks constantly.

Substitute, if you wish, for succinctness:

- The dog I bought for my son barks constantly.
- The books which I placed on the table are missing.

Substitute, if you wish, for succinctness:

- The books I placed on the table are missing.
- The person whom I just met is your friend.

Substitute, if you wish, for succinctness:

- The person I just met is your friend.

However, if the restrictive pronoun functions as the subject in its own clause, do not omit it:

- The commission that promulgated the ordinance has convened.
- The person who just left was my attorney.

Do **NOT** substitute:

- * The commission promulgated the ordinance has convened.
- * The person just left was my attorney.

The exception to this rule is that when the verb is a form of "be," both the form of "be" and the relative pronoun may be omitted, for succinctness:

- The book which is on the table .　.　.
  The book on the table .　.　.
- The person who is responsible .　.　.
  The person responsible .　.　.
- The court that is sitting .　.　.
  The court sitting .　.　.

8. How to Decide Whether to Use *Who* or *Whom*

To answer this question, you can use a fairly simple formula. Think of every sentence as a **"surface structure"** that may contain more than one

"deep structure."   A sentence containing a relative clause is really two **"deep structure"** sentences, an **outer** and an **inner sentence**.   Look at the following sentence:

- The attorney [who/whom] argued the case was the Public Defender.

This **surface structure** contains **two deep structure sentences:**

- **Outer Sentence:** The attorney was the Public Defender.

- **Inner Sentence:** [The attorney] argued the case.

Because *who,* in the **surface structure sentence** substitutes for the **subject** in the **deep structure Inner Sentence,** you need the subjective form, *who*:

- The attorney **who** argued the case was the Public Defender.

Now apply the same formula to the next sentence:

- The attorney [who/whom] the defendant requested was the Public Defender.

Here is the **deep structure** of that sentence:

- **Outer Sentence:** The attorney was the Public Defender.

- **Inner Sentence:** The defendant requested [the Public Defender].

If you were to substitute *he/him* or *she/her* for "the Public Defender" in the **deep structure Inner Sentence,** you would choose the **objective** form of these words (*him/her*).   So you would also choose the objective form of the relative pronoun (whom):

- The attorney **whom** the defendant requested was the Public Defender.

The formula works just as well when a preposition is involved:

- The prisoner did not know [who/whom] he was talking to.

Deep Structure,

Outer Sentence: The prisoner did not know [something].

Inner Sentence: He [the prisoner] was talking to [her/him].

You can now see that you need the **objective** case of the relative pronoun (whom):

- The prisoner did not know **whom** he was talking to.

In written (and formal oral usage), you will probably place the preposition (to) before the relative pronoun, re-casting the sentence as:

- The prisoner did not know **to whom** he was talking.

Note: To determine which **deep structure** is the **Inner Sentence,** look for the relative pronoun.   The clause in the **surface structure** sentence that contains the relative pronoun (who/whom) is the **Inner Sentence** of the **deep structure.**   The word that the relative pronoun refers to is part of the **deep** structure **Outer Sentence.**

9. Case of Personal Pronouns (I/Me, He/Him, She/Her, They/Them)

Someone must have strongly impressed upon many law students, somewhere in their past education, the necessity of using the subjective case of personal pronouns in sentences like the following:

- John and I are going out.
- She and I were in the library.
- We on the committee voted "yes."
- It was he whom I wanted to meet.

Many law students seem to have been so well convinced to use the subjective form of personal pronouns in constructions like those cited that they do not use the objective forms of pronouns even when they should. The following examples are incorrect:

   * Give it to Mary and I.

   * For they who wished to study, the library was open.

   * Our study group is made up of John, Mary, and we two.

To decide whether to use the subjective or objective form of the pronoun, mentally revise the sentence so as to place the pronoun next to the verb.

(1) Give it to me (and Mary).

(2) The library was open for them (or "those") who wished to study.[2]

(3) Our study group is made up of us two, John, and Mary.

After *than* or *as*, the personal pronoun takes the subjective or objective form depending upon whether it is the subject or object of the verb (in its own clause) either stated or implied. Thus:

- John admires Joe more than me.
- (John admires Joe more than John admires me.)
- John admires Joe more than I.
- (John admires Joe more than I do.)
- College students socialize more than law students; law students study more than they (do).
- Phil is younger than Jack but taller than he (is).
- Jim is as tall as I (am).

10. The Dangling Participle

Standard English requires that when a participial clause has no subject, its implied subject is the stated subject in the following independent clause.

2. *Them* is the objective form because it is the object of the preposition *for*; *who* is the subjective form because it is the subject of its own clause. These subject/object distinctions of personal and relative pronouns may in time be eliminated, but current good usage still requires they be made, especially in writing. The use of *those* avoids the problem in this locution and is a more felicitous choice.

Participles dangle when the implied subject in the dependent clause is not the same as the stated subject in the independent clause. The sentences that follow contain no dangling participles:

> (1) Being sick in bed, I missed class.
>
>   (I was sick in bed.)
>
> (2) Opening the jar, I took a pickle.
>
>   (I opened the jar.)
>
> (3) Followed by my dog, I left the house.
>
>   (I was followed by my dog.)

But in the next three sentences the implied subject in the dependent is not the same as the subject of the independent clause:

> (1) * Becoming senile, the daughter committed her mother.
>
>   (Was the daughter becoming senile?)
>
> (2) * After identifying the remains, the body was buried.
>
>   (Who identified the remains?)
>
> (3) * Being filthy and roach-infested, the plaintiff refused to rent the apartment.
>
>   (Was the plaintiff filthy and roach-infested?)

To eliminate dangling participles, just add a subject to the dependent clause; or re-word the sentence without the dependent participial clause:

> (1) Because her mother had become senile, the daughter had her committed.
>
> (2) After a relative identified the remains, the body was buried.
>
> (3) Because the apartment was filthy and roach-infested, the plaintiff refused to rent it.

In legal writing, dangling participles may be confusing. Consider the following sentences in which the missing subject of the first clause should be "the son." As written, sentence (1) says that the spouse may be convicted of murder; and sentence (2) says that "the share of his mother's estate" committed the murder. Sentence (3) clarifies the writer's intent:

> (1) * If convicted of murder, the son's spouse would inherit his share of the mother's estate.
>
> (2) * If convicted of murder, the son's share of his mother's estate would go to his spouse.
>
> (3) * If the son is convicted of murder, his spouse would inherit his share of the mother's estate.

Note: A few words that were formerly participles have become prepositions or adverbs, and are not therefore considered dangling. A common word in this group is *considering*. Some others are *conceding, barring,* and *regarding*. [3] Thus the following constructions do not 'dangle':

- Considering his lack of education, his progress has been amazing.
- Conceding the contrary argument to be valid, his point is still well-taken.
- Barring untoward events, the meeting will be held.
- Regarding your letter, the problem you discuss is being corrected.

11. Squinting Modifiers and Split Infinitives

Squinting modifiers were so-named because they "squint" in two directions, causing ambiguity. Here are a few examples:

- The trial that was postponed twice apparently will take place next month.

  Was the trial apparently postponed twice? Or will it apparently take place next month? Either of the two sentences that follow will remove the guesswork:

- The trial that was apparently postponed twice will take place next month.
- The trial that was postponed twice will apparently take place next month.
- The attorney agreed eventually to aid the plaintiff in his suit.

  Did the attorney eventually agree? Or did the attorney eventually aid the plaintiff? Read on, and find out:

- The attorney eventually agreed to aid the plaintiff in his suit.
- The attorney agreed to eventually aid the plaintiff in his suit.

Embedded in the last sentence is a split infinitive. ("to eventually aid").[4] Until fairly recently, split infinitives were considered sub-standard usage. But times have changed, and they are no longer considered anathema except by the most avid purists. They are, in fact, perfectly acceptable when, as in the last sentence above, they add clarity and smoothness to the statement. But do not insert the negatives "not" and "never" between "to" and the verb of the infinitive. Avoid the following constructions:

- * She promised to never drive without a license again.
- * He was anxious to not be conspicuous in public.

Re-write these as:

- She promised never to drive without a license again.

---

3. For a complete list, see W. Follett, *Modern American Usage,* Hill and Wang, 1984.

4. You "split" infinitives when you put an adverb between the word "to" and the verb; e.g., "to hardly move," "to apparently rely."

- He was anxious not to be conspicuous in public.

  (Or: He was anxious to be inconspicuous in public.)

12. The Possessive Apostrophe

Before learning how to use the possessive apostrophe, learn where *not* to use it.

A. Generally, avoid the possessive apostrophe to indicate possession in inanimate nouns.[5] Use the longer form instead, called the periphrastic possessive. For example, write

- the roof of the house (*not* the house's roof)
- the contents of the course (*not* the course's contents)
- the winner of the dispute (*not* the dispute's winner)
- the long form of the possessive (*not* the possessive's long form).

Like all rules, this one has an exception: certain well-known phrases like "for argument's sake" are acceptable. And inanimate nouns, if they are composed of human beings, use the possessive apostrophe. For example,

- the committee's policy (but "the policy of the committee" is also acceptable.)
- the corporation's profits (but "the profits of the corporation" is also acceptable.)
- the alumni association's program (but "the program of the alumni" is also acceptable).

B. Do *not* use the possessive apostrophe with personal pronouns. For example, the following are correct forms:

- The book is hers.
- The decision is theirs.
- The dog is ours.
- The luggage is yours.

Now for where the possessive apostrophe *is* used:

- In most singular animate nouns, add 's to form the possessive:
- the author's words
- the dog's tail
- Joe's house
- the professor's class.

In plural animate nouns ending in an *s* or *z* sound, add the possessive apostrophe after the final letter:

- boys' caps
- professors' classes

5. This rule does not apply to informal, colloquial writing.

- ladies' clubs
- geniuses' problems

In one-syllable singular animate nouns that end in an *s* or a *z* sound, add *'s*:

- the boss's request
- the horse's legs
- James's appointment

In singular nouns of more than one syllable, add only an apostrophe:

- Euripedes' plays
- Moses' leadership
- Socrates' death

But in nouns in which the second *s* or *z* sound is pronounced, add *'s*:

- Louise's deposition
- Horace's hearing
- Alice's book

You may use the periphrastic possessive, if you prefer, for animate nouns, but not for proper nouns. That is, you can say "the classes of the professor," but not, "the book of Alice."

The following compounds add *'s* to form the possessive:

everybody's	someone's
anybody's	no one's (or noone's)
somebody's	everyone's
nobody's	anyone's

When two or more nouns are used to denote possession, only the last noun in the series takes the possessive form when possession is shared by all members of the group. For example:

- John, Mary, and Bill's property (joint ownership)
- Mary and Paul's will (only one will)
- Joe and Joan's tax form (joint filing)

But when separate possession is indicated, every noun in the list must take the possessive form:

- John's, Mary's, and Bill's property (three pieces of property)
- Mary's and Paul's wills (two separate wills)
- Joe's and Joan's tax forms (separate filing)

13. Number Errors

Back in the good old days, when Latin was widely taught in high schools, speakers of English recognized the Latin plurals in words like *curricula, addenda, criteria, media,* and *data,* which have become a part of the English language. Now that Latin is no longer a part of the high school curriculum, these words are believed by many persons to be singulars, and such monsters as *criterias appear in the writing of persons you would think would know better.

To add to the confusion, English plurals have become acceptable as alternatives to the Latin plurals of some words: *curriculums* is acceptable, along with the traditional *curricula*; *mediums* is as common as *media*. Some of the English plurals have even driven out the old Latin plurals (I can hear some of you saying "Good riddance!"). How often do you read about *stadia*, which is the Latin plural for *stadiums*?

But before you decide to abandon wholesale the Latin plural forms, I should remind you that attorneys should probably adhere to the traditional forms until they are entirely replaced. As attorneys, you will use Latin words and phrases far more often than your lay friends, in your legal writing, and consistency is desirable. The following list gives the preferred singular and plural forms of some of the words you use that have Greek and Latin origins:

Singular	**Plural**
criterion	criteria
addendum	addenda
curriculum	curricula
medium	media [6]
datum	data [7]
stratum	strata
alumnus	alumni (male)
alumna	alumnae (female)
dictum	dicta

What should you do about the so-called sexist pronoun he? Although *he* is still the only correct personal pronoun to refer to a singular noun, to some persons the pronoun *he* sounds sexist in constructions like:

- Each physician is expected to comply with practices customary in **his** community.

- If one fails to pass the state bar examination, **he** may retake it.

- If a party is involved in a dispute in a state court, **he** is subject to state rules.

In each of these sentences, the masculine pronoun refers to gender—not sex. Nevertheless, since some persons find the usage offensive, you may want to avoid it as much as possible. How can you do so and still avoid the ungrammatical *they*? **One way** is to change the nouns to plural, and then you can correctly use the pronoun *they* to refer to them:

6. Ninety percent of the Usage Panel of the *American Heritage Dictionary of the English Language* (1973) calls "media" (as a singular noun) unacceptable, and the use of "medias" for the plural is even more severely condemned.

7. The singular form of the plural "data" and "strata" has all but vanished. Still, correct written usage requires the plural verb to follow. Thus, "the data are . . ."

- All physicians are expected to comply with practices current in *their* community.
- If applicants fail to pass the state bar examination *they* may retake it.
- If parties are involved in disputes in state courts, *they* are subject to state rules.

Another way to solve the problem is to recast the sentence to obviate the need for a pronoun:

- All physicians are expected to comply with current community practices.
- Applicants who fail to pass the state bar examination may retake it.
- Parties involved in disputes in state courts are subject to state rules.

Any discussion of number should contain a reminder that you should usually refer to a committee, a court, an institution, a corporation (any *entity*) as *it*:

- In Edwards v. California, the Court based *its* reaffirmation of the federal right of interstate travel upon the Commerce Clause.
- May a city limit *its* population by zoning laws?
- Congress *is* empowered to protect *its* constitutional right to travel by legislation.
- The jury arrived at *its* decision after several days.
- The defense called as *its* first witness an expert chemist.

14. Redundancy and Improper Deletion: Two Opposite Errors

Perhaps the most common redundancy in legal writing is the insertion of an **unnecessary *that*** into sentences like the following:

- * The Court ruled in the earlier case that because quantity, price, and conditions were all stated that a valid offer resulted.
- * It has been argued that because some students panic in a single final examination that several tests should be given.

In these sentences, **the second *that* is redundant; delete it** so that the sentences read:

- The Court ruled in the earlier case that because quantity, price, and conditions were all stated there was a valid offer.
- It has been argued that because some students panic in a single examination several tests should be given.

On the other hand, some legal writers tend to omit even one '*that*' in the same kind of sentences. You can delete *that* if doing so causes no lack of clarity, but in the following sentences clarity does suffer. The reader must re-read the sentence to understand it because the writer omitted *that*:

- The judge held the flowerpot could constitute a deadly weapon.
- The defendant could reasonably have foreseen the cutting of the boat line would result in the boat's sinking.

- The court found a statute that was not colorblind was unconstitutional.

The problem in each sentence is that, because the transitive verbs *hold, foresee,* and *find* take noun objects, the reader assumes that *flowerpot, cutting,* and *statute* are the objects of the verb (and not, as is the case, the subjects of their own dependent clauses). So initially, the reader understands the sentence to mean:

The judge held the flowerpot . . .

The defendant could reasonably have foreseen the cutting . . .

The court found a statute that was not colorblind . . .

If you, the writer, include the deleted *that*, however, you put the reader on notice that the object of the verb will be the entire clause that follows, not just the nearest noun:

- The judge held that the flowerpot could constitute a deadly weapon.
- The defendant could reasonably have foreseen that the cutting of the boat line would result in the boat's sinking.
- The court found that a statute that was not colorblind was unconstitutional.

Succinctness is desirable, but not when it is achieved at the cost of time and effort to the reader. When you are using the same kind of construction with a verb that could not possibly take as an object the noun that follows it, you will not confuse your reader, so you can either retain or omit the *that*:

- The juror did not think [that] the witness was telling the truth.
- City officials believe [that] the proposed development should be permitted.
- The district attorney stated [that] the persons indicted were in custody.

Because you can neither *think a witness, believe a development,* nor *state a person,* you have created no ambiguity by omitting *that.*

The omission of *that*—even when it results in ambiguity—is not a grammatical problem, so I might well have included it in the next chapter, dealing with style. Because it is closely related to the grammatically-incorrect redundant *that,* I have included it here. But other deletions do result in grammatical errors. For example, can you see the grammatical problem in the following sentences?

- * I have and always will believe in the jury system.
- * He has in the past and continues to proclaim his innocence.

Compare those sentences with the following correct sentences:

- I enjoy corporate law practice and probably always will.
- John has been employed by the city attorney, as has Mary.

The difference in the two sets of sentences is that in the last two sentences, the deleted verb is the **same** verb as the one that is present in each sentence:

- I enjoy corporate law practice and probably always will [enjoy] corporate law practice.

- John has been employed by the city attorney, as has Mary [been employed by the city attorney].

But you would not say:

* I have [believe] and always will believe in the jury system.

* He has in the past [proclaim] and continues to proclaim his innocence.

The rule is: You cannot delete a verb unless it is identical to the verb that remains in the sentence. So you would rewrite the incorrect sentences:

- I have always believed in the jury system and always will.

- He has proclaimed his innocence in the past and continues to do so.

Another kind of redundancy makes the following sentences ungrammatical:

* If the defendant would have used his rear-view mirror, he could have avoided the accident.

* If the attorney would have prevailed, he would have modified the judge's instructions.

The rule is that in conditional sentences, like those cited, you use the locution *had . . . would* (*or could*) *have*. So change the sentences to read:

- If the defendant had used his rear-view mirror, he could have avoided the accident.

- If the attorney had prevailed, he would have modified the judge's instructions.

Another redundancy, another improper deletion—both common in legal writing:

(1) **The extra *is*:**

* The fact is is that . . .

* The problem is is that . . .

These are *not* misprints; some law students and lawyers mistakenly consider that "the fact is" and "the problem is" (and similar locutions) are noun-subjects, so they tack on a verb (*is*). The misunderstanding is probably caused by one construction that does act as a noun, the common (in speech) *what it is*.

- What it is is a series of written proposals.

In this sentence the second *is* is proper, necessary grammatically, though the construction is informal and probably inappropriate for most legal writing. But the first two examples should be re-written as:

- The fact is that . . .

- The problem is that . . .

(2) **The deleted preposition:**

In a profession known for its wordiness, lawyers nevertheless frequently omit necessary prepositions:

* The defense has considered which newspaper the advertisement should appear.
* The Senate is the forum which he should make his case.
* The controversy abounds the press.
* The students browse the library.

In all of these sentences you need to add a preposition. The first two constructions may have resulted from the writer's reluctance to end a sentence with a preposition. But that rule has long been relaxed. You may recall Winston Churchill's famous, perhaps apocryphal, comment to a speechwriter who eliminated one of Churchill's terminal prepositions: "This is the sort of arrant nonsense up with which I will not put!" The only valid reason for refusing to end a sentence with a preposition is that the end of the sentence is too important a position to fill with virtually meaningless words. (For further discussion of this subject, see Chapter Two.)

Rewritten, the four sentences would read:

- The defense has considered which newspaper the advertisement should appear in.

OR

- The defense has considered in which newspaper the advertisement should appear.
- The Senate is the forum which he should make his case in.

OR

- The Senate is the forum in which he should make his case.
- The controversy abounds in the press.
- The students browse in the library.

One more comment about the verb/adverb combination in the last two sentences: English speakers are currently reducing the number of these combinations. You all have heard "airport" usage:

- Passengers should exit the plane by the rear door.
- Passengers departing the airport may take the shuttle buses.

Idiomatic usage traditionally required *exit from* and *depart from,* but—probably by analogy to *enter* and *leave,* which require no adverb accompaniment—the *from* has been deleted, at least in airport lingo. You will need to develop an "ear" for the deletion of the adverb in other verb/adverb combinations; do not be in the vanguard of the new usage. For example, though we no longer enter *into* a room, you will still enter *into* an agreement.

Finally, there is another kind of redundancy common to a profession whose members want to make themselves "absolutely clear," though to be "clear" would seem to be enough. This kind of redundancy is not grammatical, but should be mentioned here. See if you can recognize it in the following statements:

(1) The defendant acted wilfully by allowing such immoral acts to continue.

(2) Judges should not tip the scales of justice improperly.

(3) We must protect citizens from the arbitrary harassment of police officials.

In sentence (1) the defendant would have acted willfully had the acts been merely "immoral." In sentence (2), judges should not "tip the scales of justice" at all. In sentence (3), police harassment need not be "arbitrary" to be improper.

The point is that all unnecessary (and perhaps misleading) modifiers should be deleted. Try your skill at deleting excess words in the following sentences:

- The burglars were able to accomplish their crime because of the insufficient number of inadequately trained guards.
- The grading of my paper displays a too-capricious procedure.
- The inebriated passenger failed to exercise due care by playfully grabbing the steering wheel while the car was in motion.

15. Count and Non-Count Nouns

Most of you will recognize that something is wrong with the following sentences, but how may of you know what it is?

(1) The amount of students in a class depends upon the teaching skill of the professor.

(2) The feedback provided by tests are inadequate to discover what the students learned.

(3) Law students have less chances to write than their counterparts in liberal arts.

The mistake in each of these sentences involves the improper treatment of count and non-count nouns. In sentence (1), since "students" is a count noun, the word referring to it should be "number," not "amount." In sentence (2), since "feedback" is a non-count noun, it does not have a plural and must therefore take a singular verb. In sentence (3), since "less" must refer to a non-count noun, "chance" should be substituted for "chances."

(1) The number of students in a class depends upon the teaching skill of the professor.

(2) The feedback provided by tests is inadequate to discover what the students learned.

(3) Law students have less chance to write than their counterparts in liberal arts.

Count and non-count nouns are easily distinguishable. For one thing, count nouns are divisible into units and can be counted. "Cat" is a count noun: you can say "one cat, two cats, three cats." Non-count nouns are indivisible into units and cannot be counted; they have no plurals. "Information," "salt," "laziness," and "affluence" are a few examples of non-count nouns.

Another way to identify count and non-count nouns is by placing the indefinite article ("a" or "an") in front of them. You can say "a box," "a chair," or "an orange," but not "a flour," or "an information." Count nouns not only can be preceded by an indefinite article, but—in the singular—*must* have either a definite or indefinite article. In their plural form, however, count nouns like non-count nouns, can be used without an article:

* Umbrella is handy in a tropical climate.

• An umbrella is handy in a tropical climate.

• Umbrellas are handy in a tropical climate.

* Alternative is available.

• The alternative is available.

• Alternatives are available.

• Recklessness is a required element of some torts.

• Beauty is in the eyes of the beholder.

All nouns, both count and non-count, can be preceded by the definite article (*the*):

• The advice is welcome.

• The argument is valid.

• The question is moot.

• The briefs are due.

Count nouns are usually tangible: *father, church, lake, feather*. But *hope, desire,* and *ideal* are a few examples of count nouns that are intangible. Non-count nouns usually fall into one of two groups: they name bulky materials (like *dirt, butter, salt,* or *rice*) or they name states or qualities (like *peace, cheerfulness, nutrition,* or *exuberance.*) Some non-count nouns may occur as count nouns too. "Freedom," "democracy," *sin,* and *bread* are a few words that are sometimes used as non-count nouns and sometimes as count nouns:

• Freedom is precious.

• Our freedoms are precious.

• Democracy is under attack.

• One new democracy is the state of Israel.[8]

With count nouns use:	With non-count nouns use:
many	much
few, fewer	little, less
number	amount

8. Non-count nouns frequently become count nouns but count nouns seldom become non-count. In Middle English (between about 1100 and 1500 A.D.) "peas," which is now a count noun, was a non-count noun, spelled "pease." Languages differ in what nouns they consider count and non-count, and even two dialects of English, American and British, differ on the word "hospital," which is a count noun in the U. S. and a non-count noun in England.

For example, *many joys* but *much happiness*; *few lakes* but *little water, a number of dollars* but *an amount of money, fewer headaches* but *less pain, fewer chances* but *less chance.* More can be used with either count or non-count nouns.

The Appendix provides some sentences with which you can test your ability to distinguish between count and non-count nouns.

16. Hyphens

The decision of when and where to use hyphens is as much stylistic as it is grammatical. The discussion of hyphens appears here instead of in Chapter Two mainly because this is where readers probably expect to find it. Generally speaking, use hyphens for three reasons: (1) to express the idea of the unity of two or more words; (2) to avoid ambiguity; and (3) to prevent mispronunciation. Examples follow.

(1) **Hyphenate to indicate the unity of two or more words.** This rule applies to adjectives and to nouns. First, **adjectives:**

- A well-known legal rule
- A six-member law firm
- A value-added tax
- An open-and-shut case
- Four- five- and six-page pleadings
- Black-letter law

Note that in all these examples, the hyphenated adjectives modify their noun **together,** not singly. An **exception** to the rule is when the modifiers are an adverb-adjective combination and the adverb ends in **-ly:**

- An unusually negligent act
- An increasingly severe sentence
- A suddenly appearing witness

Applying the rule of unity to nouns, you should realize that hyphenation of nouns represents one stage in a process. What happens is that when two or more nouns begin to be used together, first they are considered two separate words, then they are (usually) hyphenated, and finally they become one word. This is what has happened in the following words:

First	**Later**	**Currently**
ice box	ice-box	icebox
ball park	ball-park	ballpark
mail man	mail-man	mailman
racquet ball	racquet-ball	racquetball

Because hyphenation in these compounds represents only a stage, you may disagree with the final item (current usage) in this list. Perhaps, in your usage, you still hyphenate racquetball. If so, feel free to do so; you are making a stylistic choice. English usage is more conservative than American usage, so you will find words still hyphenated in British English that Americans write as one word. Winston Churchill, who is said to have hated hyphens, urged English writers to avoid them: "My feeling is that you may run [words] together or leave them apart, except when nature revolts."

Even American writers continue to use hyphens in certain titles, for example:

- Attorney-at-law
- Editor-in-chief
- Commander-in-chief
- President-elect

The final word is that there is **no arbitrary rule** about the hyphenation of two or more words to indicate their unity. As a native speaker (and reader), you may rely on your instincts to guide your own usage.

(2) **Hyphenate to avoid ambiguity.** Here the rule is based, not upon style, but upon common sense. In each of the examples below, the lack of a hyphen would result in a change of meaning:

- A little-used sailboat (*compare* a little used sailboat)
- A hard-working attorney (*compare* a hard working attorney)
- Extra-judicial duties (*compare* extra judicial duties)
- Three-quarter-hour intervals (*compare* three quarter-hour intervals)
- A re-formed contract (*compare* a reformed contract)
- Re-covered office furniture (*compare* recovered office furniture)

(3) **Hyphenate to avoid mispronunciation.** Notice that in the last two examples, above, hyphens change the pronunciation of the compound adjective, as well as its meaning. You may wish to retain the hyphen in words like loop-hole, co-worker, and public-house, to avoid the pronunciation *pho, cow* and *cho*. Even American writers, less concerned than English writers with the possible mispronunciation of non-hyphenated words, usually hyphenate *de-ice, de-emphasize, re-issue,* and *re-analysis*. Only fairly recent is the omission of the hyphen following the prefix *co-*, when it is followed by a vowel, as in *co-educational, co-ordinal, co-incide*. You can choose to retain or remove the hyphen following *co-* and other prefixes, like *non-, ex-, pro-,* and *anti-*. With suffixes, like *-less,* frequency and familiarity are also the deciding factor. Thus, you would not hyphenate *harmless, careless,* or *meaningless*; but you might hyphenate *brain-less* or *ambition-less*.

(4) The rule regarding the hyphenation of compound numbers and fractions is more precise. **Hyphenate compound numbers from twenty-one to ninety-nine and hyphenate fractions used as modifiers:**

- Twenty-five members attended.
- Ninety-five percent of those questioned responded.
- A one-third vote of the registrants (*Compare*: One third of those registered voted.)

- A two-thirds majority (*Compare*: A majority of two thirds).

Finally, it is easier to decide when *not* to hyphenate.

Do not hyphenate when modifiers follow nouns:

- A thirty-page brief (*but* a brief of thirty pages)
- A well-known legal principle (*but* a legal principle that is well known)
- A vehicle-operator mileage restriction (*but* a mileage restriction for vehicle operators)
- A for-adults-only film (*but* a film for adults only)

CHAPTER TWO

Legal Style

One need only consider the differences in the writing styles of James Joyce, Ring Lardner, Ernest Hemingway, and William Faulkner to realize that writing style is a combination of the subject matter and the writer's personality. In creative writing, the writer's personality brightly illuminates the subject matter; in legal writing, the writer's personality should appear only dimly, if at all. Matter, in legal writing, should dominate manner.

In fact, in legal writing, style should not even intrude. The reader should be left with the thought that the arguments are complete and convincing, not that the writer's style is clever or pleasing. The story is told of the appearance of Caesar and Cicero before the Roman Senate, which had met to decide what should be done about the bothersome Gauls. When Cicero finished his oration, the senators agreed that his speech was without equal—eloquent and brilliant. When Caesar finished his speech, however, the senators cried with one voice, "Let us fight the Gauls!" Good legal writing, like Caesar's oratory, should impel to action.

Legal Writing ABC's

Since the essence of effective legal writing is communication, the ABC's are **accuracy, brevity,** and **clarity.** All of the writing techniques discussed in this chapter will make your writing more accurate, brief, and clear; all are included because they are often lacking in the writing of law students and legal professionals.

Accuracy is achieved by the most effective combination of ideas and language. The decision about what ideas to include and exclude is crucial for a written product both complete and selective. The stressing of important ideas and the subordination of less important ones may be the key to successful examinations and persuasive arguments. And the choice of the right word in the right place can change vagueness into clarity.

Brevity is equally important. Your writing will be more likely to be read, understood, and remembered if it is brief. But it takes time to be brief; a student once complained that his memo exceeded the word limit because he didn't have time to write a shorter one. To reduce verbiage, edit carefully. Your time will be well spent: constant effort to reduce wordiness helps eliminate the habit, and your readers will appreciate your succinctness.

Writing that is **brief** and **accurate** has a good start toward **clarity.** But clarity also requires **good organization.** Take the reader by the hand and lead him logically and undeviatingly from point to point. Don't leave gaps that force imaginative leaps. Don't digress unnecessarily. Clear legal writing resembles a roadmap with the route plainly charted, not a maze in which readers must search their way.

A. THE DO'S OF LEGAL WRITING

In written discourse, "every needless thing gives offense and must be eliminated. Had this always been done, many large tiresome volumes would have shrunk into pamphlets, and many a pamphlet into a single period."

(Benjamin Franklin)

1. Write With Verbs

In my legal writing classes I read to my students some ponderous legal constructions that contain a subject, a vague verb (like 'is' or 'has') and a noun or adjective. I then ask the students to put the same idea into fewer words. They can always do it—and what they do is to substitute for the vague verb-plus-noun/adjective string of words, a strong, precise verb. They are writing with verbs. The left column, below contains a typical list of ponderous legal constructions; on the right is the shorter, more precise version that you get when you write with verbs:

- It is violative of   It violates
- He has a tendency to   He tends to
- This is illustrative of   This illustrates
- It has an influence on[1]   It influences
- It has an effect on[1]   It affects
- This is wasteful of   This wastes
- It is indicative of   It indicates

• The list is by no means exhaustive; you could no doubt add items. Once you become sensitive to the improvement in your writing when you write with verbs, you will be able to edit out excess words without difficulty. Try your skill on the following paragraph:

> This paper presents an examination of the duty of a manufacturer of warning of possible risks of its product's use by consumers. The examination will be of two federal court decisions, Davis v. Wyeth Laboratories, Inc., and Reyes v. Wyeth Laboratories, Inc. These cases contain a description of the sustaining of injuries by consumers after the injection of drugs. The issue is whether there was a sufficient warning by the manufacturers of the plaintiffs as to the information about the danger of the drugs.

When you substitute the right verb for the verb-noun/adjective combination, your new paragraph will look something like this (the new verbs are in bold-face):

> This paper **examines** whether the manufacturer has a duty **to warn** consumers of possible risks they may **incur** when they **use** its product.

---

1. But even the verb form of these words is imprecise. Say *how* it influ- ences, or *how* it affects. Does it improve, worsen, aggravate, ameliorate . . .?

Two federal court decisions **will provide** examples. In both cases, consumers **sustained** injuries after they **were injected** with the manufacturers' drugs. The issue was whether the manufacturer sufficiently **informed** the consumers that the injected drugs were dangerous.

Notice that this paragraph is both clearer and more succinct than its predecessor. A RULE OF THUMB: **When you can say the same thing in fewer words, do so.**

One more point: when you fail to write with verbs, you often forget to tell your readers what the **subject** of your sentences is. Here is another paragraph from the same paper:

The court found there was a failure to meet the burden of providing a warning of the dangers involved when taking defendant's drug. The product was not of ordinary usage, so there was a duty to warn of its dangers. The court concluded that there is an absolute duty to warn that there are risks involved in the use of the product.[2]

A re-write includes subjects, verbs, and objects:

The court found that the **manufacturer failed** in its duty **to warn** the **consumers** that the **drug** might **be** dangerous. Since **consumers did** not ordinarily **use the drug, the manufacturer** had the **duty to warn them** of its dangers. **The court concluded** that the **manufacturer must warn consumers** that **they are** at risk when **they use** the **drug.**

In the re-write, you can understand **who** did **what** to **whom.** So, a RULE OF THUMB: Be sure to **tell your reader WHO did WHAT to WHOM.**

2. Prefer Active Voice

In speech and informal writing, most of us instinctively choose active voice verbs instead of passive voice verbs. You would probably say, "I threw the ball to her," instead of "The ball was thrown by me to her." Somehow, in the process of becoming lawyers, we abandon the succinct, clear, active verbs and get bogged down in passive constructions. In the **active voice**, the **subject** comes first (in the first sentence above, "I"), the **verb** comes second ("threw"), and the **object** follows ("the ball"). But in the **passive** voice, the **former object** ("the ball") becomes the subject, the **verb** changes from **active** to **passive** voice ("threw" to "was thrown"), and the **former subject** becomes the **object** of a preposition ("by me")—and sometimes is dropped out of the sentence completely.

Here are some **active voice constructions.** They are short, direct, and succinct:

- The committee decided . . .
- The court announced its holding . . .
- The plaintiff's attorney argued . . .

2. On 'there,' see Chapter 2, § 3, below.

When these statements are written in the **passive voice,** the result is less clear and more wordy:

- The decision was arrived at by the committee . . .

- The holding was announced by the court . . .

- The argument was made by the attorney for the plaintiff . . .

- The following sentence was part of a student's answer to writing problem III on page 178. See if you can re-write it using active verbs.

  - If the defendant's car is found to have been purchased for transportation to and from work, it will be found to be a necessity and the defendant's contract will not be voidable despite his minority.

When you change the passive verbs to active, your sentence will probably read:

  - If the defendant purchased his car to drive to and from his job, the court will consider the car a necessity and, despite his minority, the defendant will be unable to avoid the contract that he signed.

What is most damaging about the passive voice is that frequently the subject of the sentence is altogether omitted:

- John applied force in leaving the building. (**Active voice**)

- Force was applied by John in leaving the building (**Passive voice**)

  This sentence then is written:

- Force was applied in leaving the building.

  Who applied force? Who left? We don't know.

When you use the active voice, you usually comply with the second RULE OF THUMB in the previous section: **Tell your reader WHO did WHAT to WHOM.**

BUT do not shun the passive construction completely; use it with discrimination and it becomes a valuable writing strategy. **Use the passive voice when:**

(1) the object of the verb in your sentence is more important than the subject.

- When President John Kennedy was assassinated, newspaper headlines proclaimed, "Kennedy Assassinated." (The object of the action was more important than the subject.)

(2) the subject of your sentence is unknown.

- When traffic congestion of unknown cause is reported, the sentence might read, "Traffic was congested on Route One during rush hour yesterday."

(3) the subject of the action wishes to dissociate himself from the act:

- "The yearly subscription rate will be slightly increased beginning July 1."

3. Use Expletives Sparingly

At first glance, you probably assume that I am suggesting that you cut down on profanity, for that is no doubt the meaning of 'expletive' with which you are familiar. But the word has a grammatical meaning too, and that is the meaning I refer to. In English, grammatical expletives are added to sentences to fill a slot that syntax requires be occupied. Take the two sentences:

- There is no reason to delay.
- It is easy to draft pleadings.

In these sentences, *there* and *it* contain no meaning. They are present merely to fill the subject slot at the beginning of the sentence. The *real* subjects are *no reason* and *to draft pleadings.*

There is nothing wrong with the expletive—only with its overuse. Use the expletive construction when the subject of the sentence is unimportant or unknown. But in the following sentences, note how elimination of the expletive makes the sentence clearer and more succinct:

- There is a cause of action on behalf of the passenger, who suffered from the reckless conduct of the driver.
- **Re-write:** The passenger, who suffered from the reckless conduct of the driver, has a cause of action.
- There is a possibility that the accused man could plead intoxication as a defense, if intent and knowledge are necessary elements of the crime.
- **Re-Write:** If intent and knowledge are necessary elements of the crime, the accused man could plead intoxication as a defense.
- It was indicated in *Zell* that there is almost universal acceptance of extrinsic parol evidence.
- **Re-Write:** *Zell* indicates almost universal acceptance of extrinsic parol evidence.

4. Use Concrete Language

Surprisingly, some law students who read the last edition of this book did not know what concrete language was, and they suggested that a definition of it be added in this edition. Concrete language is easier to recognize than to describe; it is language that relates to actual or specific things that exists in reality. It is particular, not general; clear, not abstruse. Compare the following statements on the same subject:

- It is a false assumption that *every* graduate of a law school is, by virtue of that fact, qualified for ultimate confrontation in the courtroom.
- Lawyers, preachers, and tomtit eggs; there's more of them hatched than come to perfection.

The second sentence is more concrete than the first, which was written by a Supreme Court justice. The second, as you may have guessed, was written by

Benjamin Franklin. As long as abstract language is comprehensible, there is nothing wrong with it, especially if it is clarified by concrete illustrations or examples. Concrete language is, however, more vigorous, more graphic, and more memorable. It should be part of every lawyer's stock-in-trade.

But legal language is notorious for its vague abstractions. Some of the public's complaints about legal jargon are based on abstract legal language. The old story about Franklin Roosevelt is relevant: FDR instructed a legal aide to draft a memo asking White House employees to conserve energy (during World War II), and the aide came up with: "It has been suggested that we minimize the utilization of excess illumination." When the memo reached FDR's desk, he added, "That is, turn out the lights." More recently, during the Watergate era, John Dean wrote the now-famous memorandum to President Richard Nixon:

> • We should address the matter of how we can maximize the fact of our incumbency in dealing with persons known to be active in their opposition to our administration.

Then he added, in concrete language, "Stated more bluntly, how can we use available federal machinery to screw our enemies?"

Language that concrete is not recommended; but you can readily distinguish abstract from concrete language in these illustrations! The Plain Language laws passed in many states will make it necessary that lawyers draft consumer contracts in language that consumers understand. So the argument of some attorneys that the complexity of the law makes abstract language necessary will not hold weight. The following illustration of abstract language comes from a book about crime and punishment written by lawyers and law professors:

> • It may be possible to delineate the limits on magnitude better than we have done, but the foregoing should suffice to illustrate the basic idea; in deciding the magnitude of the scale, deterrence may be considered within whatever leeway remains after the outer bounds set by a scale of certain magnitude has been chosen; however, the internal composition of the scale should be determined by the principle of commensurate desserts.[3]

I will not attempt to paraphrase that passage in concrete language, for I am not certain what it means. Below are a few examples that you may enjoy paraphrasing—followed by possible re-writes. (More can be found in the Appendix.)

- • Precipitation entails negation of economy.
- • It is a human attribute to make errors.
- • The display of your entrance permit is mandatory.

---

3. Quoted by R. Goldfarb in "Lawyers and their Language Loopholes, *The Washington Post*, June 8, 1977, p. 10. (Note that the anonymous author so confused himself that he used the singular verb 'has' with his plural subject, 'outer bounds.'

- A youth, designated only as 'Jack' sustained, incident to a loss of equilibrium, a fracture of the cranium.

- Rodents, in the absence of their feline enemy, are prone to divert themselves.

Re-Writes:

- Haste makes waste.

- To err is human.

- Show your pass.

- Jack fell down and broke his crown.

- When the cat is away the mice will play.

Abstract language is not used only by lawyers. The writing of the educational establishment, for example, contains plenty of pretentious poppy-cock, as well. But its members talk largely to one another, while the legal profession must communicate with the public it serves. When you add concrete language to your writing, you may uncover banality, which the abstract language hid. That, too, is a benefit, for as Alice's King said, "If there is no meaning in it, that saves a world of trouble, you know, as we needn't try to find it."

5. Use Connectors Carefully (See also Chapter 3, § 4.)

As important as your ideas themselves are the words you use to connect and relate them. If your readers do not understand your point, they will not appreciate it. Some connectors are **conjunctions** (like *but, for, and, or* . . .); others are **adverbs** (like *hence, therefore, however, since, although* . . .); sometimes **numbers** are connectors; sometimes a **word repeated,** and preceded by **'the'** or **'this.'** Sometimes connectors are not words at all, but **punctuation marks.**

All of this may seen elementary, and indeed it is, but too often, connectors are absent in legal writing. In fact, the better you know your subject, the more apt you are to omit connectors, probably because your mind puts them in even when you have not written them down. Here is a paragraph from the thesis of an L.L.M. student who knew his subject very well—too well, in fact, to communicate it clearly:

> • Taxpayers and Congress play games with tax laws. Congress enacts a tax law disallowing deductions for certain activities. Taxpayers' lawyers find loopholes in the law so as to provide deductions for their clients. Congress promulgates an amendment to the law to close the loophole. The depreciation deduction allowed under Sections 167 and 168 permitted taxpayers to include borrowed amounts in determining the adjusted basis of property. When taxpayers reduced their tax liability by depreciation deductions through heavily mortgaged property, tax shelters resulted. Congress enacted Section 465 in 1976 to close the loophole.

The same paragraph, with connectors in boldface, is longer, but also clearer:

> • Taxpayers and Congress play games with tax laws. **First,** Congress enacts a tax law disallowing deductions for certain activities. **Then** taxpayers' lawyers find loopholes in the law so as to provide deductions for their clients. **Next,** Congress promulgates an amendment to the law to close **the loopholes. And so it continues. For example,** the depreciation deduction allowed under Sections 167 and 168 permitted taxpayers to include borrowed amounts in determining the adjusted basis of property. **This depreciation** resulted from depreciation deductions through heavily mortgaged property. **Therefore,** in 1976, Congress enacted Section 465 in order to close **that loophole.**

Here is another actual excerpt from a law student's analysis of a case in which a workman sued the manufacturer of a machine in which he injured his hand:

> • The plaintiff worked in a factory. He injured his hand while operating machinery provided by the defendant. The plaintiff sustained a crushed hand. The court stated that the plaintiff did not act out of choice. The court reasoned that the plaintiff's occupation required that he do so. The court reasoned that it was possible that plaintiff had been ordered to use machinery in the way in which he did in the course of his employment. The court said that liability for an injury belongs to the party who is in the best position to eliminate dangers, in this case, the manufacturer.

Besides the absence of connectors, you probably noticed the monotonous repetition of one kind of sentence structure in the excerpt above: Subject-Verb-Object. Variety of sentence construction is important to good legal writing, and it will be discussed in Chapter Three. Here, you will notice that variety, as well as connectors, are added in the re-write:

> • The plaintiff, a factory worker, crushed his hand in a machine he was operating **and** brought suit against its manufacturer. The court found that the plaintiff was not responsible for his injury **because** his occupation required that he operate **the machine. Thus** he did not act out of choice and may **even** have been ordered to use **the machine** in the way in which he did. In finding for the plaintiff, the court **also** stated that liability for injury belonged to the party best able to eliminate the danger, in this case the manufacturer.

The Comma as Connector:

It is both customary and grammatically correct to omit the final comma in a series. But it sometimes causes problems, and when it might, you would be well-advised to add the last comma. Here is an item from a news release:

> • The Israelis have announced the capture of five terrorists, three Lebanese, and two Syrians.

> **QUESTION:** How many individuals were captured?

- The Israelis have announced the capture of five terrorists, three Lebanese and two Syrians.

QUESTION: How many individuals were captured?

The answers are, of course, that in the first news item the total is ten; in the second, the total is five. Only the final comma signals the difference.

The absence of the final comma in the following sentence creates an absurdity:

- The director of nursing explained that the clinic had been closed because of the dilapidated condition of the building, lack of facilities and vermin.

The absence of the final comma in the next sentence raises a question about meaning:

- Professor X enjoyed fishing in the Gulf of Mexico, traveling, the study of Egyptian art and history.

One more illustration of the peril of omitting a comma, this from § 21(1) of the Restatement of Torts, defining assault:

- .   .   . an act other than the mere speaking of words which, directly or indirectly, is a legal cause of putting another in apprehension of an immediate and harmful or offensive contact .   .   .

QUESTION: For assault to lie, must the contact be immediate and harmful, or offensive? or must it be immediate, and either harmful or offensive? The definition does not tell you which—because of an omitted comma.

A re-write, with the comma added, gives you the answer:

- .   .   . an act other than the mere speaking of words which, directly or indirectly, is a legal cause of putting another in apprehension of an immediate, and harmful or offensive contact .   .   . .

Don't Use 'And' to Show Causality.

In the following sentences, **'and'** is a poor choice:

(1) If the landlord is guilty **and** violates the rule, his conduct constitutes constructive eviction.

Re-Write:

- If the landlord is guilty **because** he violated the rule, his conduct constitutes constructive eviction.

(2) If the defendant can prove that the statute was vaguely written **and** did not give adequate notice, the federal statute would override it.

Re-Write:

- If the defendant can prove the state statute was vaguely written in that it did not give adequate notice, the federal statute would override it.

6. Put Words in Their Best Order

Someone said that good writing consists of the best words in the best order. You can choose the best words by increasing your general and your legal vocabularies. But unless you know what the best arrangement is for your purposes, you may not put your words in their best order.

Placement of words in sentences is strategic. Put your **most important ideas** at the **end** of the sentence, the **next most important** ideas at the **beginning** of the sentence, and all of the qualifiers, the amplifiers, and the 'ho-hum' words in the **middle.** Here are a few examples of each:

Qualifiers: on the other hand, however, in the alternative, nevertheless, on the contrary, for the most part . . .

Amplifiers: in addition, for example, furthermore, specifically, moreover . . .

Ho-hum Words: that is to say, in fact, as a matter of fact, indeed, in effect, effectively, certainly . . .

The rule that these words belong in the middle of the sentence is subject to exception however. Notice where I have placed 'however' in the last sentence; I put it there because it is important. When qualifiers, amplifiers, and even ho-hum words, are important to your context, put them in a place of importance instead of dropping them into the middle of your sentence.

Here is how to emphasize, by placement:

- If the defendant can prove that the state statute did not give adequate notice because it was vaguely written, the federal statute would override it.

 (**Most important point**: the federal statute would override.)

- The federal statute would override the state statute if the defendant can prove that the state statute did not give adequate notice because it was vaguely written.

 (**Most important point:** the state statute may be vaguely written.)

- The federal statute would override the state statute if the defendant can prove that, because the state statute was vaguely written, it did not give adequate notice.

 (**Most important point:** the state statute might not have given adequate notice.)

In the following paragraph, the writer was attempting to argue that a tire sold by the defendant to the plaintiff's father was not defective, although it had blown out, causing a fatal crash:

- Certainly the defendant owed a duty to the plaintiff to sell him a tire which would withstand normal wear and tear. However, defendant's breach of duty was not established by the plaintiff. Here the evidence indicates the tire was not defective because a blow-out was possible due to the condition of the road.

Can you re-write the paragraph to place the important points in the proper position to emphasize them? The following re-write places the important point at the end of each sentence and moves the ho-hum word ('certainly') and the qualifier ('however') from the beginning to the middle of their sentences:

- The defendant certainly owed a duty to sell the plaintiff a tire which would withstand normal wear and tear in ordinary road conditions. Because the evidence indicates, however, that the tire may have blown out due to abnormal road conditions, the plaintiff has failed to prove that the defendant breached his duty by selling the plaintiff a defective tire.

Your re-write may differ from this one. But if you follow the RULE OF THUMB, as you write, of placing important ideas in the best places, your writing will provide the emphasis you desire. (Chapter Three discusses the organization of paragraphs.)

7. Place Modifiers Next to the Words They Modify

Your words will not be in their best order if your modifiers are misplaced. Clarity will suffer. Note the ambiguity of the following statements:

- His father, who died in 1973 at the age of 81, was a former county judge, state representative, and U.S. congressman for 22 years. (Did his father serve in all three capacities for 22 years, or only as congressman for 22 years?)

Re-write:

- His father, who died in 1973 at the age of 81, was a former county judge and state representative, and, for 22 years, a U.S. Congressman. (Now we know.)

- The cause/effect relationship cannot be assumed in the absence of some interim connection or continuity. (What does 'interim continuity' mean?)

Re-write:

- The cause/effect relationship cannot be assumed in the absence of continuity or some interim connection. (Now we understand what the author really means.)

- The solar energy expert repeatedly asserts this theme: Our energy supply is like a family which has a savings account; so we must live within its income. (This compares the energy supply to a family.)

Re-write:

- The solar energy expert repeatedly asserts this theme: our energy supply is like a family's savings account; we must live within the income from that account. (Now the intended comparison is clear.)

The problem in each of the above sentences was a misplaced modifier. The **RULE OF THUMB** is obvious: **Place your modifiers close to what they modify.** If you don't, you may achieve unintentionally funny results, as in the following sentences that appeared in the press and elsewhere:

- A bicycle messenger made his rounds Wednesday in Minneapolis despite a winter storm that dumped nearly a foot of snow on the city, which drifted into Canada yesterday.
- Tutor needed by law student proficient in verbal skills.
- In Barton, the plaintiff was a passenger on a carrier raped by a chauffeur.
- He only died last week. (He did nothing else of interest?)
- The plaintiff was probably killed by the defendant's negligence. (When will we know for sure?)
- No man should take a wife until he has a house and a fire to put her in. (This is Benjamin Franklin, speaking as **Poor Richard**, and intentionally creating humor with a misplaced modifier!)

Misplaced modifiers are often not funny, only confusing like the following:

- In *Torres*, the court sustained provisions of the Social Security Act which denied benefits to U.S. citizens who had moved to Puerto Rico. (Did the Act deny benefits? Or only some of its provisions?)
- In *Rogan*, the defendant appealed his conviction of assault with a deadly weapon on the ground that a flower-pot was not a deadly weapon. (Was his conviction . . . on the ground that; or was his appeal . . . on the ground that?)

Note: Single-word modifiers usually go before the noun they modify; but multiple-word modifiers follow the noun.

For example:

- **Related** parties . . . **but**
- Parties **related to the defendant** . . .

The Doctrine of the Last Antecedent:

Courts have been called upon to construe modifying words and phrases so often that they have given them a legal title, the Doctrine of the Last Antecedent. In applying this doctrine, courts presume that drafters intended to place modifying words and phrases as close as possible to whatever they modify. Here are two examples:

- The parties have asked us to determine whether an ad valorem tax on a leasehold interest of governmental property that is measured by income or volume of transaction . . .

  (The court interpreted this language to mean that the **governmental property was measured,** although the drafter actually intended to state that the **ad valorem tax** was measured.)
- Where injury is caused by the willful refusal of the employee to use a safety appliance or observe a safety rule required by statute . . .

  (The court held that only the **safety rule** was required by statute, not the use of a safety appliance.)

So draft documents carefully so that modifiers are properly placed.   The benefits may be in dollars and cents, to your clients and yourself.

8. Make Lists; Use Parallel Structure

Legal writing has often been criticized for its murkiness.   One way to avoid the murkiness is to make lists when you discuss complex legal doctrines, rules or definitions.   Here is the legal definition of 'negligence,' in the form of a list:

> • Negligence includes (1) the duty to use reasonable care, that is, to conform to a certain standard of conduct so that others are not subjected to unreasonable risk by your behavior; (2) the failure to conform to that standard, either by doing something you ought not do or by failing to do something you ought to do; (3) injury resulting to another because of your failure to conform to the standard set in (2), i.e., a causal connection between your conduct and the injury the other person suffers; and (4), loss or damages to another person's interests as a result of the injury.

If the definition is short and uncomplicated, you need not number your list. Below is a definition of plagiarism cited in a federal appellate court decision, and, following that, the same definition, in the form of an un-numbered list:

> • To be liable for plagiarism it is not necessary to exactly duplicate another's literary work, it being sufficient if unfair use of such work is made by lifting of a substantial portion thereof, but even an exact counterpart of another's work does not constitute plagiarism if such counterpart was arrived at independently.

This definition is flawed for other reasons as well: the use of legal jargon ('thereof'), a dangling modifier, and the failure to write with verbs (for discussion of which, see this chapter, section one).   Here is a re-write which avoids these problems and puts the definition in list form:

> • A writer is liable for plagiarism if he or she unfairly reproduces a substantial portion of another writer's literary work and passes it off as his or her own product.   But even an exact counterpart of another's work is not plagiarism if the writer independently arrives at the counterpart.

For grammatical and stylistic reasons, you should use parallel structure when you make lists.   A surprisingly large number of legal writers do not do so.   The following excerpt is from a law office definition of what constitutes a valid banker's acceptance.   Can you notice the lack of parallelism?

> • A valid banker's acceptance contains the following: (1) a time draft; (2) signature of an officer of a bank; (3) when and where the acceptance is payable; (4) statement of the underlying transaction; and (5) "accepted" written across the face of the instrument.

The list violates the two requirements of parallel structure:

(1) The word that introduces the list must be appropriate for all items on the list. (Here, the words "contain the following" are inappropriate for

item (1), since a banker's acceptance "is" (not "contains") a bank draft. The introductory words also connect awkwardly with items (3) and (5).

(2) The grammatical structure of all the items must be similar. If the first item on the list begins with a verb, all items should begin with a verb; if a noun, all items should begin with a noun. But, in the example above, items (1), (2), and (4) begin with nouns; item (3) begins with an adverbial phrase; and item (5) begins with a past participle.

An improved version of the sentence complies with the requirements noted above; the introductory words ("time draft") are appropriate for all items on the list, and each item begins with the -ing form of a verb (the present participle):

- In order to be valid, a banker's acceptance must be a time draft: (1) containing the signature of an officer of the bank; (2) stating when and where acceptance is payable; (3) referring to the underlying transaction; and (4) bearing the word "acceptance" on its face.

The inability of educated persons to utilize parallel structure was brought sharply to my attention as I read the answers to tests taken by college graduates who hoped to enter law school. The students had been asked to paraphrase the following 16th century legal rule listing three criteria for the possession of wild animals:

- Actual bodily seizure is not indispensable to acquire right to or possession of wild beasts, but . . . the mortal wounding of such beasts by one not abandoning his pursuit may . . . be deemed possession of them, since thereby, the pursuer [has] manifest[ed] an unequivocal intention of appropriating the animal to his individual use, has deprived it of his natural liberty, and [has] brought it within his certain control.

Some of the students' answers follow. Can you re-write them using parallel structure?

(1) * A general rule in possession of wild animals can be that of one's being in actual power over that wild animal, and one must have deprived the wild animal of its natural liberty.

(2) * We can also compare the elements of acquiring title to a wild animal, that an intent to possess, deprivation, reducing to a certain control must all be present.

(3) * To establish ownership of a wild animal, the hunter has to intend to capture it, deprivation of its liberty, actual possession, and all reasonable means must be used to bring the animal under control.

(4) * The criteria are (1) the animal must be deprived of its natural liberty, (2) pursuer must intend to deprive it of its liberty, and (3) be rendered to a state of certain control.

(5) * Pierson v. Post, gives a general rule of certain elements to look for in determining whether or not one has title to a wild animal. These are intent to possess, reduce to certain control, with an effort to deprive of natural liberty.

If your re-write looks something like the one that follows, you have used parallel structure. Note that the three requirements for possession are stated parallelly, introduced by a third person singular verb.

- The mortal wounding of a wild animal by one who continues to pursue the animal is deemed possession if the pursuer (1) manifests the intent to capture the animal, (2) deprives the animal of its natural liberty, and (3) brings the animal within certain control.

A diagram shows at a glance how parallelism works:

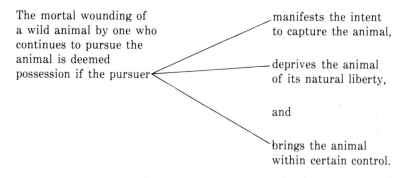

Diagramming will prevent non-parallel structures like the following:

   * A state statute requires bicyclists to either use bicycle paths or ride in the stream of traffic.

Diagrammed, the sentence would look like this:

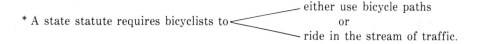

Re-casting the sentence so that "either" is the introductory word produces the following parallel sentence:

- A state statute requires bicyclists either to use bicycle paths or ride in the stream of traffic.[4]

Diagrammed, the sentence looks like this:

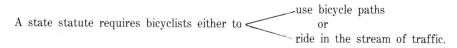

Parallelism is desirable in all good writing, not only in lists.[5]
Nineteenth century writers, particularly, took great pains to present their thoughts in balanced sentences, giving their writing a grace and cadence not

---

4. The re-cast sentence also avoids a split infinitive. See discussion in Chapter One, Section 11.

5. For more on balanced sentences, see Chapter Three, Section D–3.

often present in that of twentieth century writers. This brief excerpt from Herbert Spencer's *The Philosophy of Style* provides an illustration:

> In proportion as the manners, customs and amusements of a nation are cruel and barbarous, the regulations of their penal codes will be severe.
> . . . In proportion as men delight in battles, bullfights, and combats of gladiators, will they punish by hanging, burning, and the rack.

Balance is achieved in these two sentences by the careful placing of parallel thoughts in parallel grammatical structure:

	Nouns	**Adjectives**
Idea One	manners	cruel
	customs	barbarous
	amusements of a nation	

	Nouns	**Gerunds & Noun**
Idea Two	battles	hanging
	bullfights	burning
	combats of gladiators	the rack

Parallel statement helps to make great ideas unforgettable. Consider Ecclesiastes:

- To every thing there is a season, and a time to every purpose under the heaven: a time to be born and a time to die; a time to plant and a time to pluck up that which is planted; a time to kill and a time to heal; a time to break down, and a time to build up. . . .

On a more mundane level, Erich Fromm's statement, "It is easier to love humanity than to get along with your neighbors," obtains its force as much by the parallelism of its structure as by the sentiments it expresses. Note the effectiveness of the re-stated infinitive form in "to love" and "to get along."

B. THE 'DON'TS' OF LEGAL WRITING

"Clutter is the disease of American writing. We are a society strangling in unnecessary words, circular constructions, pompous frills, and meaningless jargon." (William Zinsser, On Writing Well, 1976.)

1. Don't Use Jargon

You may not be able to define jargon, but you probably know it when you see it. Jargon, sometimes called 'gobbledegook,' comes in many forms, a few being 'bureaucratese,' 'educese,' and 'legalese.' Legalese is what non-lawyers most frequently complain about in legal writing, and for this reason alone you should delete it from your writing whenever possible.[6] Another practical

---

6. A recent comic strip has a secretary complimenting her boss on a clear, concise contract. The boss answers, "That's be- cause the company's lawyer hasn't gone over it yet."

reason: recent legislation protects consumers from accountability for documents they sign but do not understand.

Legalese comes in several forms. One form is the language that has come down from the Middle Ages and had little meaning even then: words like 'herein,' 'therefrom,' 'same,' 'said,' 'thereof,' 'thereunder,' 'forthwith,' and many others you can probably add. Change these words to ordinary English, if you need to use them at all. Following is an excerpt from a lease, containing typical legalese (with emphasis added):

- Tenant **hereby** further agrees to use **said** premises as a dwelling and for no other use, to pay the rent **herein** reserved when **same** is due, without any deduction **therefrom,** to pay all utility bills for **said** premises when and as the **same** shall become due, and not assign or sublet **said** premises or any portion **thereof**. . . . This lease, at the option of the Landlord, shall **forthwith cease and terminate,** and **said** premises shall be surrendered to the Landlord, who **hereby** reserves the right to **forthwith** re-enter and re-possess **said** premises.

With very little effort, you can create a clearer document, minus much of the legalese:

- The Tenant further agrees to use the premises as a dwelling, to pay the rent when it is due, and to pay all utility bills when they are due. The Tenant agrees not to assign or sublet the premises. The Landlord reserves the right to terminate the lease on demand, and to re-enter and to re-possess the premises.

Legalese also comes from the use of archaic words and phrases that once had ordinary meaning but now survive only in the language of the law. The phrase 'suffer and permit' was once a compound of 'joined synonyms,' when 'suffer' meant 'permit,' as in "Suffer little children . . .;" now that 'suffer' means 'to endure pain or loss,' that phrase should be abandoned. The archaic phrase, "payment this day made" has been found ambiguous by a court, because the phrase can mean either payment *was* made 'this day' or payment *will* be made this day. Other archaic words and phrases come from Latin and Anglo-French, like 'laches,' 'cestui que trust,' and 'gifts causa mortis.' From 'estoppel' comes the verb 'estop,' which is equivalent to the common 'stop,' but is still used in its stead. The justification sometimes given for using such language is that these are 'terms of art,' but the more you can avoid them, the clearer your writing will be.

Another, even less excusable, legal tendency is to use two or more words that mean the same thing, join them together in a string, and strew them throughout your writing. In some cases, synonyms were coupled during the medieval period, as English lawyers began to abandon the use of French as the principal legal language. Others combine French and Latin (like 'cease' (French) and 'terminate' (Latin) in the excerpt above. Many of these combinations still encumber legal writing; for example:

- acknowledge and confess
- breaking and entering

- deem and consider
- keep and maintain
- peace and quiet
- give, devise, and bequeath
- goods and chattels
- free and clear [7]

This annoying habit persists, even with no excuse, as a sort of legal throat-clearing. You are familiar with what has become known in some quarters as Watergate-ese, since both the attorneys on the Senate and House Committee and those attorneys who appeared before it freely undulged in it. Some illustrations:

- in no way influenced, changed, or altered
- the duty, responsibility, or obligation
- in any manner, shape, or form
- null and void, and of no further force or effect

The problem with this legalese is that, in addition to cluttering your writing with verbiage, you are creating a seeming distinction where there is no actual difference in meaning.

Add to these another kind of throat-clearing that I call 'the long wind-up.' Here are some of them, with suggested substitutes:

For	Substitute
• The question as to whether	• Whether
• There is no doubt but that	• Doubtless
• He is a person who	• He
• In a reckless manner	• Recklessly
• This is a subject that	• This
• For the purpose of	• For
• In the same way as	• Like
• Until such time as	• Until
• During the time that	• While

Long wind-ups sometimes occur when you forget to "write with verbs"—the subject of an earlier section. For example:

For	Substitute
• It is not necessary for you to	• You need not
• It has been held by most courts	• Most courts have held
• There are many points still to take into consideration	• Many points still need considering

7. For more joined synonyms, see David Mellinkoff, *The Language of the* *Law*, Little Brown & Company (1963), at 121, 122, and passim.

For	**Substitute**
• If the error was the result of	• If the error resulted from
• There are a few courts that have stated a rejection of	• A few courts have rejected

Finally, long wind-ups sometimes contain the over-used '**the fact that**,' a phrase that you should edit out of your writing most of the time. Delete such combinations as:

- Due to the fact that
- It is a well-known fact that
- I should like to call your attention to the fact that
- It is a true fact that

The last item on the list is particularly repugnant to many persons who are sensitive to good usage, since a 'fact' is by definition 'true.' Other combinations you need to be wary of are **tautologies**, like 'new innovation,' 'old antiques,' and 'erroneous misstatements.'

The inability to make fine distinctions in language indicates an inability to make such distinctions in thinking. Some people maintain that language sloppiness is at the root of most inefficient behavior:

> To think, we must devise connected chains of predications, which, in turn, require fluency of language. Those who are fluent in no language just don't have the means for thinking about things. They may remember and recite whatever predications experience provides them, but they cannot manipulate them and derive new ones. Mostly therefore, they will think and do those things that the world suggests they think and do.[8]

Hyperbole is evident here. Nevertheless there is an obvious lesson for would-be lawyers: in a profession dependent upon the ability to think logically, practitioners must avoid the very appearance of mental confusion that sloppy language conveys. The Appendix provides some sentences, taken from actual writing, that contain awkward metaphors and impossible comparisons. These sentences should provide practice to help you avoid this kind of sloppy writing.

2. Don't Use Vague Referents

A comic strip shows a little boy holding up a cookie box so that his sister can see it and saying that if she can guess what kind of cookie is in the box, he will give it to her. Delighted, she correctly guesses, "chocolate chip," and he says, "Right!" and gives her the empty box, thus illustrating the intentional use of the vague referent 'it.' But, in legal writing, it is the unintentional use of vague referents that can cause trouble—and litigation.

8. Mitchell, *Less Than Words Can Say*, (1979), pages 157–158, and passim.

The small, unimportant-looking pronoun "it" along with its companions "this" and "which," should refer to closely adjacent antecedent nouns. If their antecedents are too far away, if they refer to some nebulous concept not actually mentioned in the sentence, or if they have no antecedent at all, *it, this,* and *which* become **vague referents**. Vague referents cause confusion in all kinds of writing, but they are dangerous in legal writing, where precision is so important. These sentences were taken from law students' writing:

(1) Since defendants were playing a practical joke on the plaintiff, **it** shows intent on their part.

What shows intent? That is, what does the referent **"it"** refer to? The writer is aware that one of the elements of battery is "intent" and wants to say that the playing of the practical joke by the defendants indicates their intention to carry out the battery. In his sentence structure, however, the noun phrase that "it" refers to is "practical joke," and practical jokes cannot possess intent. The sentence needs recasting:

- The defendants showed intent when they decided to play a practical joke on the plaintiff.

(2) If one wishes to be free of liability, **it** must be clearly stated.

The writer intends **"it"** to refer back to "wish," but "wishes" here is a verb, not a noun, so the reference is unclear. The rewrite clarifies the meaning:

- In order to be free of liability, one must clearly disclaim it.

(3) The court held that since the petitioner believed he would be repaid, **this** was enough to prove a bona fide relationship.

Again, **"this"** refers back to a non-existent noun ("belief"). A re-write provides the noun and makes the vague referent unnecessary:

- The court held that the petitioner's belief that he would be repaid was enough to prove a bona fide relationship.

(4) The loss of sleep suffered by the plaintiff's daughter was caused by the accusations of the defendant, and **this** adds support to the plaintiff's claim of intentional infliction of emotional distress. (This sentence was part of a response to Writing Problem V, on pp. 166–167.)

What adds support? **"This"** refers to nothing in particular. The sentence is grammatically improved by adding "fact" after "this," avoiding the vague referent but doing nothing to reduce the vagueness itself. In order to get rid of the vagueness, the idea of causality needs to be added:

- Because the accusations of the defendant caused the plaintiff's daughter loss of sleep, the daughter has a claim against the defendant for the intentional infliction of emotional distress.

In the re-write, it is clearly the daughter whose claim is validated by her loss of sleep. In the original sentence, the erroneous impression is that the mother's claim is based upon her daugher's sleeplessness. The claim of the daughter is given emphasis by placement, in the re-write, at the end of the sentence in the main clause, while the less important information is in a subordinate clause at the beginning of the sentence. If the accusations of the defendant were the most important information, the sentence positions would be reversed.

One more illustration; the vague referent **"which"** is the culprit:

(5) In the Senate debate there are a number of good reasons for the passage of the Equal Rights Amendment, **which** should be considered.

As the sentence is cast, the antecedent of "**which**," is "Equal Rights Amendment." But the intended referent is "reasons." Recast, the sentence becomes clear:

- In the Senate debate about the Equal Rights Amendment, a number of good reasons for its passage should be considered.

3. Don't Use Negatives

Negative statements do not assert; they only deny. Therefore affirmative statements are more forceful and direct. So **state affirmatively, when possible, even negative ideas.** Compare the following pairs, the first stated in the negative, the second in the affirmative:

- He did not carry out his responsibility.
- He abdicated (relinquished, renounced) his responsibility.
- He did not fulfill his duty.
- He failed in his duty.
- He did not carry out the contract.
- He breached the contract.

As well as lacking in force, **negatives are often ambiguous.** Here is an excerpt from the Model Penal Code § 5.01(2):

- Without **negativing** the sufficiency of other conduct, the following, if strongly corroborative of the actor's criminal purpose, **shall not be held insufficient** as a matter of law. (Emphasis added.)

With the three negatives removed, the statement is clearer:

- Although other conduct may also suffice, the following conduct, if it strongly corroborates the actor's criminal purpose, shall be held sufficient as a matter of law.

Another example, this from case law:

- Whether the case of an intrusion by a stranger who **does not have** title, on a peaceable possession, is **not one** to meet the exigencies of which the courts will recognize a still further qualification or explanation of the rule requiring the plaintiff to recover only on the strength of his own title, is a question which **has not** as yet been decided by this court. (Emphasis added.)

Not only the negatives, but the sentence structure, make this statement well-nigh incomprehensible. (For more about sentence structure, see Chapter Three, Section D.)

Negative statements are also often ambiguous. The daily newspaper was the source of the following examples; each item has three possible meanings. (The intended meaning of each was the third.)

- Billboards are not appearing along city streets due to loopholes in the law.

Possible Meanings:

1. Loopholes in the law prevent billboards from appearing along city streets.

2. Billboards are appearing along city streets, but not due to loopholes in the law.

3. Billboards are missing from city streets, but not due to loopholes in the law.

- A's breach of duty was not established because A injured B.

1. A's breach of duty was not established, for the reason given.

2. A's breach of duty was established, but not for the reason given.

3. A's breach of duty was not established, but not for the reason given.

The ambiguity in these two illustrations is due to the combination of the **negative plus causality.** The same problem is apparent in the following statement: "I was not able to save money because of the salary I receive." (Query: Was she able to save money—or wasn't she?) Remove the negative, state the idea affirmatively, and the question disappears.

Another confusing combination is **'all' plus the negative.** For example, when you say "All cats are gray," you are dealing with totality. Not so when you add the negative. When you say "All cats are not gray," you are actually saying that *some* cats are. Your assertion is now synonymous with "Not all cats are gray." To assert totality, you must say, "No cats are gray." That sentence is the opposite of "All cats are gray."

The writer of a recent bulletin board notice was unaware of this problem. The notice read:

On Tuesday, June 8 and Wednesday, June 9, all regularly scheduled classes will not meet.

What the notice *said* was that some regularly scheduled classes *would* meet. How should the notice have been worded?

However, as with all 'rules,' this one has some exceptions. The negative statement is useful when you want to convey **lukewarm enthusiasm**—or even **intentional ambiguity.** For example, when he was questioned about a former government official who was under indictment, President Reagan said, "Mr. ———— is not a dishonest man."

A law colleague tells me he responds reluctantly to requests of undeserving students for a recommendation, by writing, "I cannot recommend him too highly." The ambiguous negative is useful to damn with faint praise, to endorse with a degree of doubt. The professor of legal writing who says,

"This is not bad writing," does not necessarily mean it is *good* writing. A 1975 court, in permitting the removal of a kidney from an incompetent man, used the negative to express its reasoning that, ". . . the transplant is not without benefit to him." [9]

Perhaps the final word on the use of negative constructions should be this: Someone once defined a lady as a woman who never insulted anyone without intending to do so. Similarly, never use the ambiguous negative without intending to do so.

4. Don't Shift Your Point of View

Whenever you write, you make an implicit promise to your readers not to shift your point of view unless you let them know about it. If you change the subject or object of your sentence without notifying your readers, you are shifting your viewpoint, and that constitutes bad (and confusing) writing. Here is one illustration, from the office of an attorney (I have inserted the unanswered questions):

> • Although zoning ordinances should furnish owners of historic properties some relief from the financial burden of maintaining their property for public benefit, decline in market value [of what?] and diminished expectations [whose? about what?] are not sufficient injuries [who received? who caused?] to constitute a taking of property [who took?] without just compensation [to whom?]

Put into the sentence guideposts which clearly point out to your reader the subjects and objects of the clauses, and your readers' questions (inserted above) are answered:

> • Zoning ordinances should furnish owners of historic properties some relief from the financial burden of maintaining their property for public. However, the injury to the landowners of a decline in the market value of their property or their diminished expectation of income from the property is not sufficient for the court to find that the state has taken private property without compensation to the property owners.

Here is another actual example, again with questions inserted:

> • In order to collect exemplary damages [who collects?], the conduct causing the injury [whose conduct?] must be wanton, malicious, or grossly negligent as to show heedless or willful disregard for the rights and safety of others.

Here is a re-write, with the necessary guideposts added:

> • In order for the victim of an injury to collect exemplary damages, the conduct of the person who caused the injury must have been so wanton, malicious, or grossly negligent as to show heedless or willful disregard for the rights and safety of others.

---

9. In re Guardianship of Pescinski, 67 Wis.2d 4, 226 N.W.2d 180.

And here is an example from a student's examination answer:

- Defendant is guilty of driving recklessly, and with no opportunity to avoid the accident, the collision occurred.

Who had "no opportunity to avoid the accident"? Because he fails to insert the new subject (plaintiff), the writer is guilty of shifting his viewpoint without notifying the reader.

Earlier in this book, I stated a RULE OF THUMB: Say **who did what to whom** in each sentence. Another way to state this is to say that you should take your readers by the hand and guide them through your writing. If you do so, you will not make unannounced viewpoint shifts.

5. Don't Make Impossible Comparisons

Because legal writing should be precise, avoid the careless practice of comparing incomparable things. Notice that the following statement makes an impossible comparison because it compares New York laws to Connecticut, not to Connecticut laws, as the writer intended:

* The laws of New York, unlike Connecticut, provide for restitution as an alternative to prison for first offenders.

Either of the following re-writes will eliminate the error:

- The laws of New York, unlike those of Connecticut, provide for restitution as an alternative to prison for first offenders.

- New York law, unlike Connecticut law, provides for restitution as an alternative to prison for first offenders. (These sentences could also be crafted differently, of course, as long as the comparisons were correctly stated.)

Here are some impossible comparisons taken from law students' legal writing; each is followed by a corrected version:

* In a recent court case, the petitioners represented more than 75% of the benefits in the will.

- Correct version: In a recent court case, petitioners' interests represented more than 75% of the benefits in the will.

* Like the court in *Amsted v. Rich*, the decision here should be based on probable cause.

- Correct version: This decision, like that in *Amsted v. Rich*, should be based on probable cause.

* Unlike inter vivos gifts, the donee does not acquire full title to property until the death of the donor.

- Correct version: Unlike the donee of an inter vivos gift, this donee does not acquire full title to property until the death of the donor.

6. Don't Mix or Mangle Metaphors

The tendency to mix or mangle metaphors or to use trite or stale metaphors is not unique to members of the legal profession, but its members are at least as susceptible to it as members of other professions. Metaphors enhance your writing, but they must be fresh and appropriate. When you use metaphors that are stale, mixed, or inappropriate, your writing becomes stodgy, and sometimes unintentionally comic. Consider the following:

- State department spokesman: We are not going to play this game with all our cards face up on the deck. (Combination of poker and ship metaphors.)
- Political campaign speech: It's a new ball-game, and we're playing with a full deck. (Combination of cards and sports metaphors.)
- On voting: If we all unite, we will be a force that will be heard. (How do you "hear" a "force"?)
- On taxation: We need to bridge the battle and erase the financial gap. (But one "wages" battles and "bridges" gaps.)
- On an opponent's record: His record speaks louder than any smoke screen. (Does a smoke screen "speak"?)

Metaphors like these have a tendency to creep into writing. So be on the lookout for them and edit them out of your first draft. Follow these two rules:

- Never use trite metaphors, and indulge only sparingly in fresh ones.
- Be certain that your metaphors illuminate your message.

C. WATCH YOUR LANGUAGE

News item: A veterinarian on trial for the murder of his teenaged son worsened his chances when he admitted that after shooting the boy he dragged him from the house to the trunk of his car "by his back legs."

It has been correctly noted that the difference between the right word and the almost-right word is like the difference between lightning and the lightning bug. To convey the ideas you want to express, to get the attention they deserve, even to get the respect due you, you need to pay attention to the words you use. The almost-right word is not good enough; you need the right word.

1. Problem Words

a. Confusing Pairs

In this category are words that people tend to use interchangeably although they have different meanings. Some of these word-pairs are confusing because they look alike; others are confusing because they are often mis-used. Here are some of these confusing pairs:

- **affect/effect**

These two words are not interchangeable. The verb *affect* means *influence, change, or modify.* You can *affect* decision-making with your vote. *Affect* also means *pretend or imitate*; you might *affect* interest in something that really doesn't interest you.

The verb *effect* means *bring about or accomplish*; for example, legislation is designed to *effect* an end. Because *to effect a change* (that is, to bring about a change) contains the idea of *affecting* something, *effect* and *affect* are often confused. But if you distinguish between the words, you may *effect* a change in usage that will *affect* your writing.

• principal/principle

These words receive heavy use in the legal profession. Be sure to distinguish between them. *Principles* are basic truths, rules or assumptions. Your legal arguments will often be based upon legal rules, also called theories or *principles*. The word 'principle' is never an adjective; it is always a noun.

The word 'principal' can be either a noun or an adjective. As a noun it refers to the individual or party who is first in importance, rank, or degree. Schools employ principals and vice-principals. In contract law, reference is often made to the principal/agent relationship. The *principal* is one who empowers another (the *agent*) to act as his representative. The *principal* is one who has the prime obligation in a contract, or one who, in criminal law, commits a crime.

As an adjective 'principal' means *chief, or first, or of highest rank,* as in, *The Constitution is the principal defense of our rights.* You will also be referring to the *principal* (i.e., "main") argument for the prosecution or the defense.

• lie/lay

The discriminating writer maintains the distinction between these two words, which have become a shibboleth for educated usage. *Lay,* the word more often used, is properly a transitive verb, which means that it must be followed by a noun as object. Thus you *lay* a book on the table, *lay* down a law, and *lay* bricks to make a wall. In all these phrases *lay* means *put, place* or *set forth*. (*Lay* has many other related meanings, for which consult your dictionary, but they all have in common some sort of placement, as in *lay a wager.*)

Lie is an intransitive verb; that is, it does not take an object-noun. You *lie* on the bed, or you *lie* down, *lie* meaning, in general usage, *recline*. In legal usage, it adds another meaning, *to be admissible,* as in *an action lies in torts.* (The third meaning of *lie* is one that confuses no one: *tell an untruth.*)

The problem with *lie* and *lay* is that the past tense of *lie* is identical with the present tense of *lay*. Although last night I *lay* on my bed, today I *lay* the books on my desk. The complete paradigm for each verb is:

lay	laid	laid
lie	lay	lain

• in/into

These prepositions are not interchangeable; *in* refers to a position, condition, or location, and *into* refers to a *change* of condition, indicating movement to another location. A person is sitting *in* a room, but when she leaves the room and enters another, she goes *into* another room. Both *in* and *into* have numerous other meanings (for which consult your dictionary), but the only confusion caused by the words is in this small but important distinction.

- **bring/take**

Although these words are not look-alikes, they are often mistakenly interchanged. They are distinguishable by the orientation of the speaker. Something is *brought* to the person speaking, or to his residence (when he is there), or to a place identified with him (when he is there). Thus you, as speaker, would tell someone to *bring* his class notes to you when he comes to your home or to *bring* them to your home tonight, when you are there. But if you are at the law school you would tell him to *take* the notes to your home or to *take* them to another place. The distinction is like that between *come* and *go*. (*Come* to me; *go* anywhere else.)

- **loan/lend**

A law school colleague asked me to include this pair, noting that she is really annoyed at their mis-use. Traditionally, *loan* was always a noun, never a verb. You could make someone a *loan*, but you could not *loan* money to her. Usage has changed that, and you have no doubt heard even educated speakers use 'loan' as a verb. Meticulous users still retain the distinction, however, and I would recommend that you use 'lend' as the verb and 'loan' as the noun in your legal writing. (There is no point in irritating those who object to the more recent change in usage.)

- **imply/infer**

The distinction here is carefully observed in legal writing. The speaker/ writer *implies;* the listener/reader *infers.* To 'imply' is to intimate or to state indirectly; to 'infer' is to draw a conclusion based on what someone has said or written.

- **foregoing/forgoing**

Notice the 'e' in the first word. It indicates that the prefix ('fore') means "before." Thus the *foregoing* is something that has gone before. The prefix 'for' has nothing to do with what went before. It has the sense of 'exhaustion' (as in 'forspent'), 'giving up completely' (as in 'forsake' or 'forswear' or 'forgo'), or 'prohibition' (as in 'forbid'). *Forgoing* might appear in the sentence, "*Forgoing* the opportunity to obtain redress, the negligence victim declined to file suit."

- **credible/credulous**

'Credible' means "believable." (The witness was *credible*.) 'Credulous' means "believing too readily, thus gullible." (The victim of the swindle was *credulous*.) These words are more often used in their negative forms: 'incredible' meaning "unbelievable," 'incredulous' meaning "disbelieving, skeptical."

- **eager/anxious**

These words are not synonymous, though they are often used as if they were, and they may eventually become interchangeable due to incorrect usage. One is *eager* for something to occur, when one looks forward with pleasure to the occurrence. One is *anxious* about the possible occurrence of an event that one views with trepidation.

b. Words With More Than One Meaning

Some words, through years of use, have come to signify two different (sometimes opposite) meanings. Be sure that in your writing the context clearly denotes the meaning you intend. For example:

- **oversight:** can mean "unintentional error" or "intentional watchful supervision."

  The Brief was filed late due to an *oversight* on the attorney's part.

  (That is, the attorney made an error.)

  The Foreign Relations Committee has *oversight* over its subcommittee's proceedings.

  (That is, it has *authority* over its subcommittee's proceedings.)

- **effectively:** can mean either "well" or "actually."

  The responsibility was *effectively* discharged.

  (That is, it was carried out well or efficiently.)

  The responsibility was *effectively* discharged.

  (That is, it was actually carried out or was, in effect, carried out.)

- **sanction:** can mean "approval" or "penalty."

  The *sanction* of violence should never be government policy.

  (That is, government should never approve violence.)

  Official *sanctions* are being considered against Argentina.

  (That is, coercive measures are being considered.)

- **presently:** can mean "soon" or "right now."

  I will join the group *presently.*

  (That is, I will be there soon.)

  I am *presently* without an apartment.

  (That is, I am without one now.)

- **cite:** can mean "command," "point out," or "summon before a court of law."

  He was *cited* for his bravery.

  (That is, he was commended for bravery.)

  He was *cited* as a typical law student.

  (That is, he was pointed out as typical.)

He was *cited* for a traffic violation.

(That is, he was summoned before a law court.)

* ultimately: can mean "at the end" or "at the beginning."

She *ultimately* reached her goal.

(That is, she finally got there.)

The two words are *ultimately* cognates.

(That is, they had the same ancestor.)

* may: can indicate either *permission* or *possibility.*[10]

Students *may* adhere to the dress code.

(That is, they are permitted to do so.)

Students *may* adhere to the dress code.

(That is, it is possible that they will.)

Other words, not listed here, are perhaps candidates for addition to this list, because English usage is constantly in flux, with words adding and changing meanings constantly. In the list above, the earliest meaning appears first.

c. Vague and Vogue Words

No living language communicates perfectly because in none does each word contain only one meaning, precise and understood by all speakers. William James said, "The most immutable barrier in nature is between one man's thoughts and another's." Choosing words carefully takes effort; it is easy to use a word that is popular, current—and perhaps vague. But when a word comes to have numerous possible meanings, it can express no one meaning very well.

where

Where can mean *when, if, because, in which, that,* and perhaps other things as well. Henry Weihofen suggests that one should use *where* to express only place, as in "states where the rule is followed," but that "cases where the rule is followed," should be changed to "cases in which the rule is followed," or "cases that follow the rule." [11]

Whether you follow Weihofen's suggestion or not, you should consider substituting other words for *where* when doing so will express your idea more precisely:

* False imprisonment occurs **where** one party acts in a manner intending to confine another within fixed boundaries. (Substitute '**when.**)

10. The meaning of "may" is one issue in In re Advisory Opinion of the Governor Civil Rights, S.Ct. of Fla., 306 So.2d 529, 531 (1975).

11. In *Legal Writing Style,* 2d edition, 1979, p. 40.

- **Where** a person's house is searched without a search warrant, he has a cause of action against the officer who conducted the search. (Substitute *if.*)

- The defendant had reason to believe his life was in danger **where** the plaintiff had a knife. (Substitute *because.*)

- The burglar read in the newspaper **where** another man had been arrested for the burglary. (Substitute *that.*)

as to

This phrase is another favorite of lawyers, so often used by them that it has been called, "the lawyerly as to." Its overuse has resulted in its taking on so many meanings that it is hard to tell which one the writer has in mind. It may mean *for, about, of,*—or nothing at all, as in the phrase *as to whether.* Here are some examples:

- Suggestions **as to** improvement are welcome.

  (Substitute *for.*)

  We can only guess **as to** the reasons for the crime.

- (Substitute *about.*)

- There is no problem **as to** jurisdiction or **as to** whether to take this case. (Substitute *of* for the first *as to* and **omit** the second.)

address

This verb is generally overused. Once used mainly in the context of directing a letter to its intended recipient, 'address' has become a portmanteau word with at least the following meanings: (1) direct, (2) call attention to, (3) attempt to answer, and (4) consider. In the following sentences it is used in these ways:

(1) She **addressed** the question to the Chairperson. (That is, she asked the Chairperson for an answer.)

(2) He **addressed** the matter of the safety measures the city had adopted. (That is, he called attention to the matter.)

(3) She **addressed** the problem of unemployment. (That is, she attempted to find a solution for it.)

(4) He **addressed** the liaison between the departments. (That is, he considered the liaison.)

What applies to these vogue words applies generally. Your writing will be more clear and exact if you replace vogue and vague language with specific words. Some other overused words are '**affect**' (as a verb). It can mean 'improve,' 'worsen,' 'ameliorate,' 'retard,' and a number of other things. The current vogue words, '**go to**,' '**look to**,' and '**look at**' are similarly vague. The verb '**pursue**,' which once meant 'follow' is now approaching the same state, with '**pursuant to**' right behind.

Rule: Before you use a word, consider whether it conveys your precise meaning.

d. Words With Special Legal Meanings

Law students and lawyers should be sensitive to everyday meanings of some words, as well as their legal meanings, if for no other reason than to explain the difference to their clients. Some words whose lay and legal meanings differ are:

- cure

The everyday meaning of this verb is "heal," as in, "Medicine *cures* illness." But the legal meaning may be "correct," as in "The court held that the trial proceedings *cured* defects in the pleadings."

- constructive

The layman understands this adjective to mean "helpful," as in, "The review of the performance contained *constructive* criticism." But the legal meaning is more likely "to be considered as," as in "constructive notice," "constructive admission," "constructive fraud," "constructive possession," and other legal terms.

- facially

This refers in common speech to a portion of the human anatomy, but the legal meaning may well be "that which appears on the face of the document, with no explanation." A "facial defect" is more likely to be an imperfection in a legal document than an anatomical defect, as in, "The statute is *facially* unconstitutional."

- lie

For the everyday versus the legal meaning of this verb, see p. 54.

- issue

In everyday usage, this is a transitive verb (i.e., it must be followed by a noun-object) meaning "distribute." ("The Administration issued a policy-statement.") But in legal use it is sometimes an intransitive verb (i.e., it is not followed by a noun-object), meaning "come forth," as in, "The writ *issues.*"

- material

The layman uses this word most frequently as a noun, meaning "substance," as in "The dress was made of flimsy *material.*" To the lawyer, the word is more often an adjective meaning, "of the essence," as in, "The testimony of the eyewitness was *material.*"

- harmless

The layman understands this word as meaning "not harmful." Law adds a second meaning, "blameless, not liable," as in "The defendant was held *harmless* for the bicycle accident caused by improper signing of bicycle paths."

e. Words Denoting Useful Distinctions

This list is shrinking even as I write, for there is a "law" of linguistics that when two words mean approximately the same thing, either they acquire different meanings or one disappears from the language. In the list of words that follow, the words of each pair did acquire different meanings. But careless users ignored the distinctions in meaning, and inevitably one word of each pair will ultimately disappear from the language unless educated users maintain the distinction. Perhaps you can help save these words from extinction. Here they are:

- healthy/healthful

Only animate beings are healthy (i.e., in a state of good health); something that is good for you is healthful. *Healthy* adults need the *healthful* qualities of milk. This distinction, however, is seldom observed today.

- sensuous/sensual

"Sensuous" means "having qualities that appeal to the senses, often esthetic qualities." "Sensual" means "appealing to the sexual appetites." A garden of roses is *sensuous;* a strip-tease act may be *sensual.* (You may insult your client if you choose the wrong adjective.)

- historic/historical

An event of importance in history is a "historic event." "Historical" refers to anything concerned with history, as in "historical fiction."

- economic/economical

"Economic" is the broader of these words, meaning "relating to material wealth." Thus, inflation is viewed as an *economic* disaster. "Economical" means "thrifty." "*Economical* people put away money for a rainy day." The noun "economy" embraces the meanings of both members of this pair, contributing to the confusion regarding the difference in their meaning.

- famous/notorious

If you are famous, it is because you have done something you can be proud of. If you are notorious, you have done something dishonorable. In both cases, you become well-known as a result of your act. To be *notorious* is to be *infamous.*

- unique/unusual

"Unique" means "one of a kind." But news commentators and others have prefaced it with "rather," "very" and "most," thinking of it as an adjective meaning "unusual." Unless users change their ways, "unique" will completely lose its uniqueness.

- uninterested/disinterested

Alas, the first member of this pair is disappearing. Please join the battle to save it. When it is correctly used, if you are *uninterested* in something, you are indifferent to it, one way or another. If you are *disinterested,* you may well be concerned about it, but you are also impartial about it. Thus a *disinterested* observer may be counted upon to report what is going on, without bias; an *uninterested* person will probably not observe what is going on at all.

- farther/further

'Farther' refers to literal distance, either temporal or spatial. (Cincinnati is *farther* from New York than from Louisville.) 'Further' is used in all other senses, especially to indicate degree or figurative space or time. (America goes *further* into debt every year. Let me explain *further*.) Because of its wider application, careless writers substitute 'further' for 'farther.'

- discrete/discreet

The first word refers to individual, distinct parts. (Civil procedure includes a number of *discrete* steps.) The second word refers to a respect for reserve. (Attorneys should be *discreet* in their client relationships.)

- enormity/enormousness

If you want to comment on the mere size of something, use 'enormousness.' The word 'enormity' means "excessively wicked, outrageous in a moral sense." You might speak of the *enormity* of a crime, but of the *enormousness* of a dinosaur.

- tortuous/torturous

The first member of this pair can be either literal or figurative in meaning. It means "twisted or circuitous," as in (literal meaning) "a *tortuous* path," or as in (figurative meaning) "*tortuous* logic." The second member, an adjective formed from 'torture,' means "afflicted with or causing great physical or mental pain." It is used only with its literal meaning, as in "a *torturous* injury."

- reluctant/reticent

The first word means "hesitant or unwilling to do something." "The witness was *reluctant* to testify." "*Reticent*" means "*characteristically silent or reserved*," as residents of Maine are reputed to be. Recently, "reticent" has been substituted for "reluctant," but they are *not* synonyms.

2. Elegant Variation

The late grammarian, H. M. Fowler, gave this somewhat elaborate name to the tendency of some writers to refer by different names to the same referent. When my students do this, they explain that somewhere along the way, a teacher suggested that the practice lent variety and interest to their writing. Variation may be desirable in ordinary writing, but the confusion caused by the practice makes it undesirable in legal writing. Here is an example of elegant variation, from a law student's statement of a 16th century legal rule for possession:

- For the *hunter* to have possession of the *beast*, the *pursuer* would have to *kill* the *animal* and leave it where the *beast* was *slain*. (Emphasis added.)

Note that in this sentence, the *hunter* is also called the *pursuer*, the *beast* is also called the *animal*, and the act referred to is first *kill* and then *slain*. The result is confusion for the reader. To gain possession, how many persons must kill (or slay) how many animals (or beasts)? To avoid the confusion, simply denote one idea by one word:

- For the hunter to have possession of the beast, he would have to kill the beast and leave it where it was killed.

The following are two more examples of elegant variation:

- Students with writing deficiencies will take a *course* in basic writing before entering the regular legal writing *program*. After completing the basic *program*, they will enter the regular *course*. (Emphasis added.)

Besides calling each writing segment both a *course* and a *program*, the writer has used the designations indiscriminately. A clearer statement would be:

- Students with writing deficiencies will take a *course* in basic writing before entering the regular legal writing *program*. After completing the basic *course*, they will take the regular legal writing *program*. (Emphasis added.)

Another example of elegant variation:

- There are many *possibilities* for liability arising from this incident, but it does not appear that any of the three *options* will succeed. (Emphasis added.)

Do 'three' and 'many' refer to the same or different ideas? Are 'possibilities' the same or different from 'options'? These questions would not have to be asked had the writer assigned a single word to a single concept. For example,

- There are *three possibilities* for liability arising from this incident, but it does not appear that any of the *three* will succeed. (Emphasis added.)

Rule: Choose clarity over elegance.

3. Legerdemain With Two Senses

Grammarian H. M. Fowler has given this name to the opposite tendency in writing, in which the writer calls the same item by different names. Perhaps Fowler chose the name because it involves a sort of rhetorical sleight-of-hand. An even more exotic name for the writing fault was given it by linguists Ogden and Richards, who called it "ultraquistic subterfuge." Whatever the name, the result is confusion for the reader, who assumes that a word retains its original meaning when used a second and third time in the same tract. Some examples of legerdemain with two senses follow:

- A defendant is not *responsible* [for his act] if at the time of his unlawful conduct his mental or emotional processes or behavior controls were impaired to such an extent that he cannot be held *responsible* for his act. (Emphasis added.)

This sentence was part of a proposed jury instruction. The reader assumes that "responsible" means the same in both parts of the sentence. But this is not so: the first "responsible" means "able to discharge one's obligations"; the second "responsible" means "accountable for one's actions." Fortunately, this instruction confused no juries, for drafters of the Model Penal Code rejected it.

Another example:

- My client has a *cause* of action against the defendant because the *cause* of my client's injuries was defendant's conduct.

In this sentence, the word "cause" has two meanings, not one, as the reader would expect. A re-write might be:

- My client can maintain an *action* against the defendant because the defendant's conduct *caused* my client's injuries.

Finally, this:

- This law is unfair to the poor. For them *murder* may be punishable by execution, but the wealthy get away with *murder* in their business dealings all the time.

Here the writer hopes to strengthen his argument by using the word "murder" first literally, then figuratively. Some attorneys exploit the possibilities inherent in the multiple meanings of words. For example, the attorney for a physician charged with procuring an abortion for a patient, claimed that his client was protected from liability by the Statute of Frauds, which states that no one should be held for the debt, default or "miscarriage of another" without written evidence.[12] Awareness of the possible employment of 'legerdemain with two senses' prepares you to expose the practice and defend against it.

4. Match Nouns and Verbs

The misalliance of noun and verb, like other mismatches, causes an unhappy condition, as in the following examples of actual writing:

- The defendant's words were at a loss to express his meaning.

The verb phrase "to be at a loss" requires a *human* noun as subject: only persons can "be at a loss." A rewrite carries the intended idea:

- The defendant was at a loss to express his meaning. (The verb "express" includes the meaning of "words.")

In the next sentence the misalliance occurs because the verb requires a *sentient being* as object:

- The judge rebuked the language of the defense attorney.

The restatement makes the object of the verb a person, as it ought to be:

- The judge rebuked the defense attorney for his language.

Will a Supreme Court decision cause rapes to "disappear"? The next sentence seems to say so:

- A U.S. Supreme Court decision that will allow publication of rape victims' names may mean the disappearance of rapes reported to the police.

12. Cited in Chafee, "The Disorderly Conduct of Words," 41 *Col.L.Rev.* 381, 387 (1941).

On closer inspection, one finds that the writer intends only to predict that the number of rapes *reported* will decrease. A more exact statement would be:

- A U.S. Supreme Court decision that will allow publication of rape victims' names may mean a reduction in the number of rapes reported to the police.

In the next sentence the noun/verb mismatch occurs because the verb "discriminate" requires a *human* noun as object.

- The employer should not discriminate against an employee's religion.

The sentence needs recasting to supply one:

- The employer should not discriminate against an employee because of his religion.

A noun/verb mismatch can also occur when one verb has *two* objects, but properly applies only to *one:*

- U.C.C. section 2–207 affords advantages and drawbacks to industrial sellers.

The verb *affords* properly refers to *advantages*, but is improperly forced to apply to *drawbacks* as well. A more neutral verb would correct the statement:

- U.C.C. section 2–207 has advantages and drawbacks for industrial sellers.

The same problem arises when two verbs have only one object, and the object is appropriate for only one of the verbs:

- The evidence does conclude but does support the fact that the information conveyed to the defendants was incorrect.

Evidence can *support* but not *conclude* facts. A simple change will solve the problem:

The evidence is not conclusive but it does indicate that the information conveyed to the defendants was incorrect.

To avoid noun/verb mismatches, read over what you have written and ask yourself, "Does the verb I have chosen really fit its subject? Is the object I have selected really the appropriate object for the verb?"

CHAPTER THREE

Organization

"Just as the sentence contains one idea in all its fullness, so the paragraph should embrace a distinct episode; and as sentences should follow one another in harmonious sequence, so the paragraphs must fit on to one another like the automatic couplings of railway carriages. . . ." (Winston Churchill, A Roving Commission, 211–212.

A. THE OUTLINE

1. Why Outline?

As stated previously in this book, the most important quality of legal writing is the precise communication of ideas. That is the chief reason you must use correct grammar and punctuation, proper sentence construction, succinct and exact language. But equally important to clear communication is good organization. Unless you organize your thoughts well, they may be unappreciated or even misunderstood, and your writing will fail in its purpose.

Because a good outline is basic to good organization, this chapter begins with the outline. Many of the documents you will write in law school and during your legal career follow a prescribed style; for example, memos, briefs, pleadings and complaints must be written in a rigid formula which eliminates the need for you to outline. But you will also be writing legal theses for which you will have to furnish the outline.

In this law school, a senior thesis is a requirement for graduation, and I conduct seminars for students who are writing their senior thesis. The first question these students ask is: Where do I begin? The answer: with an outline.

What does an outline accomplish?

- It answers the question of how and where to start.
- It provides a framework for the discussion.
- It acts as a road map, showing where and how to proceed.
- It prevents gaps and digressions in the discussion.
- It indicates what should be in the body of the paper and what should be footnoted.
- It shows where transition is needed.

Although some of these advantages of an outline may overlap, they are not a complete list, only enough to show why outlining is important, so important that if you do not outline before you write your paper, you will probably find yourself doing so *afterwards*—and probably rewriting the paper. And the more reluctant you are to prepare an outline, the more you need to do so. You are reluctant because you dislike forcing yourself to organize your ideas, the very characteristic that results in a badly organized paper. An outline is like a Christmas tree. Without it, even the most beautiful ornaments end up in a heap on the floor. Without a framework, your most illuminating and perceptive ideas are ineffectively displayed.

2. How to Outline

The outline below was prepared in response to the second most frequent question I am asked in my thesis-writing seminars: What should I put into my outline? It is an all-purpose, general duty outline, which can be used for many theses and law review articles. But, because it is un-specific, it is not very useful for your *particular* purpose; it is just a starting point. If you use it, you will have to modify it to fit your needs. And you will continue to modify and perfect it as you continue to do your research.

Sample Outline [1]

I. Introduction

    A. Why you chose this subject

    B. What you intend to do with this subject

II. History

    A. The genesis of your subject

    B. The changes that have occurred during its development

    C. Why it has developed into its present state

III. Status quo

    A. Its advantages

    B. Its defects

    C. Why it cannot (should not) continue

IV. Changes suggested (attempted) by others

    A. Advantages

    B. Defects

V. Your ideas for change

    A. Advantages

    B. Defects

VI. Conclusion

    A. Predictions

    B. Summary of ideas presented in paper

3. How to Use Your Research in Your Outline (and Adapt Your Outline to Your Research)

In the "olden days" (B.C.: before copiers), to do their research authors laboriously covered large numbers of index cards with voluminous notes, indicating at the top of each card where in their manuscript the notes on that particular card applied. They had to take care to copy verbatim whatever quotations they might need to use and to summarize all of the other ideas succinctly enough to fit on the index cards. Furthermore, the source of all material had to be meticulously noted so that it could be referred to if necessary for verification later. Thus both outlining and research were time-consuming, burdensome processes. Some writers still use this method, although it is the one most apt to cause error—and writer's cramp.

Writers who take advantage of photocopiers have an easier job. They may still prefer to use index cards, one to a source, with the source of the data indicated at the top of each card. Much less writing is necessary, however, because the materials consulted can be photocopied. Index card notations will refer to the photocopied materials and the labor of notetaking is therefore minimized.

The simplest method (and the one I strongly recommend) is to apply your research directly to your outline, while at the same time adapting your outline to your research. Use a looseleaf notebook for your outline. Assign one page of the notebook to each heading and sub-heading of your outline. Then, as you do your research, label it with a few identifying phrases and put those phrases into your outline. At the same time, on the photocopied research material, indicate where in your outline it belongs. As you continue your research, you may find that the material belongs elsewhere in your outline or that your outline needs revision. If you decide, for example, that heading III is really better as heading VI, it is easy to switch the pages in the looseleaf notebook.

Another distinct advantage of this method is that, once you have placed all relevant material into each heading and subheading, you can put it into the proper order within its category and decide what transitional words or paragraphs are needed to make the ideas flow. When your outline is fully fleshed out, you will be able to add relevant material in order to fill any gaps, and to eliminate or assign to the footnotes any material that prevents a clear logical presentation of your ideas. When you have done all this, your paper will be all-but written. The first draft should be easy to write; after that, it will be just a matter of polishing.

B. THE PARAGRAPH

1. Why Paragraph?

Paragraphs break up your writing into units which, properly arranged, permit the orderly movement of ideas from the beginning of your manuscript to its conclusion. Paragraphing is therefore important in all writing, but even more important in legal writing, in which clear and logical reasoning is essential. The familiar paragraph indentation at intervals on each page of writing promise the reader that with each paragraph a new set of ideas is being introduced and developed. Conversely, large blocks of unindented print discourage even the most interested reader from making the effort to learn what the writer has to say.

So paragraphing is psychologically important to the reader. It is also important to the writer. The process forces him to develop fully the ideas he has introduced, since he knows that a paragraph of fewer than four to six sentences probably indicates incomplete idea development [1] and that a paragraph of more than half a page of print is not only a fearful bore to read but a combination of too many ideas. The four-to-six-sentence rule can (and should) be broken occasionally. One-or-two-sentence paragraphs, sparingly used, are effective for summation of arguments, interjection of contrasting ideas, transition devices, or emphasis. Here is an illustration:

> Many university students first came into contact with the word "ripoff" when, in 1971, it appeared on posters placed around campus announcing a "Ripoff Rally," at which students were invited "to see how many ways you are getting ripped off." Included in the discussion at the rally were victims of injustice (black students) and the injustices themselves (e.g., a proposed tuition hike). The context indicated that "ripped off" meant "cheated" or at least "treated with great unfairness." But to a large majority of university students in 1971, the word "ripoff" was clearly new and indefinable. Of the twenty students in my transformational grammar class, not one could provide a suitable definition.

> One year later I asked students in my transformational grammar class to define "ripoff" again; all twenty students in that class could provide a working definition.[2]

Every paragraph should contain a central idea. In most paragraphs, that idea is expressed in one sentence, usually called a "topic sentence." The topic sentence often comes first in a paragraph, sometimes following an introductory or transitional sentence. Or it comes last, expressing in general the individual points made within the paragraph. Rarely, the central idea of a paragraph is left unstated, implicit in the ideas contained in the paragraph, as in the following example:

> A factory survey of men all doing the same sort of work for the same length of time showed some were exhausted at day's end while others still seemed highly energetic. What made this difference? Analysts turned up one curious fact. The tired ones expected to do nothing but rest after work. The lively ones all had plans for the evening.[3]

1. In legal writing, in which sentences tend to be longer than in ordinary writing, the four-sentence minimum may sometimes be relaxed. Another criterion is the number of words: if your paragraphs have fewer than 50 or more than 250 words, you should check their content to see if you should combine or divide paragraphs.

2. Block, "A Year of Ripoffs," *American Speech*, Vol. 45, Nos. 3–4, 1970, p. 210.

3. *The Gainesville Sun*, April 27, 1982. The unstated topic sentence is, of course, that one's after-work plans affect the amount of energy he or she has at work. Perhaps the idea is left implicit here because it is so vulnerable to attack. It is

2. How to Organize and Develop Paragraphs:

Paragraphs can be developed by any of the following methods: definition; classification; process; illustration; cause and effect; comparison and contrast; induction; and deduction. Frequently, more than one method of development occurs in a single paragraph.

Many books on English composition imply that you should choose among the methods of paragraph development before writing each paragraph. This procedure would be stultifying and a waste of time, for you are no doubt using these methods quite intuitively as you write. However, after you have finished writing the first draft of your manuscript, if any paragraphs seem undeveloped, overdeveloped, or badly developed, consider the various methods of paragraph development as one means of improving your writing. Here they are:

a. Definition

Definition explains what something is by saying what it includes and what it excludes. The item being defined is first put into a class of similar items and then is differentiated from those items. The following paragraph exemplifies the process of definition:

> Historically, larceny was a common law felony, while embezzlement and false pretenses were statutory innovations. Larceny, the trespassory taking and carrying away of another's personal property with the intent of depriving him permanently of it, is a crime against possession, not ownership. Thus, one commits larceny by stealing the ill-gotten gains of a thief, but not by taking property from its rightful possessor when the possessor parts with it voluntarily. Therefore, larceny, under its strict definition, did not include fraud or the abuse of trust by a servant or another entrusted with one's possessions.

You can use definition, not only to explain, but to persuade, by deciding what to include and what to exclude. For example, Model Penal Code sections 221.0 and 221.1 define burglary as the entering of a building or occupied structure with the purpose of committing a crime, unless the premises are open to the public at the time, or the actor is privileged to enter. Whether the facts of the case you are considering are covered by the definition may depend on the meaning of "occupied structure." Must the occupant be in general occupancy or only present when the burglary occurred? What does "license to enter" include? (Licensees have been defined by courts as persons using premises through the owner's "sufferance," [4] or "permission," [5] or as invitees who step beyond the limits of their invitation.[6]) You can persuade your reader to your point of view by arguing for the inclusion or exclusion of one or more of these definitions.

arguable that only those workers who knew they would not be tired after work made plans for the evening.

4. Boneau v. Swift & Co., 66 S.W.2d 172, 175 (Mo.App.1934).

5. Seabloom v. Krier, 219 Minn. 362, 18 N.W.2d 88, 91 (1945).

6. Wilson v. Goodrich, 218 Iowa 462, 252 N.W. 142 (1934).

b. Classification

Classification categorizes items, either by their similarities or by their differences. In legal writing, classifications are sometimes expanded, sometimes narrowed, by court decisions. In his dissent in *Roth v. Wisconsin State University*, Supreme Court Justice Thurgood Marshall argues for the expansion of basic liberties protected by the Fourteenth Amendment so as to include the right to work. That right, he says, is "the very essence of the personal freedom and opportunity that it was the purpose of the Amendment to secure." [7]

In the following paragraph, a Supreme Court decision expands the right to privacy by placing unmarried persons in the same classification as married persons:

> If under *Griswold* the distribution of contraceptives to married persons cannot be prohibited, a ban on distribution to unmarried persons would be equally impermissible. It is true that in *Griswold* the right of privacy in question inhered in the marital relationship. Yet the marital couple is not an independent entity with a mind and heart of its own, but an association of two individuals each with a separate intellectual and emotional make-up. If the right of privacy means anything, it is the right of the *individual*, married or single, to be free from unwarranted governmental intrusion into matters so fundamentally affecting a person as the decision whether to bear or beget a child . . . [8]

Note that, to argue his point, the writer of the opinion interprets "the marital couple" not as an entity but as two individuals, who are thus classifiable with unmarried cohabiting individuals. In your own case analyses, be aware of the possibilities of classification in arguing a point.

c. Process

Process involves orderly, step-by-step explanation. The ability to describe procedures and events in the proper order and without omissions is valuable in legal writing because of the importance of detail, accuracy, and completeness in legal matters. In the following excerpt the process to be followed in a lawsuit is described:

> The first step in a lawsuit is the decision to sue someone. In making this decision intelligently, the potential litigant must discover whether the grievance he has suffered is one for which the law furnishes relief, whether it is probable that he will win the lawsuit, and whether the time, effort, and expense of bringing the suit will be worth the gain if he does win. The second step is to determine in which court to bring the action, and the choice of court will depend not only upon the preference of the litigant but upon which court has jurisdiction both over the subject matter and over the

7. 408 U.S. 564, 588, 92 S.Ct. 2701, 2714, 33 L.Ed.2d 548 (1972).

8. Eisenstadt v. Baird, 405 U.S. 438, 452, 92 S.Ct. 1029, 1038, 31 L.Ed.2d 349 (1972).

person against whom the suit is being brought, and which court has proper venue.[9]

You will find that competence in the use of process is well rewarded in law school final examinations, in which detailed and orderly explanations are demanded. (See Chapter Five, Section A.)

d. Illustration

Illustration utilizes concrete examples to explain an abstract concept or persuade the skeptic of its truth. Several examples might be used, or one striking example. The following definition of constructive possession uses several examples:

> Constructive possession is the possession that the law annexes to the title, distinguishing constructive possession from in fact or in deed possession, achieved by actual occupancy. Courts have found constructive possession to exist in several situations, as when (1) an employer delivers property to his employee; (2) the owner delivers property to another for a transaction to be completed in his presence; (3) a bailee breaks bulk; (4) a wrongdoer obtains possession but not title to the property by lies; (5) a wrongdoer finds lost or mislaid property; or (6) property is delivered to a wrongdoer by mistake.[10]

The paragraph above uses six examples. However, in some situations one striking example might suffice. For example in arguing that capital punishment is unwise, the writer might use as an example a man convicted of murder but later found innocent, who would have been executed had capital punishment been in effect.

You will find illustration not only useful but necessary in your law practice to make legal concepts comprehensible to your clients.

e. Cause and Effect

In legal writing, one way to make your argument effective is to indicate clearly and completely whatever causal relationship you consider important. Yet this method of development is often overlooked or ineptly attempted by law students.[11] Paragraphs utilizing cause and effect development raise the question of why something occurs and provide the answer. The following paragraph, for example, advances a reason for the development of the *mens rea* doctrine in criminal law:

> The concept of *mens rea* was not always part of common law. Anglo-Saxon law had held that intent was not a necessary element of crime. The

---

9. These two steps are, of course, only the first two in a long and complicated procedure.

10. LaFave and Scott, *Criminal Law*, West Publishing Company (1972), p. 622.

11. For discussion of this topic, see Chapter Two, Section A–5.

act itself was considered rather than the intent behind it, and reparation was demanded of the actor for the consequences of his act. But beginning in the ninth century, this objective standard of criminal responsibility was increasingly rejected by the church. Concern for the eternal soul of the criminal and belief in the Augustinian doctrine of free will led the church to adopt instead a subjective standard of responsibility: if the actor intended freely to commit the crime, he should be punished not only in heaven but on earth. Thus was born the modern doctrine of *mens rea.*[12]

f. Comparison and Contrast

In legal writing, comparison and contrast are often employed to show substantial similarities between things that are superficially different and to show significant distinctions between things that are seemingly similar. You will use this method of paragraph development when you analogize and distinguish cases, because the judicial system relies upon the doctrine of precedent. That is, courts "reason from precedent," basing decisions in the cases at hand upon decisions with similar facts handed down previously.[13] As law students you will do this kind of reasoning when you write interoffice memoranda, appellate briefs, and final examinations, and you will continue to utilize this method of reasoning throughout your legal career.

Since prior cases seldom contain facts exactly like those in the case you are considering, you will have to decide whether the facts in your case are similar enough to those of previous cases to warrant the same decision or whether differences in the facts are significant enough for precedent not to apply.

In applying comparison and contrast, the memo writer (or the law student writing a final examination) will attempt, without bias, to reach the appropriate conclusion. The brief writer, on the other hand, is an advocate for a client. He therefore tries to show either that despite seeming similarities, the facts of his client's case can be distinguished from those of prior cases or that despite seeming differences the facts are similar enough to warrant the same decision. Here is the way one student used comparison and contrast in his brief for a defendant businessman being sued by a visitor to the premises who had been injured. The relevant facts in the instant case were:

> A customer visiting a business was walking in the business parking lot and was hit and injured by a truck negligently operated by a driver employed by the owner of a business.

In a similar case, a superior court in the same jurisdiction had held the owner of a business liable for injuries to a pedestrian. The facts in that case were:

> A pedestrian crossing a business parking lot was hit and injured by a truck negligently operated by a driver employed by the owner of the business.

12. Block, "The Semantic Delusion of the Insanity Defense," *University of Oklahoma Law Review*, Vol. 36–561, 1983.

13. See Chapter Four for a more complete discussion of this subject.

These facts are facially similar. In the one aspect in which they differ, the relationship between businessman and visitor in the instant case seems even closer than in the prior case. Here the visitor was a customer; there a mere pedestrian crossing the premises. The brief writer, as he searched for distinguishing facts, found, however, that in the prior case construction in the parking lot created a hazardous condition, whereas in the instant case the premises were safe for visitors. Further research revealed that, in the prior case, the owner of the business knew that the parking lot was unsafe, yet failed to warn visitors of that fact. The brief writer was able, therefore, to distinguish the facts of his case from those of the earlier case, and to argue that the differences were material.

g. Induction

When you use inductive reasoning, you cite particulars in order to arrive at a general truth. The scientific researcher uses inductive reasoning when he collects sufficient experimental data to reach a generalization. The trial attorney uses inductive reasoning when he orchestrates a series of questions so that a witness will reach the conclusion the attorney desires.

As law students and as lawyers, you will use inductive reasoning to derive a general conclusion from particular details. In your reading of case law you have seen inductive reasoning used by courts in their opinions. Here is one example, from an early decision, in which the court determined, by inductive reasoning, that the plaintiff was justified in entering the property of the defendant, because of the doctrine of necessity.

There are many cases in the books which hold that necessity . . . will justify entries upon land and interferences with personal property that would otherwise have been trespasses . . ..

A traveller on a highway, who finds it obstructed from a sudden and temporary cause, may pass upon the adjoining land without becoming a trespasser, because of the necessity. [Citations omitted.]

An entry upon land to save goods which are in danger of being lost or destroyed by water or fire is not a trespass. [Citations omitted.] [In one such case] the defendant went upon the plaintiff's beach for the purpose of saving and restoring to the lawful owner a boat which had been driven ashore and was in danger of being carried off by the sea; and it was held no trespass. [Citation omitted.]

This doctrine of necessity applies with special force to the preservation of human life. One assaulted and in peril of his life may run through the close of another to escape from his assailant. [Citation omitted.] One may sacrifice the personal property of another to save his life or the lives of his fellows. [In one case] the defendant was sued for taking and carrying away the plaintiff's casket and its contents. It appeared that the ferryman of Gravesend took forty-seven passengers into his barge to pass to London, among whom were the plaintiff and defendant; and the barge being upon the water a great tempest happened, and a strong wind, so that the barge and all the passengers were in danger of being lost if certain ponderous things were not cast out, and the defendant thereupon cast out the plaintiff's casket. It was resolved that in case of necessity, to save the lives of the passengers, it was lawful for the defendant, being a passenger, to cast the plaintiff's casket out of the barge; that if the ferryman surcharge the barge the owner shall have his remedy upon the surcharge against the ferryman, but that if there be no surcharge, and the danger accrue only by the act of God, as by tempest, without fault of the ferryman, everyone ought to bear his loss, to safeguard the life of a man.[14]

This somewhat lengthy excerpt shows how meticulously the *Ploof* court used precedent cases as particular examples, in order to reach a general rule that it then applied to the case at hand. Count the number of particular cases cited. The court reasoned that : (1) In all of these previously decided cases, the doctrine of necessity applied to certain facts; (2) the facts of the case under consideration are sufficiently similar to the facts of the precedent cases to warrant the application of the doctrine of necessity to *these* facts. Thus the court utilized inductive reasoning to reach its conclusion.

h. Deduction

Deduction is the opposite of induction. As shown above, when you reach a conclusion by examining pertinent details, you are using induction. Conversely, when you reason from an accepted truth, such as a statute or a legal doctrine, you are using deduction.

The syllogism is perhaps the best-known form of deduction. As described by Aristotle, it is a three-step construction consisting of a major premise, a minor premise, and a conclusion. The major premise is a general presumption accepted as true (e.g., a legal doctrine); the minor premise identifies the item under consideration as within the class described by the major premise (e.g., a fact situation); and the conclusion then follows that the minor premise should be governed by the same reasoning that governs the major premise. Socrates' classic example bears repeating:

Major premise: All men are mortal. (Class is described.)

Minor premise: Socrates is a man. (Individual under consideration belongs to class described.)

Conclusion: Socrates is mortal. (Major premise applies to individual.)

Deductive reasoning can be applied to legal problems, e.g.:

> • Defendant drove into an empty carwash after it had closed for the night, intending to commit a theft. The carwash consisted of wash stalls open at each end, a roof, a concrete floor, and a coin box. The defendant forced open the coin box, removed the contents, and fled.

14. Ploof v. Putnam, 81 Vt. 471, 71 A. 188 (1908).

The applicable section of the burglary statute in your jurisdiction reads:

> A person commits burglary when, without authority, he knowingly enters or remains within a building, housetrailer, watercraft, motor vehicle, railroad car or any part thereof, with intent to commit therein a felony or theft.

Assuming that all other elements of burglary are present, the issue is whether a carwash is defined as a building, under the terms of this statute. If you believe it should be, you might construct the following syllogism:

Major premise: Buildings are constructions containing at least two walls, a floor, and a roof.

Minor premise: A carwash has two walls, a floor, and a roof.

Conclusion: A carwash is a building.[15]

The legal doctrines enunciated by courts as a result of inductive reasoning may then become the major premises that future courts use to reason deductively. For example, in the *Ploof* case (discussed above, **Section g**), as a result of its analysis of precedent cases, the court stated: "It is clear that an entry upon the land of another may be justified by necessity, and that the declaration before us discloses a necessity for mooring the [plaintiff's] sloop." Stated as a syllogism, this reasoning might be:

Major premise: Entry upon another's land is justified due to necessity.

Minor premise: Due to necessity, in a storm, plaintiff entered defendant's land to moor his sloop to defendant's dock.

Conclusion: The plaintiff was justified in his entry to defendant's land due to necessity.

In a 1970 English case, the court explained how it utilized both inductive and deductive reasoning. Noting that the concept of negligence is based upon "the cumulative experience of the judiciary of the actual consequences of lack of care in particular instances [induction], the court said that the relevant characteristics of the case at hand must be compared to the characteristics of earlier cases "which have been held in previous decisions of the courts to give rise to the duty of care." Thus far the method is "analytical and inductive." But the inductive analysis leads to a proposition that becomes the major premise of a syllogism:

> In all the decisions that have been analyzed, a duty of care has been held to exist wherever the conduct and the relationships possessed each of the characteristics A, B, C, D, etc., and has not so far been found to exist when any of these characteristics were absent.[16]

This statement may become the major premise of a syllogism. The characteristics of subsequent cases under consideration are then analyzed to

---

15. If you did not want the carwash to be considered a building, your major premise would define a building as having four walls.

16. *Home Office v. Dorset Yacht Co. Ltd.,* (1970) A.C. 1004 (H.L.)

ascertain whether they possess the characteristics A, B, C, D, etc. If so, they become the minor premise of the syllogism, and the conclusion follows that a duty of care arises.

The *Dorset* court thus describes the reasoning processes of induction and deduction. As an attorney, you can also use the syllogism in another manner: to expose faulty reasoning. Consider the following paragraph, from an appellate brief:

> Contracts in Florida between physicians and patients have been held legally enforceable wherein the physician agreed to withhold the use of artificial methods to postpone a patient's death, when the patient was suffering from an incurable and painful illness. Dr. X, a Florida physician, contracted with his patient, a Florida resident, to withhold, at his patient's request, artificial methods to maintain life. The patient, terminally ill, told the physician not to use artificial methods to prolong his life, and the physician complied with the patient's request. Since the physician was fulfilling the terms of a legally enforceable contract, he can not be held liable for malpractice.

To discover the fallacy in the syllogism, look at the major premise, seen in the first sentence of the paragraph. Unless the major premise contains an accepted legal principle, the entire syllogism will be invalid. The statement does not reveal whether the legal principle stated in the first sentence is valid in Florida, since we do not know whether all Florida courts, a majority or only some Florida courts have adopted the principle. Furthermore, the individual described in the minor premise may not be a member of the class described in the major premise, for the facts do not indicate that his illness was "painful."

The syllogism can also be used to expose specious logic. Suppose, for example, that a powerful group of individuals in your city wish to raze an old neighborhood so as to construct a shopping center, which you oppose. The argument this group advances is that the old buildings in the neighborhood, though not unattractive, present a hazard, old buildings often being decrepit and rodent-infested. You can discredit this argument by showing that the underlying syllogism is based upon specious logic:

Major premise: All old buildings are decrepit and rodent-infested.

Minor premise: These buildings are old.

Conclusion: These buildings are decrepit and rodent-infested.

You could point out the fallacy of the major premise and build your opposing argument on the following syllogism:

Major premise: Unless old buildings are decrepit or rodent-infested they should be preserved if they are beautiful or of historical interest.

Minor premise: These old buildings are not decrepit or rodent-infested, and they are beautiful and historically interesting.

Conclusion: These old buildings should be preserved.

If the minor premise can occur outside the boundaries of the major premise, the syllogism is also fallacious:

Major premise: Attorneys are skilled in syllogistic reasoning.

Minor premise: Jane Doe is skilled in syllogistic reasoning.

Conclusion: Jane Doe is an attorney.

Even if the major premise is a generally-accepted truth, the syllogism is faulty because persons other than attorneys may be skilled in syllogistic reasoning, and Jane Doe may be one of those persons.

Specious reasoning is most easily hidden in the **enthymeme**, a syllogism stated in a reduced form, with one step missing (usually the major premise). The comment, "He must be a panhandler: he's dirty and he's loitering on the street corner," is an enthymeme, the unstated major premise of which is fallacious: All dirty people who loiter on street corners are panhandlers. Here is an enthymeme-containing excerpt from a political speech:

> During his years in the state legislature, Representative Quagmire has often spoken out in favor of federal handouts, even though he himself has profited from the free enterprise system which is about to be undermined by federal handouts. Communists in Russia and China also favor handouts and oppose the free enterprise system upon which this nation was founded. Let's replace Quagmire with John Dogood, a man of strong ideals and get the communists out of state government.[17]

This paragraph is loaded with enthymemes that are invalid because they contain fallacious major premises. Some of these are:

- People who have profited from the free enterprise system should not speak out in favor of federal handouts.

- Federal handouts are incompatible with free enterprise.

- People with "strong ideals" oppose federal handouts.

- Handouts are bad because communists in Russia and China favor them.

- All persons who favor federal handouts are communists.

C. WITHIN AND BETWEEN PARAGRAPHS: COHERENCE

At least as important to successful writing as development by one or more of the methods just discussed is organization to provide coherence within and between paragraphs. In legal writing particularly, the natural and orderly connection between your ideas ought to be obvious. Each sentence should proceed logically from the previous sentence and logically precede the sentence that follows. Each paragraph should flow naturally from its predecessor, with no ideas repeated or omitted.

---

17. The use of slanted language, as used in this paragraph, is discussed in Chapter Five, Section A(3).

1. Use Chronological Development

If your subject lends itself to chronological development, that organization best insures coherence. Your reader follows without difficulty events discussed in the order in which they occurred. Yet often writers fail to use this simple method of development. Note the difference in the two paragraphs that follow, both taken from the "Facts" portion of memos on the same subject. The first paragraph is hard to follow, the second easy; the difference is that the second paragraph is developed chronologically: [18]

> * D. W. Indy now files a motion to suppress evidence that he refused to take a breathalyzer test in compliance with Florida's implied consent statute. D. W. I. was arrested on June 13, 1981, by Officer Gettum for driving under the influence of alcohol to the extent that his normal faculties were impaired. D. W. I. refused the breathalyzer test at the police station. He was read the *Miranda* rights and Florida Statute § 322.261, providing that a refusal to take the test would result in a three-month suspension of his driver's license. Officer Gettum says he also showed Indy the implied-consent statement on Indy's driver's license. Prior to trial, Indy filed a motion to suppress evidence of his refusal to take the breathalyzer test, claiming that Officer Gettum told him that he had the right to refuse to do so. Officer Gettum denies that he did so.

In the paragraph above, the writer discusses in sentence one the most recent event (D.W.I.'s filing of the motion to suppress evidence). But in the second sentence, the writer moves back in time to discuss the first event (D.W.I.'s arrest). Because he did not deal with the events in the order in which they happened, the writer is then forced, at the end of the paragraph, to repeat what he had said at the beginning. Repetition of this sort can be avoided by placing events in their natural order, and you will place less of a burden on your reader to understand what you are describing. The writer did this in his re-write:

> • On June 13, 1981, Officer Jones arrested D. W. Indy for driving while under the influence of alcohol to the extent that his normal faculties were impaired. When taken to the police station, D. W. I. was read his *Miranda* rights and Florida Statute § 322.261, providing that a refusal to take a breathalyzer test in compliance with Florida's implied consent statute would result in a three-month suspension of his driver's license. Officer Gettum says he also showed D. W. I. the implied-consent statement on his driver's license. D. W. I. claims, however, that Officer Gettum told him at the police station that he had the right to refuse to take the breathalyzer test. Officer Gettum denies this. D. W. I. now files a motion to suppress any evidence of his refusal to take the breathalyzer test.

18. Some students tell me that they prefer not to read "bad" examples of writing, because when they do, they tend to copy them. If you have this tendency, skip the paragraphs preceded by the asterisk; these are the "bad" examples.

Here are two more paragraphs, taken from the "Facts" sections of memos. Note how chronological development improves the second paragraph:

* K. R. owns a pawnshop in a high-crime area of El Dorado. When he arrived at his shop on October 8, 1981, he saw two teenaged girls hurriedly leaving. K. R.'s clerk said that a ring worth about $1,000 was missing from its usual place. On his car radio K. R. heard that a number of jewelry thefts had occurred in the neighborhood. This especially concerned K. R. because his insurance coverage had recently been cancelled. He pursued the girls, who were running down the street.

• While driving to his pawnshop, located in a high crime area of El Dorado, K. R. heard on his car radio that a number of jewelry thefts by teenaged girls had recently occurred in the neighborhood. This news especially concerned K. R. because his insurance had recently been cancelled. As K. R. arrived at his shop, he saw two teenaged girls hurriedly leaving his shop. K. R.'s clerk said that a ring worth about $1,000 was missing from its usual place. K. R. pursued the girls, who were running down the street.

2. Use Logical Development

Some discussions do not lend themselves to chronological development. Perhaps events do not occur in chronological sequence. Perhaps the points you need to make should be discussed in the order of their importance to your general thesis. Then you should choose logical development. As long as you discuss one point at a time, and as long as your discussion is thorough (but not repetitive), focussed (not discursive), your ideas will emerge clearly and cogently. In the following paragraphs, the first draft of a paper, the writer did not organize her ideas well, and the reader is hardput to understand just what she is getting at:

First Draft

* Much of the dispute about the purpose of the equal protection clause centers on whether it should be interpreted as prohibiting the consideration of race in governmental decision-making or whether the equal protection clause should be interpreted as imposing upon government an affirmative duty to remove the effects of past discrimination against minorities. The Supreme Court has struggled to resolve the conflict about whether illicit motive or disparate impact is the touchstone in constitutional violations, whether de jure or de facto segregation is condemned by the equal protection clause. This conflict is seen in the phenomenon of suburbia.

This paper will argue that the equal protection clause should be concerned with the substance of governmental decision-making as it affects minorities. Motivation is largely irrelevant as a constitutional basis for a violation of the equal protection clause if the effect is further subordination of victims of discrimination. As the white middle class has abandoned the cities, the tax base has decreased, and the familiar minority ghettos have burgeoned.

Placed in logical order, the writer's ideas become clearer:

Second Draft

• Much of the conflict about the purpose of the equal protection clause centers on whether it should be interpreted as prohibiting the consideration of race in governmental decision-making or whether the equal protection clause should be interpreted as imposing upon government an affirmative duty to remove the effects of past discrimination against minorities. This conflict is seen in the Supreme Court's struggle to resolve the question of whether illicit motive or disparate impact is the touchstone in constitutional violations, whether de jure or de facto segregation is condemned by the equal protection clause.

This paper will argue that, although color-blind decision-making is necessary, if the results of such decision-making nevertheless discriminate against minorities, the equal protection clause should be interpreted as prohibiting such results. In such cases, motivation is irrelevant. The phenomenon of suburbia illustrates de facto discrimination against minorities, occurring along with color-blind decision-making.

The writer has improved this second draft by logically developing her subject:

First, she has stated her topic: possible interpretations of the equal protection clause.

Second, she has narrowed the topic to the Supreme Court's effort to decide on a test for violation of the equal protection clause.

Third, she has further narrowed the topic: the impact of the problem upon minorities.

Finally, she has indicated her purpose: to argue for one interpretation of the role of the equal protection clause.

Note how the discussion leads from a broad, general statement of the topic to a narrowing of the topic by examples and qualifications. This kind of logical development helps the reader follow your reasoning and makes your argument persuasive.

But the second draft is not yet sufficiently clear. It suffers from other writing flaws that have been discussed elsewhere in these pages. Some of the writing flaws that remain are:

• The use of noun phrases instead of verbs.[19]

• Some elegant variation ("conflict/dispute"; "prohibit/condemn"). [20]

• The failure to say **who** did **what** to **whom**.[21]

---

19. See Chapter Two, Section A–1.
20. See Chapter Two, Section C–2.
21. See Chapter Two, Section A–1.

In her third draft, which follows, the writer has eliminated or reduced these flaws. Compare the third draft with the second to see how she has done so:

Third Draft

• Much of the conflict about the purpose of the equal protection clause centers upon whether the clause merely prohibits the government from considering race as a factor in making decisions or imposes upon government the affirmative duty to remove the effects of past discrimination. This conflict is seen in the Supreme Court's struggle to decide whether, in order to violate the equal protection clause, the government decision must result from an "illicit motive" or whether the equal protection clause is violated if the government decision causes a "disparate impact" upon affected minorities.

This paper will argue that the second test is the appropriate one to apply to government decision-making. The paper argues that if a government decision causes a disparate impact upon minorities, the question of whether the decision was arrived at in a "color-blind" manner (that is, whether it was prompted by an illicit motive) is irrelevant. What is relevant is whether the decision results in de facto segregation; if so, the equal protection clause should prohibit it.

The phenomenon of suburbia illustrates de facto discrimination against minorities . . . [This and subsequent paragraphs elaborate on this phenomenon.]

3. Avoid Hysteron-Proteron

The habit of hysteron-proteron produces disorganized writing. The term means "the last before the first" in Greek.[22] I am fond of it, not because of its venerable past, but because it proved very useful to me when I taught freshman English composition. Whenever I found an example of the error on a student's theme, I would write "hysteron-proteron" in the margin where the error occurred. Then I would wait. If the student did not come to me and ask "What does *that* mean?" I would know he had not taken the time to read any of my comments on his paper, but had just checked the grade at the end.

Hysteron-proteron is a device frequently used in poetry. Recall Shelley's "I die, I faint, I fail," which is effective although the order of incidents must surely have been reversed. But it is quite inappropriate, and often confusing, in legal writing, where it creates the same problem as illogical development of ideas. Here are some examples of the error from students' writing:

• Congress enacted § 666 to curb the increased use of tax shelters that followed the *Baxley* holding. Before § 666, taxpayers received all the benefits of their investments but none of the risks. That is, a non-recourse

---

22. Hysteron-proteron may occur whenever you fail to organize your material effectively. It is frequent enough (and damaging enough) to devote a section to its discussion. (See, also, Chapter Three, Section C–1.)

mortgage could be used as the basis for depreciation deductions. In order to limit the deductions the taxpayer could claim, Congress enacted § 666.

As occurred in this excerpt, when the writer falls into the trap of hysteron-proteron, he often attempts to extricate himself from the resulting confusion by repeating the idea in its proper place. Therefore, the following re-write is both shorter and clearer than the previous draft:

> • After the *Baxley* holding, taxpayers received all the benefits of their investments but none of the risks. That is, a non-recourse mortgage could be used as the basis for depreciation deductions. In order to limit the deductions the taxpayer could claim and to curb the increased use of tax shelters that followed the *Baxley* holding, Congress enacted § 666.

Here is another example of hysteron-proteron. See if you can untangle it:

> • In Jones v. Jones, involving a man and woman who had just been divorced, the man had signed a note evidencing a loan from his wife, while they were still married. Then, after the divorce, by mutual consent, the former wife released the former husband from the debt. Since she was not repaid by her former husband, she took a bad debt deduction.

Your re-write may look something like this:

> • In Jones v. Jones, a man signed a note evidencing a loan from his wife. Then the couple were divorced and, by mutual consent, the man was released from his debt. The woman took a bad debt deduction because she had not been repaid by her former husband.

The topsy-turvy character of the original paragraphs above may seem so apparent that you are saying to yourself, "I'd never get that mixed up!" But you should beware of hysteron-proteron even so, because it can occur in a subtler form. You can recognize it as a reader when you are disappointed in your expectation of what is coming next. In the following paragraph, for example, stop after sentence one and consider what you expect to follow forthwith; then read on to discover whether your expectation is fulfilled.

> • In some instances the Roman commander would delegate the authority to decide the death sentence. But in any case, the commander's *lictors* were probably the executioners. This authority would sometimes be granted to the military tribunes who were next in command to the commanders. Or the delegation of the punishment would be awarded to the *centurions.*

The first sentence promises that the author will next discuss the instances in which the Roman commander would delegate authority. Instead, he begins another idea in the second sentence, returning in the following sentences not to the *instances* of delegation, but to the groups who would administer it. (A couple of paragraphs later, the writer does get around, belatedly to telling the reader what he promises to tell him here.)

Here is another paragraph from the same paper—and it contains the same problem:

• Ancient Roman military success was based on the fact that those chosen to take part in military operations had something to fight for. The soldiers knew that the outcome of their battles would determine whether they had something to come home to. Since the Republican military establishment required, from the start, that all those in its ranks own some property and/or be citizens of Rome, the soldiers knew that battles would determine whether they kept their homeland of Rome free from external conquerors and internal subversives. They had property and positions to lose if their defense of Rome was weak.

The first sentence promises the reader he will learn what it was the Roman soldiers had to fight for. In the last sentence, the reader does learn. Why not rearrange the paragraph so that the information promised appears in sentence two? The result might look something like this:

• Ancient Roman military success was based on the fact that those chosen to take part in military operations had something to fight for. All soldiers had either property or position to lose if their defense of Rome was weak, for the Republican military establishment required from the start that all those in its ranks own some property and/or be citizens of Rome. Thus the soldiers knew that whether they had something to come home to would be determined by the outcome of their battles.[23]

When the sentences are placed in their proper order, one sentence can be omitted. This is often true when disorganized sentences are rearranged because unnecessary repetitions and *non sequiturs* are more apt to creep into illogically arranged paragraphs. The material omitted will often be found to belong somewhere else in the paper.

4. Use Transition Words and Phrases (See also Chapter 2, § 5.)

Transition language makes clear the relationship between what you have said and what you are about to say; it is the language you use to show your reader where you are taking him. We all use transition, most of us without thinking about it. Good writers probably make more use of transition. But don't overdo it. Writing replete with transition language, which insistently reiterates relationships, may seem to insult your reader's intelligence or appear simplistic. On the other hand, in legal writing, which often deals with complex subjects, proper transition is needed to make comprehensible what would otherwise be confusing. And lack of transition makes writing appear to jerk rather than to flow. If you have been told that your writing is "choppy," you probably need to add transitions.

Short, choppy sentences are usually a second-stage writing development for law students. When they first come to law school, they tend to write in long, circuitous sentences. Then they are told by their instructors that they must shorten their sentences for clarity, so they break up their long sentences into short ones. The result is short sentences that are equally unclear, because

---

23. The term "and/or" might better be avoided because some judges dislike it intensely.

the links indicating their relationship are omitted. The paragraph that follows is an example of a second draft of a paper written by a student attempting to avoid the long, cumbersome sentence structure of his first draft:

> * Taxpayers and Congress play games with tax laws. Congress enacts a tax law disallowing deductions for certain activities. Taxpayers' lawyers find loopholes in the law so as to provide deductions for their clients. Congress promulgates an amendment to the law to close the loophole. The depreciation deduction allowed under Sections 167 and 168 permitted taxpayers to include borrowed amounts in determining the adjusted basis of property. When taxpayers reduced their tax liability by depreciation deductions through heavily mortgaged property, tax shelters resulted. Congress enacted § 465 in 1976 to close the loophole.

When the student adds transitional language, he makes his ideas clear:

> - Taxpayers and Congress play games with tax laws. First, Congress enacts a tax law disallowing deductions for certain activities. Then taxpayers' lawyers find loopholes in the law so as to provide deductions for their clients. Next Congress promulgates an amendment to the law to close the loophole. And so it continues. For example, the depreciation deduction allowed under Sections 167 and 168 permitted taxpayers to include borrowed amounts in determining the adjusted basis of property. This depreciation resulted from depreciation deductions through heavily mortgaged property. Therefore, in 1976, Congress enacted Section 465 in order to close that loophole.

Although you will probably never consult a list to select transition language, here are some of the words most commonly used to express the following relationships:

- Temporal relationships: Then, meanwhile, next, before, later, in a few days, until, then, when, after, following . . .
- Spatial relationships: Above, below, nearby, beyond, opposite, adjacent to, adjoining, far from . . .
- Addition: Furthermore, moreover, besides, also, again, in addition to, further . . .
- Causal relationships: Because, since, consequently, so that, in order to, for that reason . . .
- Logical relationships: Nevertheless, however, therefore, hence, thus, despite, but . . .
- Comparison and contrast: Similarly, likewise, in a like manner, yet, but, on the contrary, notwithstanding . . .

Another way to provide transition is to repeat a word or phrase used at the end of the previous sentence or paragraph. The repetition of "theories" in the following excerpt is an illustration:

> • Several theories regarding the intent of the equal protection clause are discussed in this section of the paper. Differences in these theories,

their weaknesses and strengths, and a proposal for alternative theories to avoid the unfavorable results of these theories will also be discussed.

(This device should be used sparingly, for it can cause repetitiousness.)

Between paragraphs, transition is even more important than between sentences within a paragraph, for the reader expects that all sentences in a paragraph are somehow connected and transition merely shows him how. But the new paragraph signals either a new topic or a new direction for the previous topic. In the following excerpt, the repetition of "decision" tells the reader to expect a new direction for the previous topic:

- In its decision in *Smith v. Bagwell*, the Florida Supreme Court described punitive damages as recompense to the sufferer as well as punishment to the offender and an example to the community. It described compensatory damages as those which arise from actual and indirect pecuniary loss, mental suffering, medical expenses, and bodily pain and suffering.

The court, in this decision, seemed to confuse the principle of compensatory damages—the means of compensating the victim for injury to his person—with the principle of punitive damages—punishment for the offender and a deterrent to the community.

The first draft of any writing is apt to lack transition, particularly when the writer knows his subject so thoroughly that he is unaware that transition language is missing. The problem is compounded when, as is often true in legal writing, the subject is complex. So as you read your first draft, add guideposts so that your reader can follow you to your destination.

D. SENTENCE CLASSIFICATION

Much of this book has dealt with sentences: the arrangement of words to form them, their arrangement into paragraphs, and their eventual arrangement to create the entire writing. This section will therefore overlap with some of what has already been discussed, for it deals with the ways in which English sentences are classified. You may have learned about this before, and if you have a good memory, you may want to skip this section. But if you have forgotten what you learned in grade school, the following will serve as a quick refresher.

Sentences are classified in three ways: by **function**, by **grammar**, and by **style**. That third clasification, **style**, is of most importance to you as a legal professional. It will be discussed at some length after a brief review of the other two classifications.

1. Classification by Function

Sentences function in four ways in English: the **command**, the **question**, the **exclamation**, and the **statement**. An example of each is:

Command: Review the evidence carefully.

Question: Is the plaintiff present?

Exclamation: The circumstantial evidence is incontrovertible!

Statement: The facts indicate that the defendant is liable.

Of these, the function most used by legal writers is the statement. The command, chiefly exhortatory, may be useful when you address a jury, but should be used only sparingly in writing. The question, posed and immediately answered, seems contrived and wordy and should be rephrased as a statement. The rhetorical question (Can anyone doubt the defendant's innocence?) should also be avoided in writing, although it may serve as an effective ploy in oral argument.

2. Classification by Grammar

Grammatically, sentences are either **simple, compound**, or **complex**.[24] The simple sentence is the least complicated and usually the shortest. It is composed of a single subject-predicate unit. The following are all simple sentences:

- I know John.
- Democracy lives!
- Our neighbors and their friends are active in politics.
- Mary spends her time studying and thus has little time for socializing.

Compound sentences are merely two or more simple sentences joined by a coordinating conjunction like *and, but, for*, and *so* or by a semi-colon either with or without a conjunctive adverb like *however, moreover,* or *nevertheless.* When you want to make several points of equal importance or join ideas that are closely connected, you will probably choose compound sentences to do so. The following are some compound sentences:

- I have known John for some time, but I do not know his brother.
- Democracy lives, and it will survive its present threats.
- Our neighbors and their friends are active in politics; they urge us to get involved.
- Mary spends her time studying; therefore she has little time to socialize.

Complex sentences contain at least one **main clause** and one **subordinate clause**. The main clause could stand by itself as a simple sentence and is therefore sometimes called the "independent" clause; the subordinate clause, often introduced by an adverb (like *when, while, because,* or *since*), cannot stand alone and is therefore sometimes called the "dependent" clause. Use complex sentences when you want to stress an important idea and subordinate a less important one. The following are some complex sentences:

- Because John is ethical and considerate, [subordinate clause] he is well liked. [main clause]

---

24. See Chapter One, Sections 1, 2 and 3, for additional discussion of these kinds of sentences.

- Although Joe has retired from practice, [subordinate clause] he is still politically active. [main clause]

- After the trial ends but before sentencing the defendant, [subordinate clause] the court will consider mitigating circumstances. [main clause]

By using grammatical variety you can write effectively and communicate well. Variety adds interest, too. Constant repetition of a single grammatical construction is boring. The monotony may lull your readers to sleep or make them stop reading. Choppy writing is often due to short sentences of simple structure, one after another. Writing that lacks emphasis is often the result of compound sentence after compound sentence. The best writing employs all kinds of grammatical structure—simple, compound, and complex—in the right places.

Note how changes in grammatical structure causes changes in emphasis in the following sentences:

- Marbury's formal commission for the judgeship was signed, but it was not delivered. (The compound sentence indicates that both parts of the sentence are of equal importance.) [25]

- Although Marbury's formal commission for the judgeship was signed, it was not delivered. (The complex sentence indicates that the main clause is the important one.)

3. Classification by Style

Sentences are classified stylistically as either **loose, periodic,** or **balanced.** In a **loose** sentence, the subject and predicate are close together; the subject tells what or who the sentence is about, and the predicate tells what the subject did. The typical sentence order of a loose sentence is subject-verb-object. (The predicate is composed of the verb and object, or if the verb has no object, only the verb.) In loose sentences, subject and predicate are close together, with no interrupting language separating them. The following sentences are loose in structure, although their grammatical structure is, respectively, simple, compound, and complex:

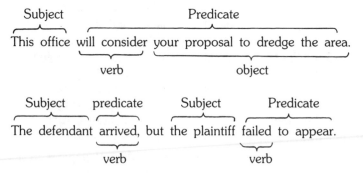

Subject   Predicate

This office will consider your proposal to dredge the area.

         verb   object

Subject   predicate   Subject   Predicate

The defendant arrived, but the plaintiff failed to appear.

         verb   verb

25. But see Chapter Two, Section A–6, for a discussion of the importance of the position of the end of the sentence.

Subject   Predicate Subject   Predicate

Although the owner had insurance, it did not cover the damages

verb object   verb   object

In legal writing, in which sentences are sometimes lengthy and often complicated, the loose sentence provides stopping points along the way, at which the reader understands what the writer means thus far. When you write long or complex sentences, use loose sentence structure as a favor to your readers.

Unlike loose sentences, **periodic** sentences provide no stopping places. Because periodic sentences contain 'interrupters,' that is clauses separating the subject from its predicate, or introductory clauses even before the subject of the sentence is stated, the reader must read the entire sentence before she knows what it is about. Here is a periodic sentence:

- On a dark night, when the moon was invisible and the stars were heavily shrouded in clouds, when only muffled earth sounds interrupted the stillness that surrounded me as I walked through the deep woods alone, deep in thought and unaware of any human presence, suddenly a raucous cry split the silence.

In the sentence above, the subject (a raucous cry), the verb (split), and the object (the silence) are delayed until the end. But the subject-matter of the sentence was probably sufficiently interesting to keep you reading. Unfortunately, the subject-matter of legal writing is usually neither exciting nor suspenseful. But legal writers seem to love the periodic sentence; certainly many of them overuse it. Consider, as a horrendous example, the following excerpt from § 25 of the Judiciary Act of 1789:

- **A final judgment or decree in any suit,** in the highest court of law or equity of a State in which a decision in the suit could be had, where is drawn in question the validity of a treaty or statute of, or an authority exercised under the United States, and the decision is against their validity; or where is drawn in question the validity of a statute of, or an authority exercised under any State, on the ground of their being repugnant to the constitution, treaties or laws of the United States, and the decision is in favor of such validity, or where is drawn in question the construction of any clause of the constitution, or of a treaty, or statute of, or commission held under the United States, and the decision is against the title, right, privilege or exemption specially set up or claimed by either party, under such clause of the said Constitution, treaty, statute or commission, **may be re-examined and reversed or affirmed in the Supreme Court of the United States upon a writ of error.** (Emphasis added.)

In this sentence, the subject (a final judgment or decree) appears in line one. But you had to read 15 lines further before you reached the verb (may be re-examined) and the remainder of the predicate. In between are dumped qualifying clauses. Neither interest nor suspense motivates you to read the sentence to the end, only the dogged determination (or need) to understand the material.

Contrast the current version of this earliest antecedent: 28 U.S.C. § 1257. The drafters of 28 U.S.C. § 1257 have substituted **loose** sentence structure for the **periodic** structure of the earlier draft and added the qualifiers in a list at the end. Note how much clearer the current version is:

- Final judgments or decrees rendered by the highest court of a State in which a decision could be had may be reviewed by the Supreme Court as follows:

(1) By appeal, where is drawn in question the validity of a treaty or statute of the United States and the decision is against its validity.

(2) By appeal, where is drawn in question the validity of a statute of any state on the ground of its being repugnant to the Constitution, treaties or laws of the United States, and the decision is in favor of its validity.

(3) By writ of certiorari, where the validity of a treaty or statute of the United States is drawn in question on the ground of its being repugnant to the Constitution, treaties or laws of the United States, or where any title, right, privilege or immunity is specially set up or claimed under the Constitution, treaties or statutes of, or commission held or authority exercised under, the United States.

If you use periodic sentence structure, you may confuse yourself as well as your readers. In the following sentence, from a student memo, when the writer reaches the end of his sentence, he uses the referent 'it' to refer back to a subject that he has forgotten to set down. Here is the sentence:

- In Peairs v. Florida Publishing Company, where the court held the newspaper publisher liable for injuries resulting from a pedestrian tripping over a wire loop left on a public parking lot by a newsboy, if the publisher was aware of the conduct of the newsboys and failed to take proper action to remedy the situation, even though the newsboys and carriers were called independent contractors, if the publisher meddled or interfered, it was deemed an agent-principal relationship; accordingly we can establish a similar relationship in the instant case.

When I read a sentence like this one, I am reminded of a dinner-table rule enforced by my mother: Never talk with your mouth full. Here the writer, his mouth full of qualifying clauses, is making an almost-unintelligible statement. He is trying to say five things:

(1) The *Peairs* court held that an agent-principal relationship existed between the defendant Florida Publishing Company and its newsboy-employee, despite the publisher's designation of its newsboy as an independent contractor.

(2) The agent-principal relationship existed because the publisher had the right to interfere in the activities of its newsboys.

(3) As "principal," the employer has the duty to remedy a dangerous situation that the newsboy as "agent" caused.

(4) Therefore the newspaper publisher is liable for the injuries of a pedestrian who tripped over a wire loop that a newsboy-employee left on a public parking lot.

(5) A similar relationship exists in the instant case.

Put these sentences together, and you will have a paragraph that is longer than the single sentence from the student memo. But the message is also clearer. You may combine the five sentences into three longer ones and retain clarity; but avoid the periodic structure that caused the problem in the first place. Here is a possible re-write in loose sentence structure.

> • The *Peairs* court held that the Florida Publishing Company, a newspaper publisher, was liable for the injuries of a pedestrian who tripped over a wire loop left on a public parking lot by a newsboy, despite the publisher's claim that newsboys were "independent contractors." The court reasoned that the relationship between the publisher and the newsboys was that of agent and principal because the publisher had the right to interfere in its newsboys' actions. Therefore the publishing company as principal should have taken appropriate action to remedy the dangerous situation of which it was aware and which was caused by the newsboy as agent. A similar principal-agent relationship exists in the instant case.

Law students who over-use periodic sentences may do so because they find them in their casebooks. Here is one from a jurisprudence text:

> • Does the **requirement** that a federal district court spend time on a property claim which would, at best, be a state small claims court matter if state-action-conferred federal jurisdiction were not implicated, **comport** with Rostow's suggestion that the Supreme Court should "avoid wasting its ammunition in petty quarrels"? (Emphasis added.)

In this periodic sentence the subject (requirement) is separated from its verb (comport) by several lines of print and several qualifying clauses and phrases. But it has another problem, also characteristic of periodic sentences. The writer, probably in order to shorten the sentence, has inserted five modifying words in front of the noun "jurisdiction." That is too many for clarity. I call this '**adjective buildup.**' It does shorten the sentence, but succinctness gained at the cost of comprehensibility is no benefit. Without the adjective buildup and with **loose** sentence structure replacing **periodic** structure, the sentence becomes easier to understand:

> • Federal district courts are required to spend time on property claims that would otherwise be state small claims court matters, at best, if state action had not conferred jurisdiction upon the federal courts; does Rostow's suggestion that the Supreme Court should "avoid wasting its ammunition in petty quarrels" comport with this situation?

Adjective build-up is a trap for all writers, not just legal writers. How does it come about? Suppose you want to write about lawyers, not all lawyers, only trial lawyers. But you want to write about the trial lawyers' association, so you add that word, and your phrase becomes

- trial lawyers' association

The association has an executive committee, so you add that language, and you get

- trial lawyers' association executive committee

The executive committee is going to form an agenda for the trial lawyers' annual meeting, so now you have

- trial lawyers' association executive committee annual planning agenda meeting

The executive committee plans to set up the agenda on Tuesday, April 6, so you add that information. Finally you add the predicate to your sentence, and you have created a periodic sentence containing adjective build-up:

- The trial lawyers' association executive committee annual planning agenda Tuesday, April 6, meeting will take place in the Empire Hotel.

Of course, you can add more information and make your sentence even harder to understand, but you get the idea. Adjective buildup forces the reader to unwind the sentence by putting the multiple adjectives into clauses and phrases. But don't place this burden on *your* readers.

The **balanced** sentence gives your writing grace and polish, and sometimes memorability. Its parallel structure and repetition of sentence patterns points up the similarity or contrast of ideas presented. When you can recall passages from literature, it is often because they contain balanced sentence structure. Here is such a passage from *Ecclesiastes:*

- To everything there is a season, and a time to every purpose under the heaven:

A time to be born, and a time to die; a time to plant, and a time to pluck up what is planted;

A time to kill, and a time to heal; a time to break down, and a time to build up;

A time to weep, and a time to laugh; a time to mourn, and a time to dance . . .

Benjamin Franklin's *Poor Richard* gave lawyers a drubbing—in balanced sentences that are still quoted:

- A countryman between two lawyers is like a fish between two cats.

- God works wonders now and then; Behold, a lawyer and an honest man!

- A good lawyer, a bad neighbor.

- Here comes the orator, with his flood of words and his drop of reason!

Good legal writing, too, benefits from the equipoise of the balanced sentence. Here is Judge Cardozo:

> • Judges have the power . . . though not the right, to ignore the mandate of a statute, and render judgment in despite of it. They have the power, though not the right, to travel beyond the walls of the interstices, the bounds set to judicial innovation by precedent and custom. None the less, by that abuse of power, they violate the law.[26]

26. B. Cardozo, *The Nature of the Judicial Process* (1921), p. 129.

CHAPTER FOUR

Case Analysis and Argumentation

"To be of any use, the language of the law (like any other language) must not only express but convey thought." **David Mellinkoff,** *The Language of the Law* (Preface, 1963).

Briefing, Analogizing, Synthesizing

As soon as law school classes begin, your professors are sure to suggest that you brief the opinions in your casebooks.[1] That is because if you brief the opinions you will understand and remember them better than if you merely read them. You can then intelligently answer the professor's questions and participate in class discussions. Unfortunately, few professors explain carefully how to brief opinions. So at the beginning of each semester a large number of students come to my office wearing the woebegone expression that immediately identifies them as first semester law students wanting to know how to brief cases.

One method of case-briefing is suggested and illustrated in the following pages. But *how* you brief is less important than *that* you brief. Briefing fixes the opinions securely in your mind; analogizing and synthesizing opinions help relate cases to one another. All are excellent preparation for final examination study. Although you can buy briefs in paperback outline form, "canned" briefs do not substitute for the do-it-yourself variety, because the ability to brief cases is an essential legal skill. You can, however, use the "canned" briefs against which to check your own.

Briefing involves three steps: (1) carefully reading an opinion, (2) selecting salient data from the plethora that the opinion contains, and (3) inserting the data in an outline. The process is explained below. The suggested outline contains nine items, but as you become experienced you may find that an outline of as few as five items is sufficient. You can start with the nine-point outline and eliminate or combine items as you gain skill in briefing.

Analogizing cases involves selecting information from your case briefs and applying it to other cases or fact situations in order to make predictions about the decision a court will reach in considering the new facts. This process is essentially what you will be doing in your final examinations in law school.

A case synthesis is a summary of two or more cases, describing their similarities and differences. Using synthesis you can discover why appellate courts sometimes reach similar conclusions in cases with seemingly different facts

---

1. As you have probably already discovered, professors and others in the legal profession use the word "case" to mean "opinion." Thus, when you are told to brief cases, you are usually being asked to brief the appellate court opinions in your "casebooks," which are actually "opinion" books.

and different conclusions in seemingly similar cases. Case syntheses also illustrate how legal rules are expanded, narrowed, or abandoned by court opinions.

A. BRIEFING

Various authors suggest different techniques for briefing cases,[2] and your law professors may have their own preferences. If you are free to choose, you should adopt the method most comfortable and helpful to you. The brief below is a suggested starting point. You may want to delete or combine some of the items. But the "briefest" brief should include at least: facts, legal theories, issues, holding, and reasoning.

The first step in briefing is to read the opinion carefully. Then list the nine items below on the left side of a legal-sized sheet, leaving enough room opposite each item for appropriate information from the opinion. Re-read the opinion, indicating in pencil in the margin what should be included opposite each item on your legal sheet. Transfer this information to your legal pad, paraphrasing it succinctly but retaining the relevant legal language. Check the meaning of any legal terms you do not know, and footnote your brief with these definitions. (See, for example, the brief for *Transatlantic Financing Corporation,* below, at 104.)

Here is the suggested outline:

1. Parties, their relationship, and how the matter reached this court
2. Legal theories (cause(s) of action and defense)
3. Facts
4. Relief requested
5. Issue(s)
6. Holding(s) and disposition
7. Reasoning
8. Resulting legal rule(s)
9. Dicta

Here is an explanation of each item:

1. *Parties, their relationship, and how the matter reached this court:*

The names of the parties usually appear in the caption at the beginning of the opinion. Their relationship also appears there, the plaintiff(s) first, followed, after the "v." (for "versus"), the defendant(s). When multiple parties are involved, list only the last name of the first litigant on each side. These are the names that appear in the body of the opinion. Even in captions reading, "In re . . ." or "In the Matter of . . ." there are at least two opposing parties, and their names should appear in your brief. In this section of your brief, indicate as well the status of each party, e.g., "employer" and "employee," "appellant" and "appellee," "petitioner" and "respondent."

---

2. For example, Statsky & Wernet, *Case Analysis and Fundamentals of Legal Writing* (Second Edition, 1984, Part Two). M. Rombauer, *Legal Problem Solving* (Fourth Edition, 1983), 10–20.

In "how the matter reached this court," briefly note any prior proceedings and explain why this court is now involved. Most of the cases you will brief are appellate court cases whose previous history appears at the beginning of the opinion. The headnote (syllabus) also contains this information, but be aware that errors may be present in this material since notes that precede the opinion are written by the reporter, not by the judge who wrote the opinion. A story, perhaps apocryphal, is told of a legal principle established over the years by *stare decisis,* whose original citation was from an erroneous headnote, the information never having appeared in the opinion itself!

2. *Legal theories (cause(s) of action and defense):*

These are the legal rules that form the basis of the plaintiff's claim. The plaintiff always advances one or more legal theories in order to obtain his desired objective. The defendant may also advance one or more legal theories if, instead of merely denying the validity of the plaintiff's cause of action, he raises a separate claim (an 'affirmative defense'), called a counter-claim.

3. *Facts:*

The fact section of your brief contains a succinct summary of the salient information, often called "key facts," of the opinion. Key facts are those facts upon which the court based its holding. Thus no facts that could be omitted or altered without changing the decision are key facts. (For example, in *Transatlantic Financing Corporation v. United States,* at 97, below, the fact that the Egyptian government had nationalized and taken over operation of the Suez Canal is not a key fact, since it could be deleted without changing the opinion of the court; however, the fact that the Suez Canal had been closed to traffic as a result of the takeover is a key fact.)

4. *Relief requested:*

The plaintiff states here what he hopes to achieve by going to court, his 'remedy.' In the cases briefed below, the relief requested is in the form of money. The kind of relief requested was a key fact in *Transatlantic Financing Corporation* (below), the court stating that the plaintiff's theory of relief was inappropriate.

5. *Issue(s):*

Issues are the precise legal questions that must be resolved by the court in order to reach its decision in the case under consideration. Often the issues are expressly stated in the opinion. If they are not, you can identify them by reading the court's holding and the reasons given to support it. The complete issue is the rule of law applied to the key facts of the case at hand.

6. *Holding(s) and disposition:*

The holding is stated as the court's affirmative or negative response to the issue. In its entirety, the holding contains the rule of law that was applied and the key facts of the case. In your own briefs of case opinions, however, you will probably include only a short answer to the issue (i.e., 'yes,' or 'no') because you have already completely stated the rule of law and key facts in the *issue* statement.

The **disposition** is whatever the court says it will do procedurally as a result of its holding. The disposition usually comes at the end of the opinion, stated in a few words (e.g., "vacated and remanded").

7. *Reasoning:*

In its reasoning, the court justifies its holding on each issue. When the case presents more than one issue, the court may intermingle the reasoning behind its holding on several issues, but you should separate the court's statements so as to apply its reasoning to each issue. To identify the reasoning of the court, look for its reasons for agreeing with one party and disagreeing with the other, for accepting some legal precedents and rejecting others, for extending or limiting other courts' opinions. Also look for the court's citation of enacted law and its interpretation of the intent of that law.

8. *Resulting legal rule(s):*

The legal rule is a broad statement of principle developed by or applied in *this* decision. The rule may then become precedent for analogous cases, in future decisions. Few decisions enunciate a new legal rule; many cite a rule previously developed, which was applied in the case at hand. This item and item 9, which follows, are often omitted from briefs, but they are helpful in placing the case under consideration into perspective with respect to cases that have preceded or will follow it.

9. *Dictum* (dicta):

Dictum (the plural of which is dicta) is official but incidental and gratuitous language, unnecessary to the decision of the case under consideration. Since courts are supposed to reach decisions only on the narrow questions before them, decisions theoretically should not contain dicta, but they sometimes do. You will recognize as dictum any statement a court makes based on facts other than those presented in *this* controversy, or any conclusion a court reaches based upon law not applicable to *this* controversy. You should identify dictum because later courts may agree with the view expressed as dictum, although dictum is not binding on subsequent court decisions any more than the minority decision is binding. (In *Transatlantic Financing Corporation*, for example, the dictum expressed by the court could result in a future court's extending this court's holding.)

Following are briefs of three cases, prepared according to the suggested ten-point outline. You may wish to use these briefs as models as you prepare briefs for the cases you are studying in your casebooks. The cases briefed are:

(1) Transatlantic Financing Corporation v. United States,

(2) American Trading and Production Corporation v. Shell International Marine LTD,

(3) Northern Corporation v. Chugach Electric Association.

A copy of the opinion of the court precedes each brief.

TRANSATLANTIC FINANCING CORPORATION
v. UNITED STATES

United States Court of Appeals, District of Columbia Circuit, 1966.
363 F.2d 312.

J. SKELLY WRIGHT, CIRCUIT JUDGE:

This appeal involves a voyage charter between Transatlantic Financing Corporation, operator of the SS CHRISTOS, and the United States covering carriage of a full cargo of wheat from a United States Gulf port to a safe port in Iran. The District Court dismissed a libel filed by Transatlantic against the United States for costs attributable to the ship's diversion from the normal sea route caused by the closing of the Suez Canal. We affirm.

On July 26, 1956, the Government of Egypt nationalized the Suez Canal Company and took over operation of the Canal. On October 2, 1956, during the international crisis which resulted from the seizure, the voyage charter in suit was executed between representatives of Transatlantic and the United States. The charter indicated the termini of the voyage but not the route. On October 27, 1956, the SS CHRISTOS sailed from Galveston for Bandar Shapur, Iran, on a course which would have taken her through Gibraltar and the Suez Canal. On October 29, 1956, Israel invaded Egypt. On October 31, 1956, Great Britain and France invaded the Suez Canal Zone. On November 2, 1956, the Egyptian Government obstructed the Suez Canal with sunken vessels and closed it to traffic.

On or about November 7, 1956, Beckmann, representing Transatlantic, contacted Potosky, an employee of the United States Department of Agriculture, who appellant concedes was unauthorized to bind the Government, requesting instructions concerning disposition of the cargo and seeking an agreement for payment of additional compensation for a voyage around the Cape of Good Hope. Potosky advised Beckmann that Transatlantic was expected to perform the charter according to its terms, that he did not believe Transatlantic was entitled to additional compensation for a voyage around the Cape, but that Transatlantic was free to file such a claim. Following this discussion, the CHRISTOS changed course for the Cape of Good Hope and eventually arrived in Bandar Shapur on December 30, 1956.

Transatlantic's claim is based on the following train of argument. The charter was a contract for a voyage from a Gulf port to Iran. Admiralty principles and practices, especially stemming from the doctrine of deviation, require us to imply into the contract the term that the voyage was to be performed by the "usual and customary" route. The usual and customary route from Texas to Iran was, at the time of contract, via Suez, so the contract was for a voyage from Texas to Iran via Suez. When Suez was closed this contract became impossible to perform. Consequently, appellant's argument continues, when Transatlantic delivered the cargo by going around the Cape of Good Hope, in compliance with the Government's demand under claim of right it conferred a benefit upon the United States for which it should be paid in *quantum meruit.*

The doctrine of impossibility of performance has gradually been freed from the earlier fictional and unrealistic strictures of such tests as the "implied term" and the parties' "contemplation." Page, *The Development of the Doctrine of Impossibility of Performance,* 18 Mich.L.Rev. 589, 596 (1920). See generally 6 Corbin, Contracts §§ 1320–1372 (rev. ed. 1962); 6 Williston, Contracts §§ 1931–1979 (rev. ed. 1938). It is now recognized that " 'A thing is impossible in legal contemplation when it is not practicable; and a thing is impracticable when it can only be done at an excessive and unreasonable cost.' " Mineral Park Land Co. v. Howard, 172 Cal. 289, 293, 156 P. 458, 460, L.R.A. 1916F, 1 (1916). *Accord,* Whelan v. Griffith Consumers Company, D.C.Mun.App., 170 A.2d 229 (1961); Restatement, Contracts § 454 (1932); Uniform Commercial Code (U.L.A.) § 2–615, comment 3. The doctrine ultimately represents the ever-shifting line, drawn by courts hopefully responsive to commercial practices and mores, at which the community's interest in having contracts enforced according to their terms is outweighed by the commercial senselessness of requiring performance.[1] When the issue is raised, the court is asked to construct a condition of performance[2] based on the changed circumstances, a process which involves at least three reasonably definable steps. First, a contingency—something unexpected—must have occurred. Second, the risk of the unexpected occurrence must not have been allocated either by agreement or by custom. Finally, occurrence of the contingency must have rendered performance commercially impracticable.[3] Unless the court finds these three requirements satisfied, the plea of impossibility must fail.

The first requirement was met here. It seems reasonable, where no route is mentioned in a contract, to assume the parties expected performance by the usual and customary route at the time of contract.[4] Since the usual and

1. While the impossibility issue rarely arises, as it has here, in a suit to recover the cost of an alternative method of performance, compare Annot., 84 A.L.R.2d 12, 19 (1962), there is nothing necessarily inconsistent in claiming commercial impracticability for the method of performance actually adopted; the concept of impracticability assumes performance was physically possible. Moreover, a rule making nonperformance a condition precedent to recovery would unjustifiably encourage disappointment of expectations.

2. Patterson, *Constructive Conditions in Contracts,* 42 Colum.L.Rev. 903, 943–954 (1942).

3. Compare Uniform Commercial Code § 2–615(a), which provides that, in the absence of an assumption of greater liability, delay or non-delivery by a seller is not a breach if performance as agreed is made

"impracticable" by the occurrence of a "contingency" the non-occurrence of which was a "basic assumption on which the contract was made." To the extent this limits relief to "unforeseen" circumstances, comment 1, see the discussion below, and compare Uniform Commercial Code § 2–614(1). There may be a point beyond which agreement cannot go, Uniform Commercial Code § 2–615, comment 8, presumably the point at which the obligation would be "manifestly unreasonable," § 1–102(3), in bad faith, § 1–203, or unconscionable, § 1–302. For an application of these provisions see Judge Friendly's opinion in United States v. Wegematic Corporation, 2 Cir., 360 F.2d 674 (1966).

4. Uniform Commercial Code § 2–614, comment 1, states: "Under this Article, in the absence of specific agreement, the normal or usual facilities enter into the

customary route from Texas to Iran at the time of contract [5] was through Suez, closure of the Canal made impossible the expected method of performance. But this unexpected development raises rather than resolves the impossibility issue, which turns additionally on whether the risk of the contingency's occurrence had been allocated and, if not, whether performance by alternative routes was rendered impracticable.[6]

Proof that the risk of a contingency's occurrence has been allocated may be expressed in or implied from the agreement. Such proof may also be found in the surrounding circumstances, including custom and usages of the trade. See 6 Corbin, supra, § 1339, at 394–397; 6 Williston, supra, § 1948, at 5457–5458. The contract in this case does not expressly condition performance upon availability of the Suez route. Nor does it specify "via Suez" or, on the other hand, "via Suez or Cape of Good Hope." [7] Nor are

agreement either through the circumstances, usage of trade or prior course of dealing." So long as this sort of assumption does not necessarily result in construction of a condition of performance, it is idle to argue over whether the usual and customary route is an "implied term." The issue of impracticability must eventually be met. One court refused to imply the Suez route as a contract term, but went on to rule the contract had been "frustrated." Carapanayoti & Co. Ltd. v. E. T. Green Ltd., [1959] 1 Q.B. 131. The holding was later rejected by the House of Lords. Tsakiroglou & Co. Ltd. v. Noblee Thorl G.m.b.H., [1960] 2 Q.B. 348.

5. The parties have spent considerable energy in disputing whether the "usual and customary" route by which performance was anticipated is defined as of the time of contract or of performance. If we were automatically to treat the expected route as a condition of performance, this matter would be crucial, and we would be compelled to choose between unacceptable alternatives. If we assume as a constructive condition the usual and customary course always to mean the one in use at the time of contract, any substantial diversion (we assume the diversion would have to be substantial) would nullify the contract even though its effect upon the rights and obligations of the parties is insignificant. Nor would it be desirable, on the other hand, to assume performance is conditioned on the availability of *any* usual and customary route at the time of performance. It may be that very often the availability of a customary route at the time of performance other than the route expected to be used at the time of contract should result in denial of relief under the impossibility theory; certainly

if *no* customary route is available at the time of performance the contract is rendered impossible. But the same customarily used alternative route may be practicable in one set of circumstances and impracticable in another, as where the goods are unable to survive the extra journey. Moreover, the "time of performance" is no special point in time; it is every moment in a performance. Thus the alternative route, in our case around the Cape, may be practicable at some time during performance, for example while the vessel is still in the Atlantic Ocean, and impracticable at another time during performance, for example after the vessel has traversed most of the Mediterranean Sea. Both alternatives, therefore, have their shortcomings, and we avoid choosing between them by refusing automatically to treat the usual and customary route as of any time as a condition of performance.

6. In criticizing the "contemplation" test for impossibility Professor Patterson pointed out:

" 'Contemplation' is appropriate to describe the mental state of philosophers but is scarcely descriptive of the mental state of business men making a bargain. It seems preferable to say that the promisee *expects* performance by [the] means . . . the promisor expects to (or which on the facts known to the promisee it is probable that he will) use. It does not follow as an inference of fact that the promisee expects performance by *only* that means . . . ." Patterson, supra Note 2, at 947.

7. In Glidden Company v. Hellenic Lines, Limited, 2 Cir., 275 F.2d 253 (1960), the charter was for transportation of materials from India to America "via Suez

there provisions in the contract from which we may properly imply that the continued availability of Suez was a condition of performance.[8]   Nor is there anything in custom or trade usage, or in the surrounding circumstances generally, which would support our constructing a condition of performance. The numerous cases requiring performance around the Cape when Suez was closed, see, e.g., Ocean Tramp Tankers Corp. v. V/O Sovfracht (The Eugenia), [1964] 2 Q.B. 226, and cases cited therein, indicate that the Cape route is generally regarded as an alternative means of performance.   So the implied expectation that the route would be via Suez is hardly adequate proof of an allocation to the promisee of the risk of closure.   In some cases, even an express expectation may not amount to a condition of performance.[9]   The

Canal or Cape of Good Hope, or Panama Canal," and the court held performance was not "frustrated."   In his discussion of this case, Professor Corbin states: "Except for the provision for an alternative route, the defendant would have been discharged, for the reason that the parties contemplated an open Suez Canal as a specific condition or means of performance." 6 Corbin, supra, § 1339, at 399 n. 57.   Appellant claims this supports its argument, since the Suez route was contemplated as usual and customary.   But there is obviously a difference, in deciding whether a contract allocates the risk of a contingency's occurrence, between a contract specifying no route and a contract specifying Suez.   We think that when Professor Corbin said, "Except for the provision for an alternative route," he was referring, not to the entire *provision* — "via Suez Canal or Cape of Good Hope" etc.—but to the fact that *an alternative route* had been provided for.   Moreover, in determining what Corbin meant when he said "the parties contemplated an open Suez Canal as a specific condition or means of performance," consideration must be given to the fact, recited by Corbin, that in *Glidden* the parties were specifically aware when the contract was made the Canal might be closed, and the promisee had refused to include a clause excusing performance in the event of closure.   Corbin's statement, therefore, is most accurately read as referring to cases in which a route is specified after negotiations reflecting the parties' awareness that the usual and customary route might become unavailable.   Compare Held v. Goldsmith, 153 La. 598, 96 So. 272 (1919).

8.   The charter provides that the vessel is "in every way fitted for *the voyage*" (emphasis added), and the "P. & I. Bunker Deviation Clause" refers to "the contract voyage" and the "direct and/or customary route."   Appellant argues that these provisions require implication of a voyage by the direct and customary route.   Actually they prove only what we are willing to accept—that the parties expected the usual and customary route would be used. The provisions in no way condition performance upon nonoccurrence of this contingency.

There are two clauses which allegedly demonstrate that time is of importance in this contract.   One clause computes the remuneration "in steaming time" for diversions to other countries ordered by the charterer in emergencies.   This proves only that the United States wished to reserve power to send the goods to another country.   It does not imply in any way that there was a rush about the matter. The other clause concerns demurrage and dispatch.   The charterer agreed to pay Transatlantic demurrage of $1,200 per day for all time in excess of the period agreed upon for loading and unloading, and Transatlantic was to pay despatch of $600 per day for any saving in time.   Of course this provision shows the parties were concerned about time, see Gilmore & Black, *The Law of Admiralty* § 4–8 (1957), but the fact that they arranged so minutely the consequences of any delay or speedup of loading and unloading operates against the argument that they were similarly allocating the risk of delay or speed-up of the voyage.

9.   Uniform Commercial Code § 2–614(1) provides: "Where without fault of either party . . . the *agreed* manner of delivery . . . becomes commercially impracticable but a commercially reasonable substitute is available, such substitute performance must be tendered and accepted." (Emphasis added.)   Compare Mr. Justice Holmes' observation: "You can give any conclusion a logical form.   You

doctrine of deviation supports our assumption that parties normally expect performance by the usual and customary route, but it adds nothing beyond this that is probative of an allocation of the risk.[10]

If anything, the circumstances surrounding this contract indicate that the risk of the Canal's closure may be deemed to have been allocated to Transatlantic. We know or may safely assume that the parties were aware, as were most commercial men with interests affected by the Suez situation, see The Eugenia, supra, that the Canal might become a dangerous area. No doubt the tension affected freight rates, and it is arguable that the risk of closure became part of the dickered terms. Uniform Commercial Code § 2–615, comment 8. We do not deem the risk of closure so allocated, however. Foreseeability or even recognition of a risk does not necessarily prove its allocation.[11] Compare Uniform Commercial Code § 2–615, Comment 1; Restatement, Contracts § 457 (1932). Parties to a contract are not always able to provide for all the possibilities of which they are aware, sometimes because they cannot agree, often simply because they are too busy. Moreover, that some abnormal risk was contemplated is probative but does not necessarily establish an allocation of the risk of the contingency which actually occurs. In this case, for example, nationalization by Egypt of the Canal Corporation and formation of the Suez Users Group did not necessarily indicate that the Canal would be blocked even if a confrontation resulted.[12] The surrounding

always can imply a condition in a contract. But why do you imply it? It is because of some belief as to the practice of the community or of a class, or because of some opinion as to policy . . . ." Holmes, *The Path of the Law*, 10 Harv.L.Rev. 457, 466 (1897).

10. The deviation doctrine, drawn principally from admiralty insurance practice, implies into all relevant commercial instruments naming the termini of voyages the usual and customary route between those points. 1 Arnould, *Marine Insurance and Average*, § 376, at 522 (10th ed. 1921). Insurance is cancelled when a ship unreasonably "deviates" from this course, for example by extending a voyage or by putting in at an irregular port, and the shipowner forfeits the protection of clauses of exception which might otherwise have protected him from his common law insurer's liability to cargo. See Gilmore & Black, supra Note 8, § 2–6, at 59–60. This practice, properly qualified, see *id.* § 3–41, makes good sense, since insurance rates are computed on the basis of the implied course, and deviations in the course increasing the anticipated risk make the insurer's calculations meaningless. Arnould, supra, § 14, at 26. Thus the route, so far as insurance contracts are concerned, is crucial, whether express

or implied. But even here, the implied term is not inflexible. Reasonable deviations do not result in loss of insurance, at least so long as established practice is followed. See Carriage of Goods by Sea Act § 4(4), 49 Stat. 1210, 46 U.S.C. § 1304(4); and discussion of "held covered" clauses in Gilmore & Black, supra, § 3–41, at 161. Some "deviations" are required. E.g., Hirsch Lumber Co. v. Weyerhaeuser Steamship Co., 2 Cir., 233 F.2d 791, cert. denied, 352 U.S. 880, 77 S.Ct. 102, 1 L.Ed.2d 80 (1956). The doctrine's only relevance, therefore, is that it provides additional support for the assumption we willingly make that merchants agreeing to a voyage between two points expect that the usual and customary route between those points will be used. The doctrine provides no evidence of an allocation of the risk of the route's unavailability.

11. See Note, *The Fetish of Impossibility in the Law of Contracts*, 53 Colum. L.Rev. 94, 98 n. 23 (1953), suggesting that foreseeability is properly used "as a *factor* probative of assumption of the risk of impossibility." (Emphasis added.)

12. Sources cited in the briefs indicate formation of the Suez Canal Users Association on October 1, 1956, was viewed in circumstances do indicate, however, a willingness by Transatlantic to assume abnormal risks, and this fact should legitimately cause us to judge the impracticability of performance by an alternative route in stricter terms than we would were the contingency unforeseen.

We turn then to the question whether occurrence of the contingency rendered performance commercially impracticable under the circumstances of this case. The goods shipped were not subject to harm from the longer, less temperate Southern route. The vessel and crew were fit to proceed around the Cape.[13] Transatlantic was no less able than the United States to purchase insurance to cover the contingency's occurrence. If anything, it is more reasonable to expect owner-operators of vessels to insure against the hazards of war. They are in the best position to calculate the cost of performance by alternative routes (and therefore to estimate the amount of insurance required), and are undoubtedly sensitive to international troubles which uniquely affect the demand for and cost of their services. The only factor operating here in appellant's favor is the added expense, allegedly $43,972.00 above and beyond the contract price of $305,842.92, of extending a 10,000 mile voyage by approximately 3,000 miles. While it may be an overstatement to say that increased cost and difficulty of performance never constitute impracticability, to justify relief there must be more of a variation between expected cost and the cost of performing by an available alternative than is present in this case,[14]

some quarters as an implied threat of force. See N. Y. Times, Oct. 2, 1956, p. 1, col. 1, noting, on the day the charter in this case was executed, that "Britain has declared her freedom to use force as a last resort if peaceful methods fail to achieve a satisfactory settlement." Secretary of State Dulles was able, however, to view the statement as evidence of the canal users' "dedication to a just and peaceful solution." *The Suez Problem* 369–370 (Department of State Pub. 1956).

13. The issue of impracticability should no doubt be "an objective determination of whether the promise can reasonably be performed rather than a subjective inquiry into the promisor's capability of performing as agreed." Symposium, *The Uniform Commercial Code and Contract Law: Some Selected Problems*, 105 U.Pa.L.Rev. 836, 880, 887 (1957). Dealers should not be excused because of less than normal capabilities. But if both parties are aware of a dealer's limited capabilities, no objective determination would be complete without taking into account this fact.

14. Two leading English cases support this conclusion. The Eugenia, supra, involved a time charter for a trip from Genoa to India via the Black Sea. The charterers were held in breach of the charter's war clause by entering the Suez Canal after the outbreak of hostilities, but sought to avoid paying for the time the vessel was trapped in the Canal by arguing that, even if they had not entered the Canal, it would have been blocked and the vessel would have had to go around the Cape to India, a trip which "frustrated" the contract because it constituted an entirely different venture from the one originally contemplated. The lower court agreed, but the House of Lords (see Lord Denning's admirable treatment, [1964] 2 Q.B. at 233), "swallowing" the difficulty of applying the frustration doctrine to hypothetical facts, reversed, holding that the contract had to be performed. Especially relevant is the fact that the case expressly overruled Societe Franco Tunisienne D'Armement v. Sidermar S. P. A. (The Massalia), [1961] 2 Q.B. 278, where a voyage charter was deemed frustrated because the Cape route was "highly circuitous" and cost 195s. per long ton to ship iron ore, rather than 134s. via Suez, a difference well in excess of the difference in this case.

In Tsakiroglou & Co. Ltd. v. Noblee Thorl G.m.b.H., supra Note 4, the difference to the seller under a C.I.F. contract in freight costs caused by the Canal's closure was £15 per ton instead of where the promisor can legitimately be presumed to have accepted some degree of abnormal risk, and where impracticability is urged on the basis of added expense alone.[15]

We conclude, therefore, as have most other courts considering related issues arising out of the Suez closure,[16] that performance of this contract was not rendered legally impossible. Even if we agreed with appellant, its theory of relief seems untenable. When performance of a contract is deemed impossible it is a nullity. In the case of a charter party involving carriage of goods, the carrier may return to an appropriate port and unload its cargo, The Malcolm Baxter, Jr., 277 U.S. 323, 48 S.Ct. 516, 72 L.Ed. 901 (1928), subject of course to required steps to minimize damages. If the performance rendered has value, recovery in *quantum meruit* for the entire performance is proper. But here Transatlantic has collected its contract price, and now seeks *quantum meruit* relief for the additional expense of the trip around the Cape. If the contract is a nullity, Transatlantic's theory of relief should have been *quantum meruit* for the entire trip, rather than only for the extra expense. Transatlantic attempts to take its profit on the contract, and then force the Government to absorb the cost of the additional voyage.[17] When impractica-

£ 7.10s. per ton—precisely twice the cost. The House of Lords found no frustration.

15. See Uniform Commercial Code § 2-615, comment 4: "Increased cost alone does not excuse performance unless the rise in cost is due to some unforeseen contingency which alters the essential nature of the performance." See also 6 Corbin, *supra*, § 1333; 6 Williston, *supra*, § 1952, at 5468.

16. Appellant seeks to distinguish the English cases supporting our view. The Eugenia, supra, appellant argues, involved a time charter. True, but it overruled The Massalia, supra Note 14, which involved a voyage charter. Indeed, when the time charter is for a voyage the difference is only verbal. See Carver, *Carriage of Goods by Sea* 256–257 (10th ed. 1957). More convincing is the argument that *Tsakiroglou & Co. Ltd.*, supra Note 4, involved a contract for the sale of goods, where the seller agreed to a C.I.F. clause requiring him to ship the goods to the buyer. There is a significant difference between a C.I.F. contract and voyage or time charters. The effect of delay in the former due to longer sea voyages is minimized, since the seller can raise money on the goods he has shipped almost at once, and the buyer, once he takes up the documents, can deal with the goods by transferring the documents before the goods arrive. See *Tsakiroglou & Co. Ltd.*, supra Note 4, [1960] 2 Q.B. at 361. But this difference is not so material that impossibility in C.I.F. contracts is unrelated to impossibility in charter parties. It would raise serious questions for a court to require sellers under C.I.F. contracts to perform in circumstances under which the sellers could be refused performance by carriers with whom they have entered into charter parties for affreightment. See The Eugenia, supra, [1964] 2 Q.B. at 241. Where the time of the voyage is unimportant, a charter party should be treated the same as a C.I.F. contract in determining impossibility of performance.

These cases certainly are not distinguishable, as appellant suggests, on the ground that they refer to "frustration" rather than to "impossibility." The English regard "frustration" as substantially identical with "impossibility." 6 Corbin, supra, § 1322, at 327 n. 9.

17. The argument that the Uniform Commercial Code requires the buyer to pay the additional cost of performance by a commercially reasonable substitute was advanced and rejected in Symposium, supra Note 13, 105 U.Pa.L.Rev. at 884 n. 205. In Dillon v. United States, 156 F.Supp. 719, 140 Ct.Cl. 508 (1957), relief was afforded for some of the cost of delivering hay from a commercially unreasonable distance, but the suit was one in which the plaintiff had suffered losses far in excess of the relief given.

bility without fault occurs, the law seeks an equitable solution, see 6 Corbin, supra, § 1321, and *quantum meruit* is one of its potent devices to achieve this end. There is no interest in casting the entire burden of commercial disaster on one party in order to preserve the other's profit. Apparently the contract price in this case was advantageous enough to deter appellant from taking a stance on damages consistent with its theory of liability. In any event, there is no basis for relief.

Affirmed.

Case Brief

1. Parties/their relationship/how matter reached this court: Transatlantic Financing Corporation, Plaintiff/Appellant/Charter Operator v. United States, Defendant/Appellee/Charterer. Appeal from dismissal of a libel action [a] by the United States District Court for the District of Columbia. 363 F.2d 312, (1966).

2. *Legal theories:*

   Breach of contract, under:

   (1) Doctrine of deviation: The usual and customary route between points is implied into commercial contracts in which the termini of the voyage are named.

   (2) Doctrine of impossibility: A thing is legally impossible when it can be done only at an excessive and unreasonable cost.

   (3) Quantum meruit: When contract becomes a nullity, recovery "for the amount deserved" is the proper remedy.

3. Facts: In July 1956, Egypt nationalized and took over the operation of the Suez Canal. In October 1956, a contract was executed between Transatlantic and the United States for a voyage from the United States to Iran. No route was stipulated in the contract, although the usual route for such a voyage was through the Suez Canal. When Egypt closed the Suez Canal to traffic in November 1956, Transatlantic delivered the cargo by travelling around the Cape of Good Hope.

4. Relief requested: Additional compensation of $43,972.00 above the contract price, representing the added cost to the appellant over its expected cost of performing its contract by its usual route.

5. Issues:

   (1) Does the doctrine of deviation imply into the contract a voyage by the usual and customary route?

   (2) Under the doctrine of impossibility, did the closing of the Suez Canal render performance by the charter-operator legally impossible?

   (3) If so, did the charter-operator confer an in *quantum meruit* benefit upon the charterer by delivering the cargo by an alternate, more costly route?

   a. Libel: an initial pleading in a suit in admiralty, equivalent to a petition.

6. Holding and Disposition:

   (1) No. The doctrine of deviation does not imply into the contract a voyage by the usual and customary route.

   (2) No. The doctrine of impossibility does not apply if the charter-operator is able to deliver the cargo by an alternate, more costly route.

   (3) No. In *quantum meruit* benefit does not apply when the charter-operator has collected its contract price, and seeks only additional compensation.

7. Reasoning:

   1. The doctrine of deviation is inapplicable, for the Suez Route was not a condition of the contract.

   2. For a contract to be rendered legally impossible, three conditions must prevail:

      (1) a contingency must occur;

      (2) the risk of the contingency must not have been allocated by agreement or by custom;

      (3) the occurrence of the contingency must render performance commercially impracticable.

      Here, only the first requirement is met. Regarding (2), no express condition of performance via the Suez Canal is a term of this contract, nor is there a constructive condition of performance either in custom or trade usage or in the surrounding circumstances generally. Nor is condition (3) present, for the crew was not subject to harm from the longer route, the vessel and crew were fit to proceed around the Cape, and appellant could have purchased insurance as easily as appellee to protect against the unexpected occurrence.

8. Legal rule:

   For legal impracticability to be based upon added cost alone, there must be significant variation between the expected and the actual cost, with no presumption that appellant accepted and could have insured against contingency.

9. Dicta:

   (1) Even an expressed expectation that the route would be via the Suez Canal may not amount to a condition of performance. (U.C.C. § 2–614(1) cited in footnote.)

   (2) If anything, owner-operators of vessels can be more reasonably expected to insure against the hazards than those who hire their services since owner-operators are in the best position to calculate the cost of performance by alternate routes and to estimate the cost of the insurance required.

AMERICAN TRADING AND PRODUCTION CORP. v. SHELL INTERNATIONAL MARINE LTD.

United States Court of Appeals, Second Circuit, 1972.
453 F.2d 939.

MULLIGAN, CIRCUIT JUDGE:

This is an appeal by American Trading and Production Corporation (hereinafter "owner") from a judgment entered on July 29th, 1971, in the United States District Court for the Southern District of New York, dismissing its claim against Shell International Marine Ltd. (hereinafter "charterer") for additional compensation in the sum of $131,978.44 for the transportation of cargo from Texas to India via the Cape of Good Hope as a result of the closing of the Suez Canal in June, 1967. The charterer had asserted a counterclaim which was withdrawn and is not in issue. The action was tried on stipulated facts and without a jury before Hon. Harold R. Tyler, Jr. who dismissed the claim on the merits in an opinion dated July 22, 1971.

We affirm.

The owner is a Maryland corporation doing business in New York and the charterer is a United Kingdom corporation. On March 23, 1967 the parties entered into a contract of voyage charter in New York City which provided that the charterer would hire the owner's tank vessel, WASHINGTON TRADER, for a voyage with a full cargo of lube oil from Beaumont/Smiths Bluff, Texas to Bombay, India. The charter party provided that the freight rate would be in accordance with the then prevailing American Tanker Rate Schedule (ATRS), $14.25 per long ton of cargo, plus seventy-five percent (75%), and in addition there was a charge of $.85 per long ton for passage through the Suez Canal. On May 15, 1967 the WASHINGTON TRADER departed from Beaumont with a cargo of 16,183.32 long tons of lube oil. The charterer paid the freight at the invoiced sum of $417,327.36 on May 26, 1967. On May 29th, 1967 the owner advised the WASHINGTON TRADER by radio to take additional bunkers at Ceuta due to possible diversion because of the Suez Canal crisis. The vessel arrived at Ceuta, Spanish Morocco on May 30, bunkered and sailed on May 31st, 1967. On June 5th the owner cabled the ship's master advising him of various reports of trouble in the Canal and suggested delay in entering it pending clarification. On that very day, the Suez Canal was closed due to the state of war which had developed in the Middle East. The owner then communicated with the charterer on June 5th through the broker who had negotiated the charter party, requesting approval for the diversion of the WASHINGTON TRADER which then had proceeded to a point about 84 miles northwest of Port Said, the entrance to the Canal. On June 6th the charterer responded that under the circumstances it was "for owner to decide whether to continue to wait or make the alternative passage via the Cape since Charter Party Obliges them to deliver cargo without qualification." In response the owner replied on the same day that in view of the closing of the Suez, the WASHINGTON TRADER would proceed to

Bombay via the Cape of Good Hope and "[w]e [are] reserving all rights for extra compensation." The vessel proceeded westward, back through the Straits of Gibraltar and around the Cape and eventually arrived in Bombay on July 15th (some 30 days later than initially expected), traveling a total of 18,055 miles instead of the 9,709 miles which it would have sailed had the Canal been open. The owner billed $131,978.44 as extra compensation which the charterer has refused to pay.

On appeal and below the owner argues that transit of the Suez Canal was the agreed specific means of performance of the voyage charter and that the supervening destruction of this means rendered the contract legally impossible to perform and therefore discharged the owner's unperformed obligation (Restatement of Contracts § 460 (1932)). Consequently, when the WASHINGTON TRADER eventually delivered the oil after journeying around the Cape of Good Hope, a benefit was conferred upon the charterer for which it should respond in *quantum meruit*. The validity of this proposition depends upon a finding that the parties contemplated or agreed that the Suez passage was to be the exclusive method of performance, and indeed it was so argued on appeal. We cannot construe the agreement in such a fashion. The parties contracted for the shipment of the cargo from Texas to India at an agreed rate and the charter party makes absolutely no reference to any fixed route. It is urged that the Suez passage was a condition of performance because the ATRS rate was based on a Suez Canal passage, the invoice contained a specific Suez Canal toll charge and the vessel actually did proceed to a point 84 miles northwest of Port Said. In our view all that this establishes is that both parties contemplated that the Canal would be the probable route. It was the cheapest and shortest, and therefore it was in the interest of both that it be utilized. However, this is not at all equivalent to an agreement that it be the exclusive method of performance. The charter party does not so provide and it seems to have been well understood in the shipping industry that the Cape route is an acceptable alternative in voyages of this character.

The District of Columbia Circuit decided a closely analogous case, Transatlantic Financing Corp. v. United States, 124 U.S.App.D.C. 183, 363 F.2d 312 (1966). There the plaintiff had entered into a voyage charter with defendant in which it agreed to transport a full cargo of wheat on the CHRISTOS from a United States port to Iran. The parties clearly contemplated a Suez passage, but on November 2, 1956, the vessel reduced speed when war blocked the Suez Canal. The vessel changed its course in the Atlantic and eventually delivered its cargo in Iran after proceeding by way of the Cape of Good Hope. In an exhaustive opinion Judge Skelly Wright reviewed the English cases which had considered the same problem and concluded that "the Cape route is generally regarded as an alternative means of performance. So the implied expectation that the route would be via Suez is hardly adequate proof of an allocation to the promisee of the risk of closure. In some cases, even an express expectation may not amount to a condition of performance." Transatlantic Financing Corp. v. United States, supra, 363 F.2d at 317 (footnote omitted).

Appellant argues that *Transatlantic* is distinguishable since there was an agreed upon flat rate in that case unlike the instant case where the rate was based on Suez passage. This does not distinguish the case in our view. It is stipulated by the parties here that the only ATRS rate published at the time of the agreement from Beaumont to Bombay was the one utilized as a basis for the negotiated rate ultimately agreed upon. This rate was escalated by 75% to reflect whatever existing market conditions the parties contemplated. These conditions are not stipulated. Had a Cape route rate been requested, which was not the case, it is agreed that the point from which the parties would have bargained would be $17.35 per long ton of cargo as against $14.25 per long ton.

Actually, in *Transatlantic* it was argued that certain provisions in the P. & I. Bunker Deviation Clause referring to the direct and/or customary route required, by implication, a voyage through the Suez Canal. The court responded "[a]ctually they prove only what we are willing to accept—that the parties expected the usual and customary route would be used. The provisions in no way condition performance upon non-occurrence of this contingency." Transatlantic Financing Corp. v. United States, supra, 363 F.2d at 317 n. 8. We hold that all that the ATRS rate establishes is that the parties obviously expected a Suez passage but there is no indication at all in the instrument or *dehors* that it was a condition of performance.

This leaves us with the question as to whether the owner was excused from performance on the theory of commercial impracticability (Restatement of Contracts § 454 (1932)). Even though the owner is not excused because of strict impossibility, it is urged that American law recognizes that performance is rendered impossible if it can only be accomplished with extreme and unreasonable difficulty, expense, injury or loss.[1] There is no extreme or unreasonable difficulty apparent here. The alternate route taken was well recognized, and there is no claim that the vessel or the crew or the nature of the cargo made the route actually taken unreasonably difficult, dangerous or onerous. The owner's case here essentially rests upon the element of the additional expense involved—$131,978.44. This represents an increase of less than one third over the agreed upon $417,327.36. We find that this increase in expense is not sufficient to constitute commercial impracticability under either American or English authority.

Mere increase in cost alone is not a sufficient excuse for non-performance (Restatement of Contracts § 467 (1932)). It must be an "extreme and unreasonable"[2] expense (Restatement of Contracts § 454 (1932)).[3] While in

---

1. This is the formula utilized in the Restatement of Contracts § 454 (1932).

2. The Restatement gives some examples of what is "extreme and unreasonable"—Restatement of Contracts § 460, Illus. 2 (tenfold increase in costs) and Illus. 3 (costs multiplied fifty times) (1932); compare § 467, Illus. 3. See generally G.

Grismore, Principles of the Law of Contracts § 179 (rev. ed. J. E. Murray 1965).

3. Both parties take solace in the Uniform Commercial Code which in comment 4 to Section 2–615 states that the rise in cost must "alter the essential nature of the performance . . . ." This is clearly not the case here. The owner relies on a

the *Transatlantic* case supra, the increased cost amounted to an increase of about 14% over the contract price, the court did cite with approval [4] the two leading English cases Ocean Tramp Tankers Corp. v. V/O Sovfracht (The Eugenia), [1964] 2 Q.B. 226, 233 (C.A.1963) (which expressly overruled Société Franco Tunisienne D'Armement v. Sidermar S.P.A. (The Messalia), [1961] 2 Q.B. 278 (1960), where the court had found frustration because the Cape route was highly circuitous and involved an increase in cost of approximately 50%), and Tsakiroglou & Co. Lt. v. Noblee Thorl G.m.b.H., [1960] 2 Q.B. 318, 348, aff'd, [1962] A.C., 93 (1961) where the House of Lords found no frustration though the freight costs were exactly doubled due to the Canal closure.[5]

Appellant further seeks to distinguish *Transatlantic* because in that case the change in course was in the mid-Atlantic and added some 300 miles to the voyage while in this case the WASHINGTON TRADER had traversed most of the Mediterranean and thus had added some 9000 miles to the contemplated voyage. It should be noted that although both the time and the length of the altered passage here exceeded those in the *Transatlantic,* the additional compensation sought here is just under one third of the contract price. Aside from this however, it is a fact that the master of the WASHINGTON TRADER was alerted by radio on May 29th, 1967 of a "possible diversion because of Suez Canal crisis," but nevertheless two days later he had left Ceuta (opposite Gibraltar) and proceeded across the Mediterranean. While we may not speculate about the foreseeability of a Suez crisis at the time the contract was entered, there does not seem to be any question but that the master here had been actually put on notice before traversing the Mediterranean that diversion was possible. Had the WASHINGTON TRADER then changed course, the time and cost of the Mediterranean trip could reasonably have been avoided, thereby reducing the amount now claimed. (Restatement of Contracts § 336, Comment *d* to subsection (1) (1932)).

In a case closely in point, Palmco Shipping Inc. v. Continental Ore Corp. (*The "Captain George K"*), [1970] 2 Lloyd's L.Rep. 21 (Q.B.1969), *The*

---

further sentence in the comment which refers to a severe shortage of raw materials or of supplies due to "war, embargo, local crop failure, unforeseen shutdown of major sources of supply or the like, which either causes a marked increase in cost . . . ." Since this is not a case involving the sale of goods but transportation of a cargo where there was an alternative which was a commercially reasonable substitute (see Uniform Commercial Code § 2–614(1)) the owner's reliance is misplaced.

4. Transatlantic Financing Corp. v. United States, supra, 363 F.2d at 319 n. 14.

5. While these are English cases and refer to the doctrine of "frustration" rath-

er than "impossibility" as Judge Skelly Wright pointed out in *Transatlantic*, supra, 363 F.2d at 320 n. 16 the two are considered substantially identical, 6 A. Corbin, Contracts § 1322, at 327 n. 9 (rev. ed. 1962). While *Tsakiroglou* and *The Eugenia* are criticized in Schegal, Of Nuts, and Ships and Sealing Wax, Suez, and Frustrating Things—The Doctrine of Impossibility of Performance, 23 Rutgers L.Rev. 419, 448 (1969), apparently on the theory that the charterer is a better loss bearer, the overruled *Sidermar* case was previously condemned in Berman, Excuse for Nonperformance in the Light of Contract Practices in International Trade, 63 Colum.L.Rev. 1413, 1424–27 (1963).

Eugenia, supra, was followed, and no frustration was found where the vessel had sailed to a point three miles northwest of Port Said only to find the Canal blocked. The vessel then sailed back through the Mediterranean and around the Cape of Good Hope to its point of destination, Kandla. The distances involved, 9700 miles via the initially contemplated Canal route and 18,400 miles actually covered by way of the Cape of Good Hope, coincide almost exactly with those in this case. Moreover, in *The "Captain George K"* there was no indication that the master had at anytime after entering the Mediterranean been advised of the possibility of the Canal's closure.

Finally, owners urge that the language of the "Liberties Clause," Para. 28(a) of Part II of the charter party [6] provides explicit authority for extra compensation in the circumstances of this case. We do not so interpret the clause. We construe it to apply only where the master, by reason of dangerous conditions, deposits the cargo at some port or haven other than the designated place of discharge. Here the cargo did reach the designated port albeit by another route, and hence the clause is not applicable. No intermediate or other disposition of the oil was appropriate under the circumstances.

Appellant relies on C. H. Leavell & Co. v. Hellenic Lines, Ltd., 13 F.M.C., 76, 1969 A.M.C. 2177 (1969) for a contrary conclusion. That case involved a determination as to whether surcharges to compensate for extra expenses incurred when the Suez Canal was closed after the commencement of a voyage, were available to a carrier. The Federal Maritime Commission

---

6. "28. Liberty Clauses. (a) In any situation whatsoever and wheresoever occurring and whether existing or anticipated before commencement of or during the voyage, which in the judgment of the Owner or Master is likely to give rise to risk of capture, seizure, detention, damage, delay or disadvantage to or loss of the Vessel or any part of her cargo, or to make it unsafe, imprudent, or unlawful for any reason to commence or proceed on or continue the voyage or to enter or discharge the cargo at the port of discharge, or to give rise to delay or difficulty in arriving, discharging at or leaving the port of discharge or the usual place of discharge in such port, the Owner may before loading or before the commencement of the voyage, require the shipper or other person entitled thereto to take delivery of the Cargo at port of shipment and upon their failure to do so, may warehouse the cargo at the risk and expense of the cargo; or the owner or Master, whether or not proceeding toward or entering or attempting to enter the port of discharge or reaching or attempting to reach the usual place of discharge therein or attempting to discharge the cargo there, may discharge the cargo into depot, lazaretto, craft or other place; or the Vessel may proceed or return, directly or indirectly, to or stop at any such port or place whatsoever as the Master or the Owner may consider safe or advisable under the circumstances, and discharge the cargo, or any part thereof, at any such port or place; or the Owner or the Master may retain the cargo on board until the return trip or until such time as the Owner or the Master thinks advisable and discharge the cargo at any place whatsoever as herein provided or the Owner or the Master may discharge and forward the cargo by any means at the risk and expense of the cargo. The Owner may, when practicable, have the Vessel call and discharge the cargo at another or substitute port declared or requested by the Charterer. The Owner or the Master is not required to give notice of discharge of the cargo, or the forwarding thereof as herein provided. When the cargo is discharged from the Vessel, as herein provided, it shall be at its own risk and expense; such discharge shall constitute complete delivery and performance under this contract and the Owner shall be freed from any further responsibility. For any service rendered to the cargo as herein provided the Owner shall be entitled to a reasonable extra compensation."

authorized the assessment since the applicable tariffs were on file as provided by section 18(b) of the Shipping Act (46 U.S.C. § 817(b)) and also on the basis of Clause 5 of the bill of lading which is comparable to the Liberties Clause in issue here, except for the language which authorized the carrier to "proceed by any route . . . ." (*Leavell,* supra, 13 F.M.C. at 81, 1969 A.M.C. at 2182). This is the very language relied upon by the Commission in finding the surcharge appropriate (*Leavell,* supra, 13 F.M.C. at 89, 1969 A.M.C. at 2191) where the carrier proceeded to the initially designated port of destination via the Cape of Good Hope. Utilization of an alternate route contemplates berthing at the contracted port of destination. There is no such language in the clause at issue. Its absence fortifies the contention that the Liberties Clause was not intended to be applicable to the facts in litigation here.

Matters involving impossibility or impracticability of performance of contract are concededly vexing and difficult. One is even urged on the allocation of such risks to pray for the "wisdom of Solomon." 6 A. Corbin, Contracts § 1333, at 372 (1962). On the basis of all of the facts, the pertinent authority and a further belief in the efficacy of prayer, we affirm.

Case Brief

1. Parties/their relationship/how matter reached this court: American Trading and Production Corporation, Plaintiff/Appellant/Owner v. Shell International Marine LTD., Defendant/Appellee/Charterer. Appeal from a judgment of U. S. District Court for the Southern District of New York, which had dismissed the claim. 453 F.2d 939 (1972).

2. Legal theories:

   Breach of Contract:

   (1) In *quantum meruit* liability for benefit conferred upon charterer by owner's performance by other than agreed-upon methods, since contract was legally impossible to perform.

   (2) Commercial impracticability excused owner from performance because delivery had to be performed by a more expensive alternate route.

   (3) "Liberties Clause" of the contract provides explicit compensation for owner's extra costs due to his longer voyage.

3. Facts: Owner entered into a contract of a voyage charter with Charterer to hire Owner's tank vessel to deliver oil from Texas to India, the freight rate to be in accordance with the prevailing rate schedule, with an additional charge per ton for passage through the Suez Canal. Closing of Suez Canal resulted in decision to travel to India via the Cape of Good Hope, resulting in a voyage of 18,095 miles instead of 9,709 miles. Owner billed $131,978.44 in extra costs.

4. Relief requested: Owner seeks $131,978.44 in extra compensation from Charterer, for additional transportation costs due to Suez Canal closing.

5. Issues:

   (1) Was contract legally impossible to perform, subsequent delivery by owner thus conferring upon charterer a benefit for which it should respond in *quantum meruit?*

   (2) Was owner excused from performance on the theory of commercial impracticability?

   (3) Did the Liberties clause of the charter party provide explicit compensation for the owner's additional costs?

6. Holdings:

   (1) No. No in *quantum benefit* is due since owner's contract was not legally impossible to perform.

   (2) No. Owner was not excused from performance due to commercial impracticability.

   (3) No. The Liberties' Clause of the contract does not apply where cargo reaches the designated port.

   Disposition of case: Lower court dismissal affirmed.

7. Reasoning:

   (1) In order for benefit in *quantum meruit* to be obtained, the parties to the contract must have contemplated or agreed that the Suez passage was to be the exclusive method of performance. No such agreement was a part of the contract here. The Cape route is well understood in the shipping industry to be an acceptable alternative route. (Citation to Transatlantic Financing Corporation, as "closely analogous.")

   (2) The theory of commercial impracticability is premised upon only extreme or unreasonable difficulty, expense, injury or loss resulting from performance. No such circumstances present here, only an increased cost to owner of less than one-third of the contracted price for performance of the contract, an amount insufficient to constitute commercial impracticability.

   (3) The Liberties Clause applies only where the master, because of dangerous conditions, deposits the cargo at a port other than the one designated. Here the cargo did reach the designated port, although by another route. Hence, the clause is inapplicable here.

8. Legal rules:

   (1) For in *quantum meruit* liability to lie, parties must have agreed in contract that the specific method of performance be one which subsequently became legally impossible to perform.

   (2) For commercial impracticability to apply, cost of performance must be extremely and unreasonably in excess of that contemplated, or there must be unreasonable difficulty or injury caused by perform-

ance. Increased cost of one-third above the contracted price is not sufficient to constitute commercial impracticability.

9. Dicta: None

NORTHERN CORPORATION v. CHUGACH ELECTRIC ASSOCIATION

Supreme Court of Alaska, 1974.
518 P.2d 76.

BOOCHEVER, JUSTICE.

We are here presented with issues concerning the alleged impossibility of performing a public contract. Northern Corporation (hereafter referred to as Northern), appellant and cross-appellee, entered into a contract with Chugach Electric Association (hereafter Chugach), appellee and cross-appellant, on August 3, 1966 for the repair and protection of the upstream face of the Cooper Lake Dam. The contract was awarded to Northern on the basis of its low bid in the sum of $63,655.

The work to be performed was described as follows:

It is required that the upstream face of Cooper Lake Dam be regraded and riprap and filter layer stone quarried, hauled and placed on the upstream face and all other appurtenant work accomplished as required, all in accordance with these plans and specification [sic] . There are about 1750 cubic yards of filter material and 3950 cubic yards of riprap to be placed. The Contractor shall furnish all labor, equipment, materials, etc. required for this project.

The contract called for completion of the work within 60 days of notice to proceed, which was given on August 29, 1966.

The major expense in performing the contract was to be the procurement and placing of riprap. The bidders on the contract were advised with respect to quarry areas from which rock could be obtained:

A quarry area, with suitable rock outcropping on the stream bank, has been located approximately 2500 feet downstream from the dam. A haul road will have to be constructed, either down the stream bed or along the left bank. The quarry area is shown on the vicinity map.

. . .

The Contractor may, at his option, select a quarry different from the site shown on the drawings. In this event, the Contractor shall pay the costs of all tests required to verify the suitability of the rock for this project.

Northern first discovered boulders in the stream bed which would be more economical than the designated quarry and received permission to use this source. According to Northern, approximately 20 percent of the contract requirements were fulfilled before Northern exhausted the supply located in the stream bed. Then in the first week of September, Northern moved to the designated quarry site and commenced shooting rock. On September 19,

1966, Northern wrote to Chugach informing them that the rock in the designated quarry was unusable, but was directed in a letter the following day from Chugach's engineering firm to proceed with further blasting and exploration of the designated areas. By September 27, however, Chugach conceded that suitable rock was not available at the designated site and reformed the agreement accordingly.

Alternate quarry sites were found at the opposite end of the lake from the dam. As a result of negotiations, Chugach wrote to Northern on September 27, 1966 authorizing completion of the contract by use of these alternate quarry sites. The authorization provided for amendments to reflect the circumstance that suitable rock was not available in the stream bed for mining, nor in the quarry which had been designated in the original contract documents. Paragraph 3 of the letter of authorization specified:

> Rock will be quarried in suitable sizes and quantities to complete the project and will be stockpiled in or near the quarry, or quarries, mentioned above for transport across Cooper Lake to the dam site when such lake is frozen to a sufficient depth to permit heavy vehicle traffic thereon.

The contract price was increased by $42,000. Subsequently, the contract was formally amended in accordance with the September 27, 1966 authorization. Work commenced in the new quarry in October 1966; and within about 30 days, all of the required rock was drilled and shot.

Although there is some question as to who first suggested it or how it came about, it was the agreement of the parties that the rock from the new quarry site would be transported in winter across the ice of Cooper Lake. In December 1966, Northern cleared a road on the ice to permit deeper freezing of the ice. By the time the ice was thought to be sufficiently thick to begin hauling, however, a water overflow on the ice one to two feet in depth prohibited crossings by the trucks. Northern complained to Chugach of unsafe conditions on the lake ice, but Chugach insisted on performance. In March 1967, one of Northern's Euclid loaders went through the ice and sank, and a small crawler tractor subsequently broke through but was recovered. Neither incident involved loss of life. Despite these occurrences, Chugach and its engineering firm continued to insist on performance, threatening default. On March 27, 1967, Chugach again threatened to consider Northern in default unless they immediately commenced hauling operations. Northern attempted to commence operations but continued to meet with difficulties, finally ceasing operations on March 31, 1967, apparently with the approval of Chugach.

On January 8, 1968, Chugach advised Northern that it would consider Northern in default unless all rock was hauled by April 1, 1968. On January 20, Northern informed Chugach that they were returning to Cooper Lake, and wrote on January 30 that they anticipated favorable conditions to start hauling rock on January 31. The ice conditions were apparently different from those encountered in 1967—there was very little snow cover and no overflow problem. The ice varied from 23½ inches to 30 inches thick, and for several days the temperature had been 30 degrees below zero and clear.

On February 1, 1968, Northern started hauling with half-loaded trucks; but within the first few hours, two trucks with their drivers broke through the ice, resulting in the death of the drivers and loss of the trucks. Northern at this point ceased operations; and on February 16, 1968, informed Chugach that it would make no more attempts to haul rock across the lake. On March 28, 1968, Northern advised Chugach that it considered the contract terminated for impossibility of performance.

Northern commenced legal action against Chugach in September 1968, seeking recovery for costs incurred in attempted completion of the contract less revenues received. The case was tried in superior court without a jury in December 1971. Northern contended that in the original contract there were express and implied warranties that the designated quarry contained sufficient quantities of suitable rock for the job, and that breach of the warranties entitled Northern to damages. In the alternative, Northern argued that the modified contract was impossible of performance, justifying an award to Northern of reasonable costs incurred in attempted performance. Chugach counterclaimed, contending that it overpaid Northern for work performed under the contract, and that it was entitled to liquidated damages for the period between the date of completion specified in the amended contract and the date of its termination by Northern. The superior court discharged the parties from the contract on the ground of impossibility of performance, but denied both parties' claims for damages and attorney's fees. From that decision, Northern appeals and Chugach cross-appeals.

The issues on this appeal may be summarized as follows:

1. Is Northern entitled to damages for breach of alleged express and implied warranties contained in the original contract pertaining to available quantities of rock?

2. In the alternative, was the contract as modified impossible of performance?

3. If the modified contract was impossible of performance, is Northern entitled to reasonable costs incurred in endeavoring to perform it?

4. Is Chugach entitled to liquidated damages for delays in performance of the contract, and to costs and attorney's fees? [1]

Our analysis of the events preceding the lawsuit leads us to the conclusion that the dispositive issues pertain to the question of impossibility of performance. It appears clear to us that the original agreement between Chugach and Northern was superseded as a result of Chugach's letter to Northern, dated September 27, 1966, and the subsequent formal amendment of the contract in accordance therewith. The amendment recognized that the quarries originally specified did not provide a sufficient quantity of riprap. The original contract price of $63,655 was increased by $42,000 to cover the additional costs incurred and to be incurred by Northern in exploration of the quarry originally

---

1. Chugach's contention that it over-paid Northern has apparently been abandoned on appeal.

designated, in securing rock at the redesignated quarries, in hauling the rock to the dam site, in stockpiling it, and in cleaning up the redesignated quarry areas. The amendment was executed by both parties to the contract. Since the amendment provided for the additional costs incurred by Northern as a result of the absence of a suitable rock supply at the quarry originally designated, we need not concern ourselves with whether express or implied warranties were breached with reference to the quantity of rock available at the originally designated quarry.[2] There is no contention here that the amended contract did not designate quarries containing suitable quantities of rock.

IMPOSSIBILITY

The focal question is whether the amended contract was impossible of performance. The September 27, 1966 directive specified that the rock was to be transported "across Cooper Lake to the dam site when such lake is frozen to a sufficient depth to permit heavy vehicle traffic thereon," and the formal amendment specified that the hauling to the dam site would be done during the winter of 1966–67. It is therefore clear that the parties contemplated that the rock would be transported across the frozen lake by truck. Northern's repeated efforts to perform the contract by this method during the winter of 1966–67 and subsequently in February 1968, culminating in the tragic loss of life, abundantly support the trial court's finding that the contract was impossible of performance by this method.

Chugach contends, however, that Northern was nevertheless bound to perform, and that it could have used means other than hauling by truck across the ice to transport the rock. The answer to Chugach's contention is that, as the trial court found, the parties contemplated that the rock would be hauled by truck once the ice froze to a sufficient depth to support the weight of the vehicles. The specification of this particular method of performance presupposed the existence of ice frozen to the requisite depth. Since this expectation of the parties was never fulfilled, and since the provisions relating to the means of performance was clearly material,[3] Northern's duty to perform was discharged by reason of impossibility.[4]

2. See Cooperative Refinery Ass'n v. Consumers Public Power Dist., 190 F.2d 852, 856–857 (8th Cir. 1951); Johnson v. Mosley, 179 F.2d 573, 588 (8th Cir. 1950); In re Swindle, 188 F.Supp. 601, 604 (D.Or. 1960).

3. The initial contract price was $63,655. Performing by the alternative method (barging) would have cost an additional $59,520.

4. Restatement of Contracts § 460 (1932) provides in pertinent part:

Where the existence of a specific thing . . . is, either by the terms of a bargain or in the contemplation of both parties, necessary for the performance of a promise in the bargain, a duty to perform the promise . . . is dis-

charged if the thing . . . subsequently is not in existence in time for seasonable performance. . . .

In accord with this rule is Texas Co. v. Hogarth Shipping Co., 256 U.S. 619, 629–630, 41 S.Ct. 612, 65 L.Ed. 1123, 1130 (1921); Parrish v. Stratton Cripple Creek Min. & Development Co., 116 F.2d 207 (10th Cir. 1940), cert. denied, 312 U.S. 698, 61 S.Ct. 738, 85 L.Ed. 1132 (1941); see especially Kansas, Oklahoma & Gulf Railway Co. v. Grand Lake Grain Co., 434 P.2d 153 (Okl.1967).

Discharge of a party for impossibility of performance abates the severity of the old common law doctrine that not even objective impossibility excused performance; see Annot., 84 A.L.R.2d 12, 22 (1962).

There is an additional reason for our holding that Northern's duty to perform was discharged because of impossibility. It is true that in order for a defendant to prevail under the original common law doctrine of impossibility, he had to show that no one else could have performed the contract.[5] However, this harsh rule has gradually been eroded, and the Restatement of Contracts [6] has departed from the early common law rule by recognizing the principle of "commerical impracticability". Under this doctrine, a party is discharged from his contract obligations, even if it is technically possible to perform them, if the costs of performance would be so disproportionate to that reasonably contemplated by the parties as to make the contract totally impractical in a commercial sense.[7] This principle was explicated in Natus Corp. v. United States,[8] where the Court of Claims, although holding that the defense was not justified on the facts of that case, went on to explain:

> In taking this position, we readily concede that the doctrine of legal impossibility does not demand a showing of actual or literal impossibility. Removed from the strictures of the common law, "impossibility" in its modern context has become a coat of many colors, including among its hues the point argued here—namely, impossibility predicated upon "commercial impracticability." This concept—which finds expression both in case law . . . and in other authorities . . . is grounded upon the assumption that in legal contemplation something is impracticable when it can only be done at an excessive and unreasonable cost. As stated in Transatlantic Financing Corp. v. United States . . .:
>
> > . . . The doctrine ultimately represents the ever-shifting line, drawn by courts hopefully responsive to commercial practices and mores, at which the community's interest in having contracts enforced according to their terms is outweighed by the commercial senselessness of requiring performance . . . [citations omitted].[9]

Sec. 465 of the Restatement also provides that a serious risk to life or health will excuse nonperformance.[10]

---

5. See generally 84 A.L.R.2d at 35–36.

6. Restatement of Contracts § 454 (1932) states:

Definition of Impossibility.

In the Restatement of this Subject impossibility means not only strict impossibility but impracticability because of extreme and unreasonable difficulty, expense, injury or loss involved.

7. For example, one California case applied this result where it was about ten times as expensive to perform as was contemplated by the parties. Mineral Park Land Co. v. Howard, 172 Cal. 289, 156 P. 458 (1916).

8. 371 F.2d 450, 178 Ct.Cl. 1 (1967).

9. *Id.* at 456. See also Transatlantic Financing Corp. v. United States, 124 U.S. App.D.C. 183, 363 F.2d 312 (1966).

10. Restatement of Contracts § 465 states:

When Apprehension of Impossibility Excuses Beginning or Continuing Performance.

(1) Where a promisor apprehends before or during the time for performance of a promise in a bargain that there will be such impossibility of performance as would discharge or suspend a duty under the promise or that performance will seriously jeopardize his own life or health or that of others, he is not liable, unless a contrary intention is manifested or he is guilty of contributing fault, for failing to begin or to continue performance, while such apprehension exists, if the failure to begin or to continue performance is reasonable.

Alaska has adopted the Restatement doctrine whereby commercial impracticability may under certain circumstances justify regarding a contract as impossible to perform. In Merl F. Thomas Sons, Inc. v. State,[11] this court was confronted with an appeal from a grant of summary judgment against a contractor who alleged in defense of nonperformance that the contemplated means of performing a clearing contract was to move equipment across the ice on the Susitna River from Talkeetna to the job site. Due to thin ice, this means of performance was impossible. Despite the state's contention that the equipment could be transported across the ice at Hurricane, some 70 miles to the north, we reversed the grant of summary judgment, holding that the contractor's allegation that all parties contemplated that equipment would be moved across the ice at Talkeetna raised a question of fact material to the defense of impossibility of performance. We quoted with approval Professor Williston's analysis of the concept of impossibility:

> The true distinction is not between difficulty and impossibility. As has been seen, a man may contract to do what is impossible, as well as what is difficult. The important question is whether an unanticipated circumstance, the risk of which should not fairly be thrown upon the promisor, has made performance of the promise vitally different from what was reasonably to be expected (footnote omitted).[12]

In the case before us the detailed opinion of the trial court clearly indicates that the appropriate standard was followed. There is ample evidence to support its findings that "[t]he ice haul method of transporting riprap ultimately selected was within the contemplation of the parties and was part of the basis of the agreement which ultimately resulted in amendment No. 1 in October 1966," and that that method was not commercially feasible within the financial parameters of the contract. We affirm the court's conclusion that the contract was impossible of performance.[13]

DAMAGES

The court below found that the decision to utilize the alternate riprap source and the ice haul method of transporting it "was the joint decision of the parties reached in arm's length bargaining and was mutually agreed." Because adequate evidence supports that finding, the cases appellant cites permitting a contractor to recover under an implied warranty of specifications

(2) In determining whether a promisor's failure to begin or to continue performance is reasonable under the rule stated in Subsection (1), consideration is given to

    (a) the degree of probability, apparent from what he knows or has reason to know, not only of such impossibility but of physical or pecuniary harm or loss to himself or to others if he begins or continues performance, and

    (b) the extent of physical or pecuniary harm or loss to himself or to others likely to be incurred by at-

tempting performance as compared with the amount of harmful consequences likely to be caused to the promisee by non-performance.

11. 396 P.2d 76 (Alaska 1964).

12. Id. at 79, quoting from 6 Williston, Contracts § 1963 at 5511 (rev. ed. 1938).

13. Affirmance of this holding disposes of Chugach's contention that it was entitled to liquidated damages for delay. Only if the contract were held to be possible to perform could a right to damages for delay arise, for otherwise the legal duty to perform would be discharged.

theory are not applicable. Since Chugach did not unilaterally specify the ice haul method, it no more warranted that method than did Northern.

Commencing in February 1967, Northern both orally and by letter began to question the feasibility of the ice haul method. On March 16, it advised of the loss of its Euclid loader, and suggested that an alternate method of hauling the rock be considered and the contract modified. Northern requested authority to demobilize its equipment so as to reduce continuing rental costs. On March 21, 1967, Northern asked to be released from responsibility for loss of life or equipment if an attempt was to be made to haul rock across the lake. On March 22, 1967, it stated:

> We cannot morally require any employee of ours or of our subcontractor's [sic] to operate equipment on the ice any longer this spring. We feel extremely fortunate that we did not lose a life when we lost the L–30 Loader. . . . We are ready to negotiate an alternate method of hauling the rock . . . .

Subsequently, an additional letter was sent, emphasizing in detail the impossibility of hauling rock across the ice.

Despite Northern's verbal and written protestations, Chugach implacably insisted on performance of the contract as agreed upon. Repeated demands by Chugach culminated in a January 1968 letter threatening to declare Northern in default, and to take such further steps against its surety as might be necessary, unless all rock was hauled by April 1. As a result, the final and ultimately fatal, effort was undertaken in February.

It is Northern's contention that if it is not entitled to recover under an implied warranty theory, it should be awarded compensation under the so-called "changes" clause of the contract. Under that clause, Chugach reserved the right to make changes in the contract plans and specifications; but if the cost of the project to Northern was increased as a result of the modification, the contract price would be increased by an amount equal to the reasonable cost thereof.[14]

14. Art. I, sec. 2, of the Chugach-Northern contract specifies:

Changes in Construction. The Owner, acting through the Engineer and with the approval of the Administrator, may from time to time during the progress of the construction of the Project, make such changes, additions to or subtractions from the Plans and Specifications which are part of the Proposal as conditions may warrant; provided, however, that if substantial change in the construction to be done shall require an extension of time, a reasonable extension will be granted if the Bidder shall make a written request therefor to the Owner within ten days after any such change is made. If the cost of the Project to the Bidder to make the change shall be increased or decreased, the contract price shall be amended by an amount equal to the reasonable cost thereof in accordance with a construction contract amendment signed by the Owner and the Bidder and approved by the Administrator, but no claim for additional compensation for any such change or addition will be considered unless the Bidder shall have made a written request therefor to the Owner prior to the commencement of work in connection with such change or addition. The reasonable cost of any increase or decrease in the contract price covered by contract amendment as outlined above, in the absence of other mutual agreement, shall be computed on the basis of the direct cost of materials, f. o. b. the site of the Project, plus the direct cost of labor necessary to

Under comparable clauses in government contracts, contractors have been awarded their additional costs in endeavoring to meet faulty specifications that were impossible to comply with, even when such costs were incurred prior to a negotiated modification. For example, in Hol-Gar Mfg. Corp. v. United States [15] the Government solicited proposals for the manufacture and delivery of electric generator sets in accordance with an elaborate set of specifications drafted by the Air Force Air Research and Development Command. On the basis of Hol-Gar's proposal, a fixed-price contract was negotiated. Upon testing, pre-production samples were found not to comply with the Government specifications. At subsequent meetings, Hol-Gar's representative stated that they did not believe that the engine which they had selected could meet the Government's performance requirements, and that the specifications should be changed to permit a substituted engine. The contract was then amended, relaxing the size and weight limitations in the existing specifications. Hol-Gar submitted a claim for costs incurred in trying to perform within the requirements of the original specifications. It had initially been agreed that if, as a result of testing, changes in the specifications were required, such changes were to be processed in accordance with the "changes" clause of the contract (which was very similar to the "changes" clause of the Chugach contract). The court held:

> Since the necessity for the change was not due to plaintiff's fault, but to faulty specifications, an equitable adjustment requires that plaintiff be paid the increase in its costs over what they would have been had no change been required.

The Armed Services Board of Contract Appeals has recognized the correctness of the allowance of costs incident to an attempt to comply with defective specifications. See, e.g., J. W. Hurst & Son Awnings, Inc., 59–1 BCA ¶ 2095 at 8965 (1959), where the Board stated:

> . . . Where, as here, the change is necessitated by defective specifications and drawings, the equitable adjustment to which a contractor is entitled must, if it is to be equitable, i.e., fair and just, include the costs which it incurred in attempting to perform in accordance with the defective specifications and drawings. Under these circumstances the equitable adjustment may not be limited to costs incurred subsequent to the issuance of the change orders [citations omitted].[16]

In Maxwell Dynamometer Co. v. United States,[17] the Court of Claims relying on *Hol-Gar,* also found that the plaintiff was entitled to recover increased costs

incorporate such materials into the Project (including actual cost of payroll taxes and insurance, not to exceed ten percent of payroll cost of labor), plus fifteen percent of the direct cost of materials and labor. Labor cost shall be limited to the direct costs for workmen and foremen. Costs for Bidder's main office overhead, job office overhead and superintendence shall not be included.

15.   360 F.2d 634, 175 Ct.Cl. 518 (1966).

16.   Id. at 638. The court additionally based its decision on a finding of breach of implied warranty of the specifications. Judge Davis in concurring, however, evaluated the record as indicating that neither party warranted the specifications, a situation analogous to that of Chugach and Northern.

17.   386 F.2d 855, 181 Ct.Cl. 607 (1967).

and expenses which were incurred in attempting to comply with a specification requirement that was impossible to meet.[18]

Closely analogous to the Chugach situation is the decision of the Armed Services Board of Contract Appeals in *Landsverk Electrometer Co.*[19]   A manufacturer of dosimeters entered into a contract, thinking that an electrical leakage requirement could be met; but recognizing that it would be necessary for him to "stretch the state of the art" to comply.   When, after vain attempts, the contractor advised the Government that it could not meet the specification, the Government relaxed the specification.   Although it was held that the contractor was not entitled to extra compensation for the work performed in attempting to meet the specifications before notification to the Government, because the parties had contemplated the necessity of substantial research efforts to meet the required specifications and the contractor had not expended substantially more effort to that end than it was reasonable to anticipate, the Board went on to state:

> There was here no insistence by the Government that the contractor perform, or continue to try to perform, in the face of the contractor's protests that performance was impossible and it should be relieved of its obligation to meet that portion of the specification.   On the contrary, within two hours of the appellant's telling the Government that it had become convinced that it simply was unable to perform to the upgraded specification, the Government relaxed the specification and permitted performance at the old, lower level.   Had the Government, after it had, or should have, become aware that performance could not be achieved, continued to direct further efforts by a contractor, that direction would certainly constitute a compensable change in the contract, the understanding of the parties [sic].[20]

Unlike the Government in the *Landsverk* case, Chugach continued to demand performance, and we hold that its insistence after it was, or should have been, aware that performance could not be accomplished by the ice haul method constituted, in effect, a compensable change in the contract.   Notions of equity and fairness compel this result.   If liability for increased costs under the "changes" clause of Government contracts has been predicated on the defectiveness of Government specifications, of which the Government has no actual knowledge, then surely one must hold Chugach liable here, for it had been informed not once but repeatedly that the contract was impossible of performance by the ice haul method.

If Chugach, on being advised of the unfeasibility of the ice haul method, and of its hazards to life and property, had issued a change order prior to the fatal accident of February 1968 but at some time after it knew or should have known that performance was impossible, Northern would have been entitled to the extra costs incurred by it in seeking to perform by the impossible method after Chugach had, or should have, become aware of this impossibility.   In

18.   See also Bell v. United States, 404 F.2d 975, 186 Ct.Cl. 189 (1968); Jack Heller, Inc., 72–1 BCA ¶ 9341 (ASBCA 1972).

19.   67–2 BCA ¶ 6649 (ASBCA 1967).

20.   Id. at p. 30,823.

fact, Chugach apparently recognized this principle of law, for it had agreed earlier to pay Northern an additional sum for its abortive efforts to obtain rock from the initially-designated quarry. Once alerted to the impossibility of performance by the agreed-upon ice haul method, Chugach's adamant insistence on such performance and its refusal to issue a change order should not be permitted to bar Northern's claim under the "changes" clause. It would indeed be anomalous to hold Chugach liable for such extra costs previously incurred if it belatedly provided for a change order after ascertaining the impossibility of utilizing an ice road, while absolving it from such liability when it continued to insist on an impossible and highly hazardous performance. Despite the fact that no change order was actually issued by Chugach, we hold that it should be held liable for Northern's increased costs incurred after such time as Chugach was reasonably placed on notice that it was not feasible to perform the contract by means of the ice haul method. At that time, it should either have agreed to a termination of the contract or issued a change order providing for some other method of hauling the rock. Those costs incurred by Northern thereafter in its vain attempts to perform the impossible in accordance with Chugach's demands should have been recompensed.

The case is remanded for further proceedings in accordance with this opinion. Upon remand, the court should determine when Chugach knew or should have known of the impossibility of performance by the ice haul method; and if that date is ascertained to be prior to the actual termination of the contract, Northern should be awarded its costs incurred thereafter, the amount to be determined in accordance with the "changes" clause of the contract.[21]

Affirmed in part, reversed in part and remanded.

ERWIN and FITZGERALD, JJ., not participating.

Case Brief

1. Parties/their relationship/how matter reached this court: Northern Corporation, Appellant/Contractor v. Chugach Electric Association, Appellee/Owner. The Superior Court, Third Judicial District, Anchorage, discharged parties from contract on ground of impossibility of performance, but denied both parties' claims for damages and attorney's fees. Contractor appeals and owner cross-appeals.

2. Legal theories relied upon:

   (Appellant) (1) Breach of warranty: Express and implied warranties that the designated quarry contained enough rock for the job; thus breach of warranties entitles appellant to damages.

   (Appellant) (2) (Alternatively) Impossibility of contract: The modified contract was impossible to perform, justifying an award to appellant of reasonable costs incurred in attempted performance.

21. Our decision makes it unnecessary to consider Chugach's contention on its cross-appeal that because it was the pre- vailing party, it was entitled to costs and attorney's fees.

(Appellant) (3) Change of contract: The increase in costs to appellant constitutes a compensable change in contract under the changes clause of the contract.

(Appellee) (1) Breach of contract: Liquidated damages for delays in performance of the contract and for costs and attorney's fees.

3. Facts: Appellant and appellee entered into a contract for the procurement and hauling of rock from a designated area within a quarry, the rock to be transported across a specified lake to a certain dam site when the lake had frozen enough to permit heavy vehicle traffic. When suitable rock was not found at the originally-designated site, the agreement was reformed to permit a new site and the contract price was increased by $42,000. All the required rock was procured and prepared for transporting. Although both parties had agreed that the rock was to be transported across the lake, appellant soon discovered that the ice was too thin to permit this arrangement, appellant losing a loader and a tractor through the ice. Nevertheless, appellee insisted upon performance, threatening, in January 1968, to hold appellant in default of contract unless the rock was transported by April 1, 1968. On February 1, 1968, appellant began hauling rock with half-loaded trucks; nevertheless two trucks and their drivers broke through the ice, resulting in the death of the drivers and the loss of the trucks. Appellant then ceased operations, informing appellee that it would make no more attempts to haul rock and that it considered the contract terminated for impossibility of performance.

4. Relief requested: Recovery by appellant for costs incurred in the attempted completion of the contract, less revenues received. Appellee counter-claimed, contending that it had overpaid appellant for work performed under the contract and thus was entitled to liquidated damages for the period between the date of completion specified in the amended contract and the date of its termination by appellant. (Appellee's claim of overpayment was abandoned on appeal.)

5. Issues:

(1) Is appellant entitled to damages for breach of alleged express and implied warranties contained in the original contract pertaining to available quantities of rock?

(2) (Alternatively) was the contract as modified impossible of performance? [a]

(3) If the modified contract was impossible of performance, is appellant entitled to reasonable costs incurred in attempting to perform it?

(4) Is appellee entitled to liquidated damages for delays in performance of the contract and costs and attorney's fees?

a. Court calls this the "focal issue."

6. Holding:

(1) No. Appellant is not entitled to damages where the contract was formally amended by later letter.

(2) Yes. The contract as modified was impossible to perform when appellant suffered loss of life and property in attempting to perform the contract.

(3) Yes. Because the contract was impossible to perform, appellant is entitled to reasonable costs incurred by attempting to perform it and for attorney's fees.

(4) Previous holdings make it unnecessary to consider this issue.

Disposition of Case: Lower court decision affirmed in part (Issues 1 and 2), reversed in part (Issue 3), and remanded.

7. Reasoning:

(Issue 1) Since the original agreement was superseded by an amendment executed by both parties to the contract and since the amendment provided for additional costs incurred by the appellant, the court need not be concerned with whether warranties were breached with reference to the quantity of rock available at the originally-designated quarry. Appellant does not contend that the amended contract did not designate quarries containing suitable quantities of rock.

(Issue 2) Since the contract specified that the rock be hauled across the ice by truck, and since this method required ice frozen deeply enough to support such passage, and since this unfulfilled provision was material to its performance, appellant's duty to perform was discharged by reason of impossibility. Appellant is also excused under the principle of commercial impracticability, which has superseded the original harsh rule of impossibility. Under the doctrine of commercial impracticability, a party is excused from contract performance if an unanticipated circumstance, the risk of which should not be borne by the promisor, has made performance of the contract vitally different from what could reasonably have been expected.

(Issue 3) Upon remand, the Court should determine when appellee knew or should have known performance was impossible and if that date preceded actual termination of the contract, appellant should be awarded costs incurred thereafter. Notions of equity and fairness entitle appellant to its extra costs incurred in seeking to perform by the required but impossible method after such time as appellee was reasonably placed on notice that it was not feasible to perform the contract by the means required.

(Issue 4) See Holding, above.

8. Legal Rules:

   (1) The doctrine of impossibility has been expanded to include the principle of commercial impracticability.

   (2) A party to a contract is entitled to recover increased costs incurred in attempting to comply with a specific requirement in the contract that is impossible to meet, if such requirement is insisted upon by the other party to the contract.

9. Dicta: None

B. ANALOGIZING

Your case briefs will be useful as the basis for analogizing, the process of reasoning from case to case. Analogizing, pointing out the similarities and differences among cases, is the primary form of legal reasoning.[3] It is of great importance to legal argument because of the doctrine of precedent (*stare decisis*),[4] which rests upon the presumption that justice requires the law to treat persons in similar circumstances similarly. The use of precedent helps prevent court decisions based upon influence, bias, or sentimentalism, and to avoid the whimsical or random application of law. The use of precedent therefore promotes the uniform application of the law to all persons.

Reliance upon precedent also provides legal adjudication consistent in time. It helps assure that the law will be applied today as it was applied yesterday and will be applied tomorrow. Thus precedent provides a guide for conduct, assuring that conduct legal today will not be illegal tomorrow.

You will rely on precedent when you compare your case or fact situation to earlier cases or fact situations. You cannot apply precedent to the facts of your case, however, unless:

   (1) Your case is analogous in significant respects to the case you are comparing it with, and

   (2) the opinion in the earlier case is either binding upon your case or persuasive to it.

Regarding condition (1), a case is considered analogous to a previous case if its key facts [5] and the rule of law to be applied are similar. Conversely, if either the key facts or the applicable rule of law is different, the case can be "distinguished" from the preceding case and the doctrine of precedent will not apply.

With regard to condition (2), analogous previous court decisions may be either binding, persuasive, or not binding upon the court deciding the instant case. Only when the previous court decision is binding is it mandatory for *your* court to follow it. Analogous decisions of superior courts in each judicial

---

3. Analogizing is often used more narrowly to mean "showing similarities" as opposed to "distinguishing." The legal meaning of "analogy"—like its non-legal meaning—is "comparison made possible by similarities."

4. Precedent and *stare decisis* are usually used interchangeably by legal writers. (*Stare decisis* is Latin for "to stand as decided.")

5. For the definition of "key facts" see p. 95.

system are binding upon inferior courts in that system. Analogous decisions of the United States Supreme Court are binding on all other courts. Analogous decisions of the highest state court are binding upon a trial court in the same state. But higher courts in a jurisdiction are not bound by analogous lower court decisions in that jurisdiction, though they may consider those decisions persuasive. And although analogous decisions of a court in one judicial system are generally not binding upon a court in another system, they also may be adopted as persuasive.[6] Dictum is never binding, but may be persuasive when it appears in the opinion of a higher court of the same jurisdiction. Dicta in decisions of the United States Supreme Court are often accorded great weight by lower courts.

After ensuring that key facts of the previous cases are similar to those of the case under consideration and that the legal rule applied in the previous case is either binding or persuasive, you can apply analogy. To do so:

(1) Compare and contrast the key facts of the earlier cases with *your* facts.

(2) If the key facts are similar, extract from the earlier cases the legal principle(s) upon which those cases were decided.

(3) Apply those principles to your case.

(4) Arrive at a conclusion based upon (3).

These three steps may seem mechanical, but the results of analogizing are far from cut-and-dried because the decision of whether facts are similar or different is a subjective one. Only if the facts of your case are "on all fours" can you assume that a court will find your case exactly like the previous one. Hardly ever are facts of one case exactly like those of another; that situation is about as rare as a final examination question containing exactly the facts of a case studied in your casebook! Similarity is a matter of degree: other relationships between cases may be expressed as "applicable," "analogous," "dissimilar," or "inapposite."

Because opinion-forming is a subjective process, courts may variously interpret prior decisions. What an earlier case really *means* can thus be determined only in subsequent court opinions. An illustration of this assertion is the ancient case that established the "insanity defense," which provides that insanity is a total defense to behavior that would otherwise be criminal. More than 400 years ago, the court in *Beverley's Case*[7] held that no felony or murder could be committed without felonious intent and that a person deprived of reason could not possess such intent. Later courts might well have interpreted this rule to require a determination about whether the accused person did or did not have the requisite intent. Instead, later courts asked what degree of incapacity would excuse the accused person from criminal conduct. As a result of that interpretation, today a person is not guilty of a crime he committed with specfic intent to do so if his mental

---

6. The legal doctrines of *res judicata* and "full faith and credit" are exceptions. Statsky and Wernet, *Case Analysis and Fundamentals of Legal Writing* (1977), have a comprehensive treatment of analogization (281–322).

7. 76 Eng.Rep. 1118, 1121 (K.B.).

(See discussion in G. Block, "The Fallacious Presumptions of the Insanity Defense," *A Review of General Semantics*, Vol. 39, No. 3, Fall 1982.)

capacity is judged to preclude his forming general intent.[8]   Had courts interpreted the legal principle in *Beverley's Case* differently, the modern insanity defense would not exist in its present form.

The case of *Laird v. State,* which follows, illustrates the subjective quality of judicial analogizing.   Note how, in the majority opinion, earlier cases are used to justify the decision, while the same cases are cited in the dissent as justification for a different conclusion.   The paragraphs of the majority decision are numbered for easy reference.

LAIRD v. STATE

Supreme Court of Florida, 1977.
342 So.2d 962.

SUNDBERG, JUSTICE.

(**1**) This is an appeal from a judgment entered in the Circuit Court of the Seventeenth Judicial Circuit, in and for Broward County.   We have jurisdiction under Article V, Section 3(b)(1), Florida Constitution.

(**2**) Appellants John Laird and Lorraine Coffey were charged by information with one count of possession of cannabis in excess of five grams and one count of possessing paraphernalia.   After pleading not guilty, appellants filed a motion to dismiss the information on the grounds that Section 893.13(1)(e), Florida Statutes, and related portions of Chapter 893, proscribing possession of marijuana, are unconstitutional as violative of the right to privacy.   Appellants urged that the statutory provision, by including the private, noncommercial possession and/or use of marijuana in a private home, did not bear a substantial relationship to a proper governmental purpose.

(**3**) After denial of their motion to dismiss, appellants moved to withdraw their pleas of not guilty and enter pleas of *nolo contendere* to the possession count, while reserving the right to appeal the denial of the motion to dismiss. Appellant Laird admitted having the marijuana in his apartment on the day in question, and appellant Coffey admitted being present at the apartment.   The trial court accepted appellants' pleas, withheld adjudication, and placed Laird and Coffey on two and one-half years' probation.   The State entered a *nolle prosequi* as to the paraphernalia possession charge.

(**4**) Notice of appeal to the District Court of Appeal, Fourth District, was timely filed, but on appellants' motion, the cause was transferred to this Court by order of the District Court dated February 4, 1976.

(**5**) Appellants see this case—which raises the narrow issue of whether the State can prohibit private possession of marijuana in the home—as a clash between a basic constitutional right to privacy and the State's police power.   It is urged upon us that appellants enjoy the constitutional right to smoke marijuana in the privacy of Laird's domicile.   The reasoning of cases such as Griswold v. Connecticut, 381 U.S. 479, 85 S.Ct. 1678, 14 L.Ed.2d 510 (1965), and Eisenstadt v. Baird, 405 U.S. 438, 92 S.Ct. 1029, 31 L.Ed.2d 349 (1972),

8.   The trial of the attempted assassin of President Reagan illustrates this point.

is said to be applicable to the instant controversy. Appellants argue that a decision of the Supreme Court of Alaska, Ravin v. State, 537 P.2d 494 (Alaska 1975), provides persuasive authority for the position which they advance.

(**6**) For the reasons discussed herein we are unable to accept appellants' contention. We reject the notion that smoking marijuana at home is the type of conduct protected by the constitutional right to privacy and, on this record, affirm the trial court.

(**7**) In *Griswold v. Connecticut,* supra, the United States Supreme Court determined that a Connecticut statute which made the use of contraceptives a criminal offense was invalid as an unconstitutional invasion of the right to privacy of married persons. Mr. Justice Douglas, writing for the majority, found "that specific guarantees in the Bill of Rights have penumbras, formed by emanations from those guarantees that help give them life and substance." 381 U.S. at 484, 85 S.Ct. at 1681. The marital relationship was held to lie "within the zone of privacy created by several fundamental guarantees." Id. at 485, 85 S.Ct. at 1682. Justice Douglas placed heavy emphasis upon the marital relationship of the *Griswold* parties:

> "We deal with a right of privacy older than the Bill of Rights—older than our political parties, older than our school systems. Marriage is a coming together for better or for worse, hopefully enduring, and intimate to the degree of being sacred." Id. at 486, 85 S.Ct. at 1682.

(**8**) *Griswold's* protection of the privacy of the marital relationship was extended to certain intimate aspects of the lives of single persons as well in Eisenstadt v. Baird, supra, and Roe v. Wade, 410 U.S. 113, 93 S.Ct. 705, 35 L.Ed.2d 147 (1973). *Eisenstadt* invalidated a Massachusetts statute which made it a crime to sell, lend, or give away any contraceptive drug, medicine, instrument, or article. The statute permitted physicians to administer or prescribe contraceptive drugs or articles for married persons and allowed pharmacists to fill prescriptions for such items for married persons. The Court determined that the Massachusetts law could be upheld neither as a deterrent to fornication nor as a health measure nor as a prohibition on contraception. The third justification was dismissed on privacy grounds:

> If under *Griswold* the distribution of contraceptives to married persons cannot be prohibited, a ban on distribution to unmarried persons would be equally impermissible. It is true that in *Griswold* the right of privacy in question inhered in the marital relationship. Yet the marital couple is not an independent entity with a mind and heart of its own, but an association of two individuals each with a separate intellectual and emotional makeup. If the right of privacy means anything, it is the right of the *individual,* married or single, to be free from unwarranted governmental intrusion into matters so fundamentally affecting a person as the decision whether to bear or beget a child. . . .. 405 U.S. at 453, 92 S.Ct. at 1038.

(**9**) In *Roe v. Wade,* supra, an unmarried pregnant woman who wished to undergo an abortion sought a declaratory judgment that the Texas criminal abortion statutes, which proscribed all abortions except those procured or attempted by medical advice for the purpose of saving the life of the mother, were unconstitutional. The Supreme Court held, inter alia, that the right to privacy encompasses a woman's decision whether or not to terminate her pregnancy, but that a woman's right to an abortion is not absolute and may to some extent be limited by the State's interest in safeguarding her health, in maintaining proper medical standards, and protecting potential human life. After listing some decisions in which the Court or individual justices had discerned the existence of the constitutional right to privacy, Mr. Justice Blackmun, writing for the majority, declared:

". . . These decisions make it clear that only personal rights that can be deemed 'fundamental' or 'implicit in the concept of ordered liberty,' Palko v. Connecticut, 302 U.S. 319, 325, 58 S.Ct. 149, 82 L.Ed. 288 (1937), are included in this guarantee of personal privacy. They also make it clear that the right has some extension to activities relating to marriage [citation omitted]; procreation [citation omitted]; contraception [citation omitted]; family relationships [citation omitted]; and child rearing and education [citations omitted]."   410 U.S. at 152–153, 93 S.Ct. at 726.

This statement of the scope of the constitutional right to privacy remains the definitive statement of the law in this area.

(**10**) Appellants argue that another United States Supreme Court decision, Stanley v. Georgia, 394 U.S. 557, 89 S.Ct. 1243, 22 L.Ed.2d 542 (1969), controls the instant controversy. In *Stanley*, the Court reversed a conviction for possession of obscene matter in violation of a Georgia statute. The appellant in *Stanley* merely owned certain allegedly obscene films for showing in his own home; these films were seized from his residence incident to a search undertaken to find evidence of bookmaking activities. It is true that, in reversing the defendant's conviction, the Court found the right to privacy to exist in a context outside of the intimate personal relationships at issue in *Griswold, Eisenstadt,* and *Roe v. Wade,* supra. But in so doing the Court, speaking through Justice Marshall, laid special emphasis on Stanley's First Amendment rights:

". . . [Appellant] is asserting the right to read or observe what he pleases—the right to satisfy his intellectual and emotional needs in the privacy of his own home. He is asserting the right to be free from state inquiry into the contents of his library. Georgia contends that appellant does not have these rights, that there are certain types of materials that the individual may not read or even possess. Georgia justifies this assertion by arguing that the films in the present case are obscene. But we think that mere categorization of these films as 'obscene' is insufficient justification for such a drastic invasion of personal liberties guaranteed by the First and Fourteenth Amendments. Whatever may be the justifications for other statutes regulating obscenity, we do not think they reach into the privacy of one's own home. If the First Amendment means anything, it means that a State has no business telling a man, sitting alone in his own house, what books he may read or what films he may watch. Our whole constitutional heritage rebels at the thought of giving government the power to control men's minds."   394 U.S. at 565, 89 S.Ct. at 1248.

And in a footnote concerning contraband articles, the Court carefully limited its holding:

> "What we have said in no way infringes upon the power of the State or Federal Government to make possession of other items, such as narcotics, firearms, or stolen goods, a crime. Our holding in the present case turns upon the Georgia statute's infringement of fundamental liberties protected by the First and Fourteenth Amendments. No First Amendment rights are involved in most statutes making mere possession criminal." 394 U.S. at 567, n. 11, 89 S.Ct. at 1249.

(**11**) In two recent cases the United States Supreme Court has declined to extend further the scope of the constitutional right to privacy. The Court recently affirmed the constitutionality of Virginia's anti-sodomy statute even as applied to two consenting adult male homosexuals. Doe v. Commonwealth's Attorney, 425 U.S. 901, 96 S.Ct. 1489, 47 L.Ed.2d 751 (1976), aff'g, 403 F.Supp. 1199 (E.D.Va.1975). In Paul v. Davis, 424 U.S. 693, 96 S.Ct. 1155, 47 L.Ed.2d 405 (1976), respondent's name and photograph were included in a flier of "active shoplifters," after he had been arrested on a shoplifting charge in Louisville, Kentucky. After that charge had been dismissed, Davis brought an action against petitioner police chiefs, who had distributed the flier to area merchants, alleging that petitioners' action under color of law deprived him of his constitutional rights. The Supreme Court, in denying Davis relief held, inter alia, that his contention that the defamatory flier deprived him of his constitutional right to privacy was meritless. Mr. Justice Rehnquist, writing for the majority, suggested:

> ". . . [O]ur other [1] 'right of privacy' cases, while defying categorical description, deal generally with substantive aspects of the Fourteenth Amendment. In *Roe* the Court pointed out that the personal rights found in this guarantee of personal privacy must be limited to those which are 'fundamental' or 'implicit in the concept of ordered liberty' as described in Palko v. Connecticut, 301 U.S. 319, 325, 58 S.Ct. 149, 82 L.Ed. 288 (1937). The activities detailed as being within this definition were ones very different from that for which respondent claims constitutional protection—matters relating to marriage, procreation, contraception, family relationships, and child rearing and education. In these areas it has been held that there are limitations on the States' power to substantively regulate conduct." 424 U.S. at 713, 96 S.Ct. at 1166.

Thus, as indicated ante pp. 963–964, Justice Blackmun's articulation in *Roe v. Wade* of the limited scope of the right to privacy remains the current state of the law.

(**12**) The foregoing discussion should suggest the inappositeness of the leading Supreme Court cases on the right to privacy and the case we decide today. Here we do not face the intimacies of the marital relationship or of

---

1. The Court had just distinguished Roe v. Wade, supra; Terry v. Ohio, 392 U.S. 1, 88 S.Ct. 1868, 20 L.Ed.2d 889 (1968); and Katz v. United States, 389 U.S. 347, 88 S.Ct. 507, 19 L.Ed.2d 576 (1967).

procreation. There is no clear First Amendment issue posed by the question of whether appellant may legally smoke marijuana in his own home. Thus, we are not persuaded by the Alaska Supreme Court's resolution of this issue in *Ravin v. State,* supra. We note further that the *Ravin* court in part based its decision on state constitutional provisions which have no analogue in Florida.[2] 537 P.2d at 500–504.

(**13**) Appellant has presented to this Court a sampling of scientific authority to the effect that marijuana poses no significant public health problem. The State, recognizing the limitations of the procedural posture in which this cause reaches us, has made no effort to counter this material. In a proper case appellate courts may take judicial notice of such expert opinions, and, as noted by appellants, scientific authority on the subject of marijuana's harmfulness has been discussed in several such decisions. See, e.g., *Ravin,* supra; State v. Kantner, 53 Haw. 327, 493 P.2d 306 (1972); People v. Sinclair, 387 Mich. 91, 194 N.W.2d 878 (1972).

(**14**) This Court is ill-suited to make such a *de novo* judgment in a case, such as this one, which comes to us on a denial of a motion to dismiss. The record before us is simply inadequate to support a determination of whether the health hazards of smoking marijuana justify its proscription to the general public. None of the parties really argued whether the legislature lacks a "rational basis" for its decision to ban private possession of cannabis.[3] (Since we have determined that there is no fundamental right to smoke marijuana, the test becomes whether there is a "rational basis" for outlawing such an activity as opposed to a "compelling state interest" in the subject matter of the legislation.) [4] Thus in affirming the trial court, we do not foreclose the possibility of making such a determination on a properly-developed record wherein both sides have had an opportunity to present evidence of competing expert authorities before an impartial tribunal.

The judgments are affirmed.

ENGLAND, HATCHETT and DREW (Retired), JJ., concur.

OVERTON, C. J., and BOYD, J., concur in result only.

ADKINS, J., dissenting with an opinion.

ADKINS, JUSTICE, dissenting.

2. Art. I, § 22, Alas.Const., reads:

"The right of the people to privacy is recognized and shall not be infringed. The legislature shall implement this section."

See also Justice Boochever's concurring opinion in *Ravin,* supra, at 513–516.

3. "Left to another day is the question of regulation or prohibition of marijuana possession or sale in public and the issue of denial of equal protection, as more harmful recreational drugs [alcohol and tobacco] are not similarly prohibited." Brief of Appellant, pp. 7–8.

4. For a critical discussion of this two-tier model, see Massachusetts Bd. of Retirement v. Murgia, — U.S. —, 96 S.Ct. 2562, 2568, 2573, 49 L.Ed.2d 520 (Marshall, J., dissenting).

I respectfully dissent.

A constitutional right to privacy has been clearly established by the United States Supreme Court in Griswold v. Connecticut, 381 U.S. 479, 85 S.Ct. 1678, 14 L.Ed.2d 510 (1965); Eisenstadt v. Baird, 405 U.S. 438, 92 S.Ct. 1029, 31 L.Ed.2d 349 (1972); Roe v. Wade, 410 U.S. 113, 93 S.Ct. 705, 35 L.Ed.2d 147 (1973), and Stanley v. Georgia, 394 U.S. 557, 89 S.Ct. 1243, 22 L.Ed.2d 542 (1969). In *Stanley v. Georgia,* supra, this right was one basis on which the court allowed private possession of materials which the State could properly prohibit an individual from selling. The basis of the regulation considered by the court in *Stanley* was the exercise of the State's police power to protect the public morals and public decency. The court held that, although exercising the police power to these ends was proper, such power could not be validly extended to punishing private possession of obscene materials. The First Amendment rights of the individual were a second basis for the decision in *Stanley;* however, allowing regulation of these rights in public while condemning such regulation in private indicates that the right to privacy was the paramount justification for the decision.

No other constitutional rights were coupled with the right to privacy in the other cases cited above. They are clearly applicable to this case since they establish the individual's right to privacy with regard to birth control and abortion, which directly affect the individual's control over his or her bodily functions.

Brown v. Board of Education, 347 U.S. 483, 74 S.Ct. 686, 98 L.Ed. 873 (1954), establishes that the court may determine and take judicial notice of the facts which form the basis for legislation. The scientific information provided by appellant and discussed in Ravin v. State, 537 P.2d 494 (Alaska 1975); State v. Kantner, 53 Haw. 327, 493 P.2d 306 (1972); and People v. Sinclair, 387 Mich. 91, 194 N.W.2d 878 (1972), shows that the existence of the alleged harmful effects of marijuana have not been scientifically proven. It is questionable whether marijuana causes physical or moral damage, while the harmful effects of legal recreational drugs—alcohol and tobacco—have been well documented.

As in *Stanley,* however, the private possession of an object may be acceptable while the sale or use in public of the same object may not. The right to privacy is the only fundamental right which can reasonably be seen as infringed by the marijuana laws. No justification is shown for invalidating the statutes as they relate to sale. The regulation of this substance other than in the home is clearly a proper exercise of the State's police power.

Note how the majority in *Laird* analogizes and distinguishes precedent cases in reaching its decision.

In paragraph (5): The *Laird* majority considers those cases that the appellants offer to show that the constitutional right of privacy applies to the smoking of marijuana. The Florida court cites first to *Griswold* and *Eisen-*

stadt, Supreme Court decisions binding on the Florida court unless they can be distinguished.

In paragraphs (6) and (7): The Florida court distinguishes *Griswold,* reasoning that *Griswold* differs from *Laird* because *Griswold* dealt with marriage, a relationship within the "zone of privacy created by several fundamental guarantees." No such fundamental guarantees apply to the smoking of marijuana at home, says the *Laird* court.

In paragraph (8): The court distinguishes *Eisenstadt* by the same reasoning: the zone of privacy logically extends to extra-marital relationships, the subject of *Eisenstadt,* for privacy rights are due individuals in such relationships, regardless of their marital status. In both *Griswold* and *Eisenstadt* the individuals in the relationship have the right to be free from governmental intrusion into fundamental rights like bearing or begetting children. The majority again distinguishes *Laird* on the basis of the *kind* of privacy protected by fundamental guarantees.

In paragraph (9): The *Laird* majority cites to *Roe v. Wade* for the principle that the only personal rights deemed fundamental are those of marriage, procreation, contraception, family relationships, child rearing, and education. The court says that *Roe v. Wade* limits the scope of personal rights protected by the right to privacy, excluding the *Laird* facts.

In paragraph (10): The court considers *Stanley v. Georgia,* a Supreme Court decision that the appellants urge is controlling in *Laird.* The majority decision then distinguishes *Stanley,* on the ground that, while it extends the right to privacy beyond intimate personal relationships, the *Stanley* decision laid special emphasis on first amendment rights, and (in a footnote) carefully limited its holding.

In paragraph (11): The court analogized *Doe v. Commonwealth's Attorney* and *Paul v. Davis,* both cases in which the Court had declined to extend further the scope of the right to privacy.

In paragraph (12): The Florida majority declined to find persuasive the Alaska *Ravin v. State* opinion, which appellants had advanced as persuasive authority. Because *Ravin* is a decision handed down by another state supreme court, it is only persuasive (not binding), and the *Laird* majority was able to dismiss it with only a few words.

In paragraph (13): The majority declines to consider scientific authority about marijuana's harmfulness in this case, which comes to the court on a denial of a motion to dismiss.

What You Can Learn From *Laird*

The *Laird* majority opinion provides a good example of the methods of analysis that appellate courts use in reaching their decisions. Note, in *Laird,* the references to binding (controlling) and persuasive precedent. Since *Griswold* and *Eisenstadt* are United States Supreme Court decisions, they would be binding on the Florida Supreme Court if not carefully distinguished. So, too, would *Roe v. Wade* and *Stanley v. Georgia.* Thus, in all of those cases, the *Laird* court takes pains to distinguish the *Laird* facts.

But *Ravin v. State,* an Alaska Supreme Court opinion, is not binding, only persuasive, and the Florida court therefore makes short shrift of that case.

To use *Laird* to best advantage in studying case analysis, read Judge Adkins' dissent to see how, on the same facts and with almost identical precedent, Judge Adkins reaches an opposite holding. What the majority distinguishes, Judge Adkins analogizes as binding or persuasive, by a different interpretation of the facts and legal rules of those cases. And whereas the majority leaves for later consideration the subject of the harmfulness of marijuana, Judge Adkins finds this subject due "judicial notice" here and cites to the Supreme Court decision in *Brown v. Board of Education* as precedent.

Study carefully the process of analogization. You will use it frequently during law school and during your professional career.

C. SYNTHESIZING

A synthesis is a comparison of the key facts, legal theories, issues, holdings, reasoning, and legal rules of two or more opinions. In a synthesis you will analogize and distinguish key facts, much as the *Laird* court did, above.

In writing a case synthesis:

I.   Make an introductory statement broad enough to include all of the cases you are comparing, but narrow enough to exclude other cases.

II.   Show, by analyzing your briefs of the cases, how the cases resemble each other and how they differ. (That is, analogize and distinguish the cases.) In your analysis, discuss (1) the causes of action; (2) the issues raised; (3) the holdings of the courts; (4) the rule(s) formulated, applied, expanded, narrowed, or overturned; and (5) the reasoning of the courts.

III.   Come to some conclusion(s) as a result of your analysis. For example, what legal rule or rules result from these decisions? What trend do the decisions indicate? Can you predict the outcome of similar or somewhat similar cases? (That is, will the legal rule be retained intact, expanded, narrowed, or abandoned in subsequent cases?)

SAMPLE CASE SYNTHESIS

(of three cases briefed, at pages 97 to 125.)

The application of the doctrines of impossibility and its offshoot, commercial impracticability, is demonstrated in the opinions of two federal circuit courts and a state supreme court. The cases are *Transatlantic Financing Corporation* (1966), *American Trading and Production Corporation* (1972), and *Northern Corporation* (1974). The first two cases involve contracts to ship oil from the United States to the Mideast. In each of those cases the carrier was forced, through no fault of its own, to take an alternative, longer route instead of its customary route via the Suez Canal, in order to deliver its cargo. In *Transatlantic,* the carrier owner requested relief for its additional delivery costs (about 15% over the contract price), and in *American Trading,* the carrier requested relief in additional compensation (about 33% over the contract price) for its additional delivery costs.

The third case, *Northern Corporation,* involved a contract to procure and haul rock. The contractor, through no fault of its own, was unable to complete its contract to haul rock, and sought relief in payment for additional expenses incurred in attempting to do so, less revenue received.

In *Transatlantic,* the court rejected the carrier's argument that the doctrine of deviation implied into its contract a voyage by the usual and customary route and that when it was forced to take an alternative route, the contract became legally impossible to perform. The court listed three requirements necessary for the doctrine of impossibility to apply, only the first of which was present in *Transatlantic:* (1) a contingency; (2) allocation of the contingency by agreement or custom; and (3) occurrence of the contingency, rendering performance commercially impracticable. The court held that the risk of the contingency had not been allocated to the charterer and might more properly be allocated to the carrier, who might have purchased insurance to cover the contingency. Finally, the court rejected the carrier's argument that, by delivering the oil, it had conferred an in *quantum meruit* benefit for which it deserved payment. The court said that no in *quantum meruit* benefit is conferred when a carrier has collected its contract payment and seeks only additional compensation.

The court also rejected the application of the commercial impracticability doctrine to *Transatlantic,* since neither its crew nor cargo were harmed by the longer voyage. The court added that to justify relief under the impracticability doctrine there must be more variation than was present between the expected and the actual cost of contract performance. The *Transatlantic* court did not specify how much variation in cost was necessary to trigger the impracticability doctrine, but cited in a footnote an English case in which even twice the cost was insufficient for the doctrine to apply.

The *American Trading and Production Corporation* court also held that the carrier's contract to deliver oil to the Mideast was not rendered legally impossible despite the contract specification of transit through the Suez Canal, for the specification stated that the Suez Canal was the "expected" not the "required" route. Therefore, the court rejected the claim that the carrier conferred upon the charterer an in *quantum meruit* benefit, when it took an alternate, more costly, route. The court also rejected the carrier's argument that the doctrine of impracticability applied; the court noted that the requirements of "extreme and unreasonable difficulty, expense, injury or loss" were absent. In *American Trading,* the additional cost to the carrier was about one-third over the contract price, and this amount was held insufficient to trigger the doctrine of commercial impracticability. Nor was the additional length of the carrier's voyage (twice the expected distance) sufficient to constitute commercial impracticability.

However, in *Northern Corporation,* a state court did apply the doctrine of commercial impracticability when the contractor suffered the loss of two employees' lives and two trucks in his effort to haul gravel as specified in his contract, upon the demand of the other party to fulfill the contract. In applying the doctrine of commercial impracticability, the court said that a party is discharged from contract obligations if the costs of performance are so disproportionate to those contemplated by the contracting parties as to make performance "totally impractical in a commercial sense." In *Northern,* the "extreme and unreasonable difficulty," which is missing from *Transatlantic* and *American Trading,* was present. *Northern* also differs from the other two cases in that attempted performance was demanded by one party despite unreasonable and excessive losses to the other party.

In the three cases discussed, courts have defined the scope of the doctrines of legal impossibility and commercial impracticability. The *Transatlantic* court stated three criteria for legal impossibility: (1) a contingency not allocated to either party, (2) the occurrence of which (3) makes the contract performance commercially impracticable. This formula is consistently applied in the three cases. The facts of *Transatlantic* and *American Trading* failed to meet all criteria, courts in both cases noting that the variation between the carriers' contract price and the actual delivery cost was not great enough to constitute commercial impracticability.

The difference in *Northern,* where the contractor succeeded in his suit, were (1) the court found that the contractor's losses were excessive and unreasonable enough to trigger the commercial impracticability doctrine, and (2) the contractor suffered these losses attempting to perform the contract that the other party insisted upon despite losses to the contractor's property in his previous efforts. Thus, *Northern's* losses satisfied the "excessive" requirement, and the demands by the other party satisfied the "unreasonable" requirement for commercial impracticability.

Based upon the holdings in these three cases, the application of the commercial impracticability doctrine results in the same damage awards as application of the legal impossibility doctrine. For commercial impracticability to succeed, the plaintiff must suffer both excessive costs and physical harm in attempt to perform the contract. Because commercial impracticability requires only two criteria, plaintiffs whose losses meet these criteria would be well advised to rely upon that legal theory instead of the doctrine of legal impossibility.

Applying the results of your synthesis to hypothetical problems:

In your law school legal writing classes you will probably be assigned two or more court opinions to synthesize. Then you will be given a hypothetical problem about which you must make a prediction, based upon your synthesis. Later, in your legal writing course, you will be required to find precedent cases by your own research, then apply them to a hypothetical problem.

The chart on page 138 was used to prepare the synthesis of the three cases discussed above (*Transatlantic Financing Corporation, American Trading and Production Corporation,* and *Northern Corporation*). A chart like this is useful when you prepare a synthesis that you will then use for your hypothetical problem. You can brief the hypothetical problem, add it to the chart, and see at a glance the relationships between it and the precedent cases.

To test your ability to apply synthesized cases to a hypothetical problem, apply the relevant data from the synthesis of *Transatlantic Finance Corporation, American Trading and Production Corporation,* and *Northern Corporation* to the following hypothetical problem. Analogize and distinguish. Then, if you can, predict the likelihood of success for your client, Produce Packing House, in a suit against Frost Brothers.

HYPOTHETICAL PROBLEM

Produce Packing House (PPH), a firm which prepares large volumes of fresh fruit for shipment in carload lots, contracted with Frost Brothers (Frost), a company which installs ice-making equipment, to install and maintain in the PPH plant ice-making equipment to prepare ice needed in PPH's operation. In return, PPH agreed to purchase the total ice-making capacity of Frost's equipment from October 1 to June 30, each year, paying $8.00 a ton for the ice. Both parties signed a written contract to this effect on June 29, 1981.

Deficiencies in the equipment developed soon after it was installed, and PPH complained to Frost that it was not supplying the amount of ice needed. Frost attempted to remedy the situation, installing additional equipment, but these efforts were unsuccessful, according to the Chancellor, whose finding is binding upon the Court.

On March 26, 1982, PPH rescinded its contract, under the theory of impossibility of performance, alleging that Frost had assured PPH that its machinery would furnish all the ice needed by PPH, and the machinery was not capable of filling these needs. Frost contends that it should be reimbursed for the expenses it incurred in installing the equipment in the PPH plant, as well as for loss of contract.

Directions:

Assume that *Transatlantic Financing Corporation, American Trading and Production Corporation,* and *Northern Corporation,* analogized above, (see synthesis chart, below), are opinions binding on this jurisdiction. In a written synthesis, apply the relevant facts of these three opinions to the following hypothetical problem, analogizing and distinguishing them as appropriate. Then, if you can, predict the likelihood of success for your client, PPH, in a suit against Frost.

(This hypothetical problem is an adaptation of Crown Ice Machine Leasing Co. v. Sam Senter Farms, Inc., 174 So.2d 614 (Fla.App.1965). You might want to read the opinion to see whether your prediction is accurate.)

Synthesis Chart

	Transatlantic Financing Corp.	American Trading and Production Corp.	Northern Corp. v. Chugach El. Ass'n
Facts	Contract for shipment of oil to Mideast via alternative route, intended route being unavailable through no fault of either party.	Contract for shipment of oil to Mideast via alternative route, intended route being unavailable through no fault of either party.	Contract to procure and haul rock. Appellant paid additional costs in futile effort to fulfill contract, on demand of appellee.
Relief Requested	Payment for additional expenses incurred.	Payment for additional expenses incurred.	Payment for additional expenses incurred, less revenue already received.
Legal Theories	Breach of contract, under Doctrine of Deviation (Usual and customary route is implied.) Doctrine of impossibility (A thing is legally impossible when it can be done only at excessive cost.) *Quantum meruit* (When contract becomes a nullity, recovery for amount deserved is proper remedy.)	(1) In *quantum meruit* benefit conferred upon appellee for performance, since contract was legally impossible to perform through no fault of either party. (2) Commercial impracticability, which excused appellant from performance. (3) Contract (Liberties Clause) provides expressly for compensation in these circumstances.	(Appellant) (1) Breach of implied and express warranties entitles appellant to damages. (2) (Alternatively) contract impossibility justifies award of costs in attempting performance. (3) Increased costs to appellant constitute compensable change under the changes clause of the contract. (Appellee) (1) Breach of contract: liquidated damages for delays in contract performance and for costs and attorneys' fees.
Issues	(1) Does the doctrine of deviation imply into the contract a voyage by the usual and customary route? (2) Under doctrine of impossibility, did closing of Suez Canal render charter operator's performance legally impossible? (3) If so, did charter-operator confer in *quantum meruit* benefit upon charterer when he delivered cargo by an alternate, more costly route?	(1) Was contract legally impossible to perform, so as to confer benefit upon appellee for performance, payable in *quantum meruit*? (2) Was performance by appellant excused due to commercial impracticability? (3) Does Liberties Clause of contract expressly require compensation under these circumstances?	(1) Is appellant entitled to damages for breach of alleged express and implied warranties contained in the original contract? (2) (Alternatively) was the contract as modified impossible of performance? (3) If so, is appellant entitled to reasonable costs incurred in attempting to perform it? (4) Is appellee entitled to liquidated damages for delays in performance of the contract and for costs and attorneys' fees?
Holdings	(1) No. (2) No. (3) No.	(1) No. (2) No. (3) No.	(1) No. (2) Yes. (3) Yes. (4) Not applicable.
Reasoning	(1) Doctrine of deviation does not apply, for the Suez Canal route was not a condition of the contract. (2) Only one of the three conditions necessary for the doctrine of impossibility was present: unforeseen contingency. (3) In *quantum meruit* doctrine applies only when contract is a nullity; here charter-operator seeks relief only for additional expenses incurred in performance.	(1) Performance of contract did not require route through Suez Canal; thus no in *quantum meruit* liability. (2) No extreme or unreasonable difficulty proved by appellant; thus no excuse due to commercial impracticability. (3) Liberties Clause inapplicable since appellant did reach designated port.	(1) Contract was legally impossible to perform since conditions necessary to performance were not present. (2) If, on remand, appellee is found to have insisted on performance, when it knew or should have known of impossibility, appellant is entitled to costs incurred in attempting performance.

CHAPTER FIVE

Expository Techniques

"I have never been able to understand why it is that just because I am unintelligible nobody understands me." (Milton Mayer)

A. EXAMSMANSHIP

The skills of case briefing, analogization, and synthesis are of far-reaching importance to attorneys, but for most law students, the critical exercise of those skills is provided in law school final examinations. These examinations, upon which the entire grade for the course often depends, are approached with dread and foreboding by all neophyte law students. For this reason, suggestions for preparing for and taking final examinations seem in order.

1. Preparing for the Final Examination

The process of preparing for the final examination begins with the very first day of class. The groundwork is laid by day-by-day reading of the assigned material, note-taking in class, and briefing of the court opinions in your casebooks. For in order to succeed in law school, you must (1) know the subject matter, (2) be able to communicate your knowledge within a stipulated time (that never seems long enough), and (3) express your ideas in appropriate legal language (including the favorite legal terms your instructor has used in class).

This kind of preparation would surely have guaranteed an "A" in your undergraduate courses. But, alas, not in law school. Here you are all "A" students, all determined to continue making "A's." And since the quantity of material to be learned—though formidable—is finite, all highly-motivated law students will obtain a thorough grasp of it. Therefore, writing skill becomes disproportionately important in grade-determination.

Besides containing correct and complete information, the "A" examination must be clearly stated, well-organized, and succinct. Writing that rambles, discussions that begin somewhere out in left field and never quite make it back to home base, and arguments so unfocused that they seem to miss the point leave the instructor with the impression of ineptitude, no matter how salient the (badly expressed) ideas may be.[1] So a student may be as knowledgeable as his friend and get a "C" while his friend gets an "A."

---

1. When I first began to read law students' final examinations, I assumed that if "missing" material was actually present in the examination—though hidden by ineffective writing—and if the student, in a post-examination interview, pointed it out

But cheer up! Once you have mastered the amenities of grammar, the skills of organization, and the techniques of case analysis—discussed in previous chapters—all you will need is practice. Practice by writing course outlines in standard English, using complete sentences and appropriate legal language. Practice by analogizing and synthesizing lines of cases from your casebooks. Practice by tracing the development of the legal doctrines learned in the course, indicating their change during the years and their current status in various jurisdictions. And practice by writing essay answers to questions of the sort that you will be asked in final examinations. This last writing practice helps to put you at ease when you reach the moment of truth in the form of final examinations. Familiar with the answering of similar test questions, you will be able to relax and give them your best effort.

That is the reason for the essay questions and answers in this book.[2] You can model your own answers after the sample answers provided—or perhaps write even better answers. Some law professors place their previous examinations on file in the law library. Ask about them at the Reserve Desk, and practice writing answers to those questions. The more writing you do, the better you will write.

2. Taking the Final Examination

The fateful day arrives. You have, by studying and writing answers to practice essay problems, avoided exam-panic that can be so stultifying that it prevents adequate performance. Now that the examination lies before you, what is the first thing to do? The obvious answer is also the wrong answer. Do *not* begin to write immediately, assuming that your ideas will fall into order. Instead, quickly read the entire examination, orienting yourself to the job at hand and deciding how much time to spend on each question. Often the professor has done the latter for you, either by suggesting a time limit for each question or by allotting a specific weight for each question. If he has given no indication of the value of each question, assume that they are all of equal weight and allot equal time to each.

Having done so, do not cheat: when the time has expired for the question you are answering, leave some space so that you can return to it later, then jot down briefly the points you must still cover, and go on to the next question. If you have time at the end, you can finish writing your answer; if not, your professor will at least know by your jottings that you could have done so had there been time.[3]

As you assess the questions, you may find the first one very difficult. A later question might seem easier to deal with. Especially if they are both of

to the professor, the professor would then change the student's grade. I was soon set straight by students who reported to me that the professor's reaction was invariably something like, "Oh, yes, well, that's a shame." No grade change.

2. You will find them in Chapter Six.

3. Sometimes a professor writes an examination that no one in the class can complete in the time given. If you indicate how you *would* have completed your answer had you had time, you are better off than the students who merely leave blank spaces.

roughly the same weight, do not waste valuable time wrestling with the difficult question. No one says you must answer the questions in order. Go on to the first equally-weighted question that seems more manageable. "Warming up" is part of the game. Once you have warmed up on a less difficult question, you will probably find the previously intractable one easier to manage. Furthermore, in the midst of answering another question, you may suddenly receive an insight that will help you answer a previous question. If you do, stop long enough to write down that insight, lest it disappear as suddenly as it arrived.

Once you select the question you will answer first, read it again, slowly, underlining all of the language that seems significant.[4] Look carefully at the final directions so that you will be sure to comply with them. Then list on your scratch pad the **major issues** that must be resolved before the question can be answered. Leave room between **major issues** for **subissues**, **legal doctrines**, and **analysis**. Arrange the issues in the order in which you will discuss them.

Several arrangements are possible. Perhaps the most natural is **chronological**, as in a hypothetical problem like the following, in which a single individual is beset by a series of difficulties. The words in boldface are those you would have underlined as you read the problem:

A, an **adult, rented a boat** from a **small business** at the side of a lake, and was happily fishing when a **heavy tropical rainstorm** occurred. As A hurriedly began to row toward shore, one of the two oars broke, slowing his progress substantially. He finally reached land, soaked and shivering, pulled the boat onto the beach and dashed toward a house, owned by H, which was **unoccupied and unlocked.** As he went inside to get out of the rain, the floor boards, which were **rotten,** gave way, and A **fell and twisted his ankle.**

A remained in the house, in pain, until the rain subsided, then he managed to row back to the **rental shop. Entering the shop,** A fell on a **broken step** and **banged his head.** The **shopowner,** B, sympathized with A about his fall and A told him that his ankle was very painful. B thereupon told A that he had had **much experience with broken ankles,** and that A's ankle was clearly broken and should be splinted and strapped. Luckily, said B, he had some ace bandage for sale, so A bought the bandage, and B **strapped and splinted A's ankle.**

Several days later, since the ankle continued to be painful and turned blue, A consulted a physician who found that A had a **sprained ankle, worsened by B's ministrations,** a mild **concussion,** resulting **from having struck his head,** and **bronchial pneumonia,** probably from **exposure** to the **rain and cold weather.** Discuss A's possible claims against H and B.

---

4. From the underlined language you can extract the key facts. For the definition and discussion of key facts see Chapter 4.

Probably the most effective way to deal with A's several claims is **chrono-logically**. At issue, first, is A's status with regard to H, and H's consequent rights and duties vis-a-vis A. The answer to these questions will depend on the key language that you have underlined in your reading. After you have thoroughly discussed A versus H and reached a conclusion, you will move on to A versus B.

In some fact situations, on the other hand, one issue is the **threshold issue**—that issue, a decision about which will obviate any further discussion. When this is the case, you should discuss the threshold issue first. The Illinois Supreme Court decided a threshold issue in a case involving two children who were struck by an automobile while walking home from school.[5] One child was killed and the other severely and permanently injured. The children's father brought an action against (among others) the used car dealer who had sold the automobile, alleging that at the time it left the dealer's control it was defective and not reasonably safe for driving and operation. Two issues arose in the appeal: first, whether as a matter of law, strict liability extends to the seller of a used car and, second, whether a bystander who has been struck by a defective, unreasonably dangerous car may sue under a theory of strict liability.

The court first considered the issue of whether the dealer could be held strictly liable, noting that because this issue was answered in the negative, the second issue need not be considered. The first issue, then, was the threshold issue, its disposition making consideration of the second issue unnecessary.

When you are writing your answer to an examination question, however, you do not have the luxury of discarding the other issues even if the answer to the first issue would normally dispose of the other issues. Instead, you should point out that in the event that the first issue should be decided differently you will now go on to discuss the other issues.

A third method of organization can best be used when one event occasions a number of possible actions by one victim. **The action most likely to succeed** should probably be discussed first, then the others, in order of diminishing likelihood of success. Similarly, if one victim has possible claims against a number of individuals, the individual against whom the victim has the strongest claim should be dealt with first. Other factors being equal, priority should be given to the claim against the individual with the "deepest pocket."

Another procedure is to use reverse order, dispensing first (briefly) with the claims least likely to succeed, and so labeling them. For example, when you are discussing a claim of battery, and the only element in question is the intent of the defendant, you might briefly discuss why and how all of the other elements are not in question and then explore fully the issue of intent.

Whatever your decision about the order of the major issues, you will use the space you have left under each one to list **subissues, legal principles**,

5. *Peterson v. Lou Bachrodt Chevro-let Co.* 61 Ill.2d 17, 329 N.E.2d 785 (1975).

and **precedents** that you must apply to come to a conclusion about the major issues. If enacted laws apply, show whether they govern the facts of your case.[6] If cases provide precedent, show that the facts of your case resemble (or differ from) the facts of the precedential cases. It is unlikely that your case will precisely fit either under legal principles or common law precedent. Your job will be to decide whether the hypothetical problem you have been given fits closely enough for the principles and common law precedent to apply. That will require an educated guess about whether the differences between your facts and the precedent are material enough to prevent the application of the legal doctrine governing the precedent or whether the differences in the facts are not material enough to remove your case from the application of the rule.[7]

Beginning law students tend to think that their conclusions should always be unequivocal: a firm "yes" or "no." In fact, professors seldom present in final examinations hypothetical problems that require such conclusions. So a cautious "perhaps" may turn out to be the proper response—or "probably yes" or "probably no." Your final decision, moreover, whatever it is, will be less important than the thoroughness of your analysis.

What you have jotted down on your scratch pad should not have taken you more than one-fifth of the time you have allotted to the question you are answering. If your efforts have been effective, the result of your jottings will resemble the results of the well-known formula for examination-taking, called IRAC. More law students can repeat the formula than can successfully use it, so I have described how the formula works before naming it. IRAC stands for "issue," "rule," "analysis," and "conclusion." You should check your outline against these steps.

- Have you included all relevant issues and none that are irrelevant?
- Have you arranged them in the best order for discussion?
- Have you utilized all applicable legal authority ("rules")?
- Is your analysis of that authority, as it applies to your facts, complete and objective?
- Have you satisfactorily analogized and distinguished your facts and those of the cases which are most similar to yours?
- Does your conclusion follow logically from these steps?

If so, your answer should be logical, well-structured, and complete.

Consider the following hypothetical fact situation:

A, a college professor, carrying his briefcase in his rear bicycle basket, was bicycling carefully along the bike path parallel to B's house. A loudly barking dog leaning out of a passing car startled A causing him to veer and hit the curb, catapulting A into B's flower garden, bending A's bicycle

---

6. Enacted laws include constitutions and charters, statutes and ordinances, and court rules that govern procedures to be followed in litigation.

7. This is the process of analogizing and distinguishing, discussed in Chapter Four.

frame and ruining B's flowers. B observed the incident from his front window, and while A went back to pick up his eyeglasses from the bike path where they had fallen, B snatched A's briefcase. Carrying the briefcase toward his house, B yelled, "When you pay for the damage, you'll get this back." A dashed after B and grabbed back his briefcase so roughly that B fell down, angry but unhurt. A left, carrying his briefcase and dragging his bent bicycle. Discuss possible tort actions of B against A and A against B.

Using a chronological approach, you may decide that the first issue to be resolved is whether B has a cause of action in trespass against A for A's first entry onto B's property. The applicable rule is that a non-volitional entry upon property is no trespass unless the entry is preceded by negligence. A's entry can be characterized as non-volitional by reference to the given facts. You will probably recall similar cases in your casebook that may provide precedent and indicate how the legal rule was interpreted by the courts.

Now you must decide whether to continue with the claims of B against A or to switch to the possible claims of A against B, thus maintaining the chronological approach. Either procedure is acceptable, as long as you are consistent in your development and clearly indicate your procedure.

When you begin to discuss the conduct of A as he grabbed his briefcase from B, you may decide to state the rule that reasonable force necessary to recover possession of chattel after wrongful taking is permissible after fresh pursuit. You should then follow immediately with the issues of whether the degree of force used to retrieve his briefcase was reasonable and whether A's pursuit will be considered "fresh." Reversal of the order of issue and rule will not change the sequence of the other steps, analysis and conclusion.

The IRAC formula may be modified to suit your purpose. You may choose, for example, to begin with the conclusion. If you do, you will be using the deductive method of reasoning.[8] You may choose to reverse the issue and rule in an entire question or in part of the question. If you do, the formula you use will be RIAC. And in questions in which the legal rule is supplied, you will extract the issues from the fact situation and apply the rule.

Although you can thus re-arrange the IRAC formula to suit your needs in each situation, be sure to clothe IRAC in appropriate attire. That is, the IRAC skeleton should not be apparent, for IRAC is a structure on which to build, not a final product. Without complete documentation, adequate development, and clear transition, the IRAC formula will be ineffective.

3. Some Caveats

During my tenure at this law school, I have read many essay examinations on numerous legal topics. One would assume that the errors made on these examinations would be of "infinite variety." Not so: the same types of errors

8. For a discussion of deduction, see Chapter Three.

appear over and over, regardless of the subject matter. Those errors have prompted the following caveats:

(1) You have read the question and outlined your answer. Now, one last time before you begin to write, re-read the question. The reason? Too many clever answers have been provided to questions that were not asked. That last glance at the question will avoid this error, which is usually heavily penalized by the professor. His assumption is that you have chosen to answer a different question because you could not answer his. However, some students tell me that this is not the case. They have answered the "wrong" question unwittingly; they could have answered the professor's question had they only looked at it that final time before starting to write.

(2) In your answer, be sure to adopt the stipulated point of view. For example, if your role is that of a junior partner advising a senior partner about a prospective client's chances of bringing suit or defending against a suit, be objective and exhaustive in your analysis. Avoid polemic and rhetorical flourishes.

   Even if you are asked to be partisan (e.g., as attorney for the defense), do not emulate Perry Mason addressing a jury. Do not minimize or ignore opposing arguments. Acknowledge weaknesses in your client's case and attempt to deal with them. When possible, show that deficiencies in one area are offset by strengths in another. Make your points by careful analysis, not by omitting, twisting, or exaggerating the given facts. If you are making a presumption that is not in the fact situation, say so.

(3) Do not be misled by a question that seems obvious to you. Professors are too devious to select problems whose solutions are obvious. Look carefully for points on both sides of all issues; the more one-sided the question seems, the more you should suspect that your analysis—not the question—is simplistic.

(4) Therefore, avoid dogmatic assertions. Never begin your analysis with words like "obviously," "clearly," or "certainly." These are almost sure to irritate your professor, who has carefully fashioned questions that he believes are neither obvious, clear, nor certain. Even in the final paragraph, it is unwise to use such absolutes; after all, you could be wrong!

(5) Use unslanted language. Avoid what are sometimes called "purr" and "growl" words, used in persuasive writing to induce readers to adopt desired views. The professor will not be duped by slanted words. You can best impress him by clear thinking and logical reasoning.

(6) Avoid hyperbole. One student wrote, "This was a bald, unmitigated lie." She would have been better advised to write, "This was a lie," or, even better, "This was not true." For hyperbole, although it is intended to make the writing more forceful, actually has the opposite effect.

The more it is used, the more deadening it is to the reader's sensibilities. Worse, hyperbole creates a gushy effect, damaging to legal writing.

(7) For the same reason avoid using intensifiers, adverbials to support weak adjectives. Choose the proper adjective instead, and it will stand alone. For example, for "excessively often," substitute "excessive"; for "extremely important," "important"; for "very grave," "grave." In fact, "very" can be edited out of any sentence, to advantage, as can "perfectly" (as in "perfectly clear"), and "absolutely" (as in "absolutely certain"). The same holds true for "clearly," "certainly," and "definitely." And the ubiquitous "rather," which has little meaning and is used mostly as an affectation, should almost always be omitted.[9]

(8) Unless otherwise requested, base your argument only on legal grounds. The layman is entitled to approach a fact situation intuitively, emotionally, morally, ethically: as a neophyte attorney, you must approach it legally. The layman can ask, is this right, fair, moral? You must ask, is this legal? Your concern is with what the law *can* do, not what it *ought* to do.

(9) Be sure to complete your analysis: do not state the law and fail to relate it to your facts; do not state law and facts and forget to analyze and conclude from them; and do not state your conclusion without showing how you reached it.

(10) Avoid postures of arrogance or humility in your writing. A note of condescension is implicit in locutions like "it is evident that," "without question" and "obviously." On the other hand self-deprecation is unwise, as in, "I am not sure I have included everything . . ." or "(sp?)" after legal terms you think you may have misspelled. A good maxim might be: Don't assert your superiority; your instructor may not agree. Don't advertise your shortcomings; he may not notice them.

(11) Properly highlight and subordinate. Nondiscriminating treatment of facts and issues may not be enough to get you the grade you want. Remember also that too much emphasis on minor issues takes precious time and space and may prevent you from properly emphasizing major issues. Even if space and time are not limited, your instructor wants to see major issues dealt with first and most extensively.

(12) Say what you mean, exactly and only once. Do not adopt the oral rhetorical device of saying what you intend to say, saying it, then saying you have said it. Sentences that begin, "In other words," or "Again," indicate that you have failed to make your point with one try and are trying again. Redraft the original statement so that your point is clear;

9. "Rather," currently a fad word, was at one time used to reduce the effect of the following adjective, as in "rather warm." Now, however, it is often tossed into a sentence, without any such reason. A television celebrity, in one sentence, admitted that he was "rather horrified" and "rather amazed" at a "rather unique" occurrence.

then edit out the repetition. (Your professor may have been prolix orally, but he will expect you to be succinct in writing.)

(13) Do not ask rhetorical questions (e.g., "Should anyone have to suffer such indignity?"). Do not ask a question, then immediately answer it, (e.g., Is the defendant guilty as charged? He is not.") The first is pompous, the second patronizing. Both are wordy.

(14) To achieve style, affect none. Try instead for orderly, logical presentation. Treat even complex ideas with clarity, succinctness, and simplicity of statement. Affectation, elegance, and the appearance of profundity will not mask a paucity of ideas; call attention to what you are saying, not to how you say it.

(15) In general, avoid levity. Use formal, standard English. Your professor may have adopted a fraternal attitude in class. He may have made jokes at which you dutifully laughed and he may even have laughed at your jokes. But sitting in his lamplit, lonely study, grading tests, he is a different person. His only interest is to get through the stack of examinations, and to assess the knowledge of each student and be reasonably certain he has not erred in his judgment. Jokes are the last things he is interested in, and your efforts at levity may even be punished. The same goes for folksiness, slang, colloquialisms. At best, these waste your space, his time.

(16) Keep your own personality out of your writing. Write with ideas instead. Therefore avoid the first person approach, as in "I think," "I believe," "I would suggest." Worst of all is "I feel," an expression anathema to many law professors, who expect a cerebral rather than a visceral response to their examination questions. Almost as annoying is the folksy "we" approach, as in "we must consider carefully," or "we will next discuss."

Instead of the first person use third person, as in "the defendant is probably liable" (not "I think the defendant is liable"). The effect of your writing will be less biased, the writing more succinct with the third person approach.[10] Some examples follow:

This	**Not This**
The facts indicate	I have found that the facts indicate
The courts concur	In my research, I find that courts concur
The next issue	Let us consider the next issue
The evidence suggests	It is my opinion, based on the evidence

10. But avoid referring to yourself in the third person (as, "The writer believes . . ."). If you find it necessary to refer to yourself, use the first person.

(17) Finally, a few general suggestions about the writing itself, some new, some appearing elsewhere, in this book but worth reiterating. There may be exceptions, but the following advice is usually reliable:

(a) Choose a framework: deal with the events in your problem chronologically, or with one party at a time. Your decision will vary with the facts.[11]

(b) Generally, do not start by summarizing the hypothetical fact situation stated in the examination question. Your professor does not want to read a paraphrase of his fact situation; he wants to read your answer. But do use the key facts, by applying the applicable law to them so as to reach a conclusion.

(c) Use a separate paragraph for each issue. The first sentence of each paragraph is usually the topic sentence. Deal with subordinate issues immediately following the main issues from which they arise.

(d) Place arguments in their most effective order, with those most likely to succeed up front. Or dispense with less cogent arguments first, but briefly, and so label them.

(e) Write in paragraphs of about four to six sentences. Fewer sentences indicate incomplete development of ideas. More sentences than six probably indicate the inclusion of unrelated ideas—or redundance. Proper paragraphing makes your writing appear well organized.

(f) Separate and clearly label pro and contra arguments, e.g., liabilities and defenses to liabilities.

(g) If space is no problem, leave some room after each answer for possible later inspiration. In allocating time, leave a few minutes at the end for editing.

(h) Be sure there are no gaps in your reasoning. Have consideration for the professor if you expect consideration from him: don't force him to make leaps of faith. (He may not like to leap, and have little faith.) The difference between a "B" student and a "D" student may only be that the former is a "putter-inner" and the latter a "leaver-outer."

(i) Finally, bear in mind the theory of the Greek Anaxagoras, teacher of Socrates, about the origin of the universe: "All things were in chaos when mind arose and created order." Socrates, hearing this, reasoned that man, thinking for himself, could bring similar order to human affairs. Your job is to bring order to the mass of unorganized data presented in your essay examinations—and awaiting you in your legal practice.

---

11. For a further discussion of methods of development, see Chapter Three.

B. LOGICAL FALLACIES

A marvelous short story by Max Shulman, called "Love is a Fallacy," should be on the reading list of every law student. It deals with the sad denouement of a love affair between a clever, logical law student and a beautiful-but-dumb coed whom he decides to transform, by the discipline of logic, into an intellectual giant worthy of himself. To avoid revealing the ending of the tale, I shall add only that along the way the author defines and illustrates the logical fallacies that law students—and others—often fall into.[12]

In writing final examinations and as practicing attorneys, you should recognize and avoid logical fallacies, some of the most common of which are discussed below:

a. The *Post Hoc Fallacy,* more accurately, *Post Hoc Ergo Propter Hoc,* means, "After this, therefore on account of this." This form of fallacious reasoning assumes that because an event or action occurs after another event or action, the second is caused by the first. A homely example is "Every time I do my wash, it rains." Or, "Every time I brag about my child's good health, he gets sick." (Therefore to avoid rain, do not wash clothes; to ensure your child's good health, do not brag about it.) This fallacy should be recognized and exposed when it is utilized by shrewd attorneys in litigation. And it goes without saying that the Post Hoc fallacy should be avoided in one's own legal arguments for, as the Sahakians point out, "[R]easoning without committing error is an obvious asset for all persons, regardless of their walk in life."

b. *Dicto Simpliciter* involves the application of a general rule to cases that are actually exceptions to the rule. For example, "Smoking does not cause cancer. My Uncle Charlie smoked two packs a day, and he lived to be 90." "My Webster's Dictionary does not list the word 'inumbrate.' Therefore you should not use it in your brief." ("My" Webster's may be a *circa* 1900 edition!)

c. *Hasty Generalization,* the converse fallacy, involves jumping to a conclusion without adequate sampling; e.g. "Professor Brown frequently forgets to call roll; college professors certainly are absent-minded." (The conclusion may be correct, but it cannot be deduced without much broader and more representative sampling.)

d. *Non Sequitur* (literally, "it does not follow") consists of a conclusion which does not logically follow from its supposed proof. The "proof" may have no relationship to the "conclusion" which depends upon it: "No nation can survive without an all-powerful leader, for without a strong captain a ship would flounder." Is a ship analogous to a nation?

e. In the *Ad Hominem* fallacy, the speaker or writer attacks the person of his opponent rather than his opponent's ideas or arguments. Al Smith, when he was candidate for president, was opposed by some, not because of his

---

12. For a more serious discussion of these and other fallacies, see William S. and Mabel Lewis Sahakian, *Ideas of Great Philosophers,* 1966, 11–23.

experience, ideology, or actions, but because of his religion. President Ford's political detractors joked about his supposed physical clumsiness, hoping thereby to imply mental ineptness too. And recently, a vegetarian food bar in the local airport was declared unsuitable by some local residents because its manager "looked like a hippie."

f. Closely allied to the *Ad Hominem* attack is a fallacy called "poisoning the well," the question "When did you stop beating your wife?" being the classic example. By basing his question upon the presumed guilt of his adversary the speaker puts him in the untenable position of acknowledging guilt no matter how he answers the question. Unethical attorneys have been known to use such questions in order to trap a witness into making incriminating statements.

g. The rhetorical question also becomes a logical fallacy when it is used as an indirect attack. "Is our do-nothing President ever going to take a firm stand on inflation?" is an example. As in "poisoning the well," the rhetorical question is a form of question begging: it fails to prove the presumption on which it rests.

h. Another form of question begging is the use of circular reasoning: "What is a sentence?" "A sentence begins with a capital letter, ends with a period and expresses a complete idea." "How do you know whether the idea expressed is complete?" "Because it begins with a capital letter and ends with a period." The problem with circular reasoning it that it seems to provide an answer but actually does not.

i. Perhaps because our language and manner of looking at reality impose an "either/or" attitude, the Either/Or fallacy is sometimes successfully utilized in law by a clever attorney who hopes that his opponent will feel compelled to choose between two offered alternatives. The English language seems to suggest polar choices by setting up dichotomies like "right/wrong," "good/bad," "black/white," instead of considering the various possibilities in between. A foreign student in one of my English classes fell into such a trap. In order to obtain a scholarship, he was required to answer the following question (among others): "Have you ever plotted to overthrow the U.S. government or engaged in any subversive activity against the U.S. government?" The unfortunate foreigner thought he had to choose between the two alternatives, and after much soul-searching, selected one. (Needless to say, he did not get the scholarship.)

j. *Argumentum ad Populum* (Appeal to the Masses), is handy to unscrupulous politicians. Perpetrators of this fallacy appeal to the prejudices of the masses instead of discussing the issues. Their appeal might be to racial bias, to religious prejudice, to patriotism, or to their listeners' perception of superiority or inferiority—whatever can be expected to cause in the audience an immediate, unthinking, emotional reaction. During the Florida senatorial election campaign of 1950, George Smathers was running against the incumbent Claude Pepper, a liberal who had held the Senate seat for many years. Smathers was widely quoted as telling rural audiences consisting largely of ultra-conservative voters, that Pepper was a believer in Pragmatism and that Pepper's sister was a well-known Thespian. These revelations, made to voters innately suspicious of "-isms" and who perhaps confused "thespian" with "lesbian," may have helped achieve Smathers' resounding victory over Pepper at the polls.

k. In the *Tu Quoque* (You Do It Yourself) fallacy, the argument is that if one group or individual has the right to do something, all other similar groups of individuals should also have that right. But this argument is fallacious if (1) the groups are not identical, (2) the situations involved are not alike, or (3) the "right" is inappropriately held by the first party. For example, university students argue that they should have the right, as does the university faculty, to choose curricula and appoint new deans. But does the fact that students are invariably transient dwellers in the university while faculty are relatively permanent affect this argument? If so exceptions (1) and (2) should be applied, and the argument is fallacious.

l. Finally, the *Fallacy of Misplaced Authority* depends upon the assumption that because a person excels in one area, he also holds credentials in other, unrelated matters. Thus, film stars like Jane Fonda are considered expert in political matters, writers of best-selling books on baby care are authorities in the anti-war movement, and winners of Olympic medals are thereby knowledgeable about breakfast cereals. Of course, the opinions of celebrities about subjects outside their fields of competence are no more valuable than the opinions of the average man in the street. Suspect also should be the opinion of a bona fide authority, with credentials in the field being discussed, whose objectivity is in question. Thus the president of an oil company can hardly be expected to discuss without bias the taxation of excess profits of oil companies; nor can a food scientist who is a paid consultant to a hamburger chain be expected to be unbiased on the subject of fast foods.

The Appendix provides illustrations of logical fallacies for you to identify.

CHAPTER SIX

Problems and Answers for Writing Practice

This book thus far has largely been composed of rules and guidelines for legal writing, along with exercises to help you follow the rules. But rules and guidelines, though useful, cannot be applied without writing practice, and unfortunately the law school curriculum provides little writing practice. In law school, your writing is usually in the context of a final examination, dead earnest writing, in competition with your colleagues for grades. With each writing, your academic career hangs in the balance. And, as everyone knows, your legal career also may hang in the balance, for the good positions go to those who do well in law school.

So writing practice is not only helpful: it is vital. This chapter provides opportunity for that practice. You can use the rules and strategies of the first five chapters to write well-organized, cogent essay answers to the problems in this chapter. The relevant legal rules to apply are provided at the beginning of each set of problems so that you will not have to review the law in order to write your answers. Thus even non-law students, after reading the legal rules, can write competent answers to the legal problems presented.

An important caveat: the legal rules provided are not necessarily the actual rules of your jurisdiction, nor are they complete. They are for use only, and specifically, in these exercises and are therefore simplified for this purpose. Using them you can by-pass research and concentrate on your writing.

Be aware, too, that the legal fact situations presented here may be less complex than those you will find in your law school examinations, although a few of the problems approach that level of complexity. The problems in this book are simpler so that law students can develop their writing and analytical skills by dealing with less-complex problems and can then apply those skills to deal with the more difficult problems of typical final examinations. The strategies needed to attack simple and difficult problems are the same; the difference is not in kind, but in degree of complexity.

Do not take too seriously the time limitations suggested for answering the problems. But if you find that you need longer than the suggested time to write the answers, you will know that you need to speed up. Conversely, if you finish much before the suggested time, you may have missed some issues, and you will know you need to spend more time on analysis.

The answers provided are not model answers, in the sense that they are perfect solutions, perfectly written. They are merely competent answers, produced by students like yourself. Perhaps you can do a better job!

Finally, after writing answers to the problems that follow, you should proceed to your school law library where your own law professors may have placed on reserve "real" final examinations for you to use in studying for the final examination. Tackle those questions so that you can test your writing skills: if you understand the subject matter, you should be well prepared to cope with them.

Using only the following legal principles, write answers to the hypothetical legal problems below. You should take about 40 minutes to read the facts and write your answer. These legal rules should not be considered complete or for use in problems other than those presented here. You may not need to use all the rules for each problem. A sample answer, written by a student, follows each problem.

WRITING PROBLEMS, SET I

Legal Rule

Burglary: Breaking and entering into the dwelling of another in the nighttime with the intent of committing larceny.

Definitions

1. "Dwelling": Someone must live therein or have lived there and intend to return.
2. "Nighttime": Between an hour after sunset and an hour before sunrise.
3. "Breaking": Force, however slight, must be used in entering, and the entry be without the consent of the occupant. Some part of the body must enter, or an implement which is then used to effect the crime.
4. "Larceny": The taking and carrying away, with the intent to steal, of the personal property of another.

Problem I

The E. Z. Marks had bought a new home. They moved all their possessions into it, but left the premises at 6 P.M. to stay overnight at a motel because their electricity had not yet been connected. Atilla Z. Hun entered the house through an open window. He carried out silver and china, leaving through the back door, which he had unlocked from the inside. Is Hun guilty of burglary?

Answer to Problem I

A. Z. Hun's conduct fulfills one of the elements of burglary: by taking silver and china from the Marks' house with the intent to steal, he has committed larceny. The intent to steal can probably be imputed to Hun since he entered without the consent of the owners and through an open window.

Three questions remain, however. The first is whether Hun's action occurred at night. Since the facts indicate that the Marks ceased moving their possessions into the house because of darkness, Hun probably entered the house after dark, and thus an hour or more after sunset, thus satisfying the definition of "nighttime." Even if that requirement is satisfied, however, there is a second question of whether Hun's entry was into a dwelling. The rule states that in order to be a dwelling, someone must live there. Since the Marks had not yet moved in, the house may not qualify under this definition. The court must decide whether a house, prepared for next-day occupancy, qualifies as a dwelling.

The third issue is whether Hun's action meets the definition of "breaking." Since his entry was through an open window, it does not, for some force must be used to achieve the entry, and Hun used no force. The unlocking of the door might meet the definition of "force, however slight," but Hun unlocked the door to leave, not to enter.

Hun will therefore probably not be found guilty of burglary, since his behavior fails to satisfy at least one of the required elements.

Problem II

At 10 P.M., while Ben Zene was at the movies, Ken Twin climbed the high fence surrounding Zene's house and entered the porch through the unlocked porch door. He then loaded all of the porch furniture onto the back of his pickup truck. Although the living room windows which opened onto the porch were locked, Ken was able to maneuver one open by using a long wire. He climbed through that window, intending to take items from the house, but, hearing a noise, decided to leave hurriedly instead. Discuss.

Answer to Problem II

Ken Twin is probably guilty of burglary for his first act of removing the porch furniture and putting it into his truck. He had the requisite intent to commit larceny, and his entry through the unlocked porch door will probably constitute "force, however slight." Whether the porch will be considered a dwelling under the given rules is a second issue. If it is so defined, Twin has committed burglary even before he entered Zene's house itself.

Twin is also guilty of burglary for his second act, entry into Zene's house. (1) He had, as he entered, the intent to commit larceny; (2) he used force (the wire) in gaining entry; and (3) he entered without the occupant's consent. The actual absence of the owner does not change his occupant status, nor the status of his home as a dwelling. Twin's change of mind about the burglary does not nullify the "intent" requirement; the intent must only be present at the time of the entry.

Problem III

At 2 A.M., M. I. Tired, intoxicated and seeing a house that appeared empty, broke a window, climbed through it into the house, and went to sleep on the livingroom rug. The house is unoccupied, since its owner, Fig Nuton, is away on reserve military service. When M. I. awakens four hours later, he notices— with the first rays of daylight—Nuton's valuable coin collection and decides to take it. He leaves with the coins through the back door. Has M. I. Tired committed burglary?

Answer to Problem III

M. I.'s conduct satisfies some of the elements of burglary. He has committed larceny after breaking and entering a dwelling. The absence of the owner does not change the status of the house as a dwelling, if the owner intends to return, and the facts indicate that he does. M. I.'s breaking of the window satisfies the breaking requirement, and the owner has not consented to the entry. The nighttime requirement is satisfied despite the actual occurrence of the larceny during the daytime, since M. I. entered at night, and intent on entry is relevant under the rule.

However, the "intent" requirement for burglary is absent here. M. I. broke into Nuton's house only to sleep, not to commit larceny. The requirement of intent is not met when he later changed his mind. The jury may, however, infer intent from M. I.'s behavior, disbelieving M. I.'s claim that he did not intend to take the coin collection at the moment he entered the house. If so, M. I. will probably be found guilty of burglary.

Problem IV

Ima Thief worked as a cleaning woman for the D. Zasters. They regularly provided her with a key by which she could enter to clean during their absence. She had secretly taken that key to the L. Icit Key Company and had a duplicate key made.

Since she knew that the Zasters were away on vacation, Ima entered the house with her duplicate key, broke the lock on a wall safe, and exited with the contents. The time at which this occurred is uncertain. Ima says that the incident occurred at 3 P.M., but a neighbor of the Zasters says she saw Ima in the yard of the Zaster house at 9 P.M., although she did not see Ima entering or leaving the Zaster house. Is Ima guilty of burglary?

Answer to Problem IV

Ima Thief's conduct fulfilled some of the elements of burglary:

She intended her act, and she committed larceny. The Zasters' house, though empty at the time, was a dwelling according to the legal definition, and Ima's entry was without the consent of the Zasters.

The crucial issues to be determined are (1) whether entry by a duplicate key, achieved illegally, constitutes a "breaking" and (2) whether the jury will believe Ima's statement that the incident occurred at 3 P.M.

Entry by an illegally-gained key will almost certainly constitute "breaking," the slight force being Ima's using the key to open the lock and pushing the door (or pulling it) open. With regard to the second issue, the jury will have to decide whether the neighbor really saw Ima in the Zasters' yard at 9 P.M. If the jury believes the neighbor, it may well conclude that the incident occurred at night and not, as Ima asserts, at 3 P.M. The jury will then probably find Ima guilty of burglary.

Before answering the next two problems, add the following legal rules:

I. Burglary is a felony of the second degree if, in the course of committing the offense, the actor

    A. purposely, knowingly, or recklessly inflicts or attempts to inflict bodily injury upon another, or

    B. is armed with explosives or a deadly weapon.

(An act is defined as "in the course of committing the offense" if it occurs in an attempt to commit the offense or in flight after the attempt or commission.)

II. Otherwise, burglary is a felony of the third degree.

Problem V

A. Felon was in the habit of stealing from houses while the people who lived there were away. He never carried a gun while comitting his crimes.

For some time, Felon had carefully been observing the home of the Victims and had seen the Victim family leaving the premises after loading their station wagon with suitcases and gift-wrapped packages. It was the day before Christmas, and Felon assumed that the Victims had gone away for the holiday. The Victim family had indeed left for the holiday, but their eldest son John had, on the day of their departure, returned from college to study for his final examinations.

That night, while John was sleeping in his bedroom upstairs, Felon pried open the front door lock of the Victims' house, intending to enter and steal whatever valuables he could find. John, hearing Felon, jumped out of bed and found Felon standing in the livingroom. Felon turned to flee. John yelled "Stop!" He then descended the stairs and ran toward Felon. When Felon saw John approaching, he grabbed a poker from the fireplace, and brandishing it threateningly at John, he made good his escape, without taking anything from the Victims' house. What is Felon guilty of, if anything?

Answer to Problem V

Felon is guilty of burglary, either in the second or third degree. All of the elements of the crime are present: (1) Felon has forcefully entered the house of another; (2) the house is a "dwelling" because the Victims' son is occupying it (and even if he were not, they intend to return); (3) the entry was at night; and (4) Felon intended to commit larceny. These are the elements of third degree burglary.

Whether Felon is guilty of burglary in the second degree will depend upon two issues: whether the poker he has armed himself with is considered a "deadly weapon"; and whether, when he brandished the poker he intended to inflict bodily injury upon John or just to scare John enough to insure Felon's escape.

If the poker is considered a deadly weapon, Felon is guilty of second degree burglary whether or not he intended to use it to harm John. Irrelevant also is the fact that Felon was unarmed when he entered the Victims' house;

he has armed himself while committing the crime. Since a poker is made of iron and is heavy enough to cause substantial injury, it may well be considered a deadly weapon, especially since pokers have been used to kill during the commission of crimes.

Even though the poker is not judged to be a deadly weapon, Felon may still be charged with second degree burglary if the jury believes that he attempted to use it to inflict bodily harm upon John Victim, although Felon did not actually do so. Felon may argue, in his defense, that he has never carried a gun in the commission of a burglary and that his intent, in brandishing the poker, was only to escape, not to harm John. He may also be able to show that he was too far away from John in the room to make such an attempt possible. If the jury believes him, Felon will be found guilty of third degree burglary.

Problem VI

John and Mary Proprietor live in quarters above their store. After Mary had retired for the night, John Proprietor went down to the store to take inventory. He unintentionally left open the door to the stairs leading to the Proprietors' apartment.

Ken Robb, passing by, sees John at work; he also notices that the door leading up to the apartment is ajar. Thinking that he might pick up some useful or valuable items, he walks up the stairs and into the apartment livingroom.

Mary hears Ken and calls out, "John, is that you?" Receiving no answer, she gets out of bed and goes into the livingroom. Ken has hidden behind the livingroom door and when Mary comes past, he grabs her in a karate hold and throws her on the floor. Then he dashes down the stairs and out through the door. Ignoring any other crimes that Robb may be guilty of, discuss whether he has committed burglary and if so, of what degree.

Answer to Problem VI

In order for Robb to be guilty of burglary in either degree, he must have, using some force, entered a *dwelling, without* the occupant's *consent,* at *night,* with the *intent* to commit larceny.

All the requisites of burglary are present except one. The Proprietors' apartment meets the definition of a dwelling, despite its being situated above their store. Robb entered at night, without Mary Proprietor's consent, and, on entering, had the intent to commit larceny. (That he subsequently changed his mind is no defense.)

If Robb were guilty of burglary, and if his karate attack upon Mary Proprietor caused her any bodily injury, he would be guilty of burglary in the second degree, because he attacked Mary intentionally. That he was not engaged in burglary but was trying to escape when he attacked Mary would be no defense, because the attempt to escape is held to be a part of the commission of the crime.

However, one requisite of burglary is that the entry to the dwelling be accomplished with some force, however slight. John Proprietor had left the door ajar. The question is therefore whether the door was open sufficiently that Robb was able to enter without pushing it open farther or making any physical contact with the door that would be definable as "slight force." If the trier of fact believes that Robb was able to enter the house using no force whatsoever, he is not guilty of burglary.

WRITING PROBLEMS, SET II

Using only the following legal principles, write answers to the hypothetical legal problems below. You should take about 30 minutes to read the facts and write your answer. The legal rules should not be considered complete or accurate. All the rules may not be needed in answering each problem. A good answer, written by a student, follows each problem.

Legal Rules

1. Because there is a duty to conduct oneself with the care for others that a "reasonable man" would take, negligent conduct is that which imposes an unreasonable risk upon others.

II. A causal link must exist between a negligent act and the harm suffered by the victim of it (the act is the cause-in-fact, "but for" which no harm would have occurred).

III. If customary practice is dangerous, conforming to that practice may not prevent one's conduct from being negligent.

IV. If a person contributes proximately to his own injuries, he is barred from recovery (contributory negligence); if a person, voluntarily, with knowledge of the hazard, places himself in a position of danger, he assumes the risk and is barred from recovery (assumption of risk).

V. If a person fails to exercise a "last clear chance" to prevent injury to another, he is liable despite contributory negligence by the other person.

VI. Violation of a state statute constitutes negligence per se.

Problem I

Spectators at college football games held in Rah-Rah Stadium customarily use their programs to make small paper airplanes which they sail through the air toward the playing field. Abel attended the Paluka U. versus Rah-Rah U. game, and after a Rah-Rah touchdown he and other fans hurled these airplanes, with some vigor, downward through the air. At that moment Baker stood up, turned around, and waved to friends in the stands above. Abel's airplane struck Baker's eye, causing considerable damage to the cornea and necessitating surgery.

Discuss Baker's claims and his chance for success against Abel.

Answer to Problem I

Baker (B) may have a cause of action in negligence against Abel (A) because the tossing of paper airplanes in a crowded football stadium may be considered to impose unreasonable risk upon other persons. If so, the argument that A was engaging in a customary activity along with others will not succeed. Courts have held that, even when the custom, dangerous activity may be considered negligent.

B would not have suffered harm except for A's act; thus there is a causal link between B's injury and A's tossing of the airplane. A may argue, however, that B assumed the risk of injury from flying paper planes when he attended the football game. Unless A was an out-of-town visitor who did not know of the Rah-Rah custom, this argument may succeed.

A may have another argument under the theory of contributory negligence. "But for" B's standing up and looking up into the stands, the airplane may have struck him on the back of his head, without harm. The question, then, is whether B's act contributed to his injury when, aware of the airplanes floating through the air all around him, he stood up and looked upward. If so, B will be barred from recovering.

B's chance for success in his claim will depend on (1) whether A's conduct in tossing paper airplanes violated the duty of care for others, (2) and if so, whether B assumed the risk of injury by attending the game, (3) or whether B negligently contributed to the accident by looking back and upwards while airplanes were being tossed. The court may well find that B's contributory acts bar him from recovering from A's behavior.

Problem II

I. Ken Duit drove his car to his eye doctor's office for an eye examination. The doctor put drops in Ken's eyes, blurring Ken's vision, and suggested that Ken wait for two hours before driving home in order for his eyes to return to normal. After half an hour Ken grew bored and decided to leave, although his vision was still somewhat blurred. As he drove along slowly and carefully, he came to a section of the road where construction was taking place and crews of workers were working, having parked their trucks in the bicycle path along the side of the road.

At this time I. Mae Student was bicycling home from classes. Seeing the construction trucks parked on the bicycle path and the crews at work next to them on the edge of the roadway, she decided she would be safer biking on the left side of the road facing oncoming cars than on the right side of the road in the stream of traffic. (A state statute requires that bicyclists either use bicycle paths or ride in the stream of automobile traffic.)

Ken, driving as far as possible to his right in order to leave plenty of room for oncoming vehicles on his left, failed to see Mae and hit her bicycle, causing injuries to Mae. Discuss Mae's negligence claim against Ken.

Answer to Problem II

Ken has the duty to conduct himself with the care that a reasonable person would have for others. In driving with blurred vision despite his doctor's advice, Ken fails in this duty. If his action is the cause-in-fact of Mae's injury Ken will be liable for negligence, according to the given legal rules.

In addition, although the facts do not so indicate, if a statute prohibits persons with impaired vision from driving, Ken may be in violation of it and therefore negligent per se.

Otherwise, Mae's negligence claim may fail because the "but for" link between Ken's behavior and Mae's injury is not established. Mae's own actions may have contributed to her injury. By bicycling on the left side of the road she was, in fact, negligent per se because she was in violation of a state statute. However, Mae can defend against that charge by arguing that it was necessary for her own safety to ignore the statute. In this case, with trucks parked on the bikeway, Mae may have been within her rights to choose what seemed to be a safer alternative.

Her choice may bar her from recovery, however. By riding her bicycle facing traffic, Mae placed herself in a position of danger. She thus "assumed the risk" and contributed toward the harm that she received. She could have instead dismounted from the bicycle and walked it along in whatever paths were provided for pedestrians. If, in so doing, she had been forced to use the roadway and had been struck by Ken, her claim against him would have been much stronger, for vehicle drivers should expect pedestrians to walk on the left and drivers have a duty of care to avoid hitting them.

As it is, Mae's likelihood of success is small. Even if Ken is held negligent for driving with blurred vision, Mae will probably be barred from recovery because of assumption of risk and contributory negligence.

Problem III

Rae C. Driver is driving south in a 35-mile-an-hour zone at 35 miles an hour. The traffic light at the intersection is red as she approaches it, but it suddenly turns green and she continues through it without slowing down. Meanwhile, D. E. Termind is approaching the same intersection, driving east at 35 miles an hour. He sees Rae coming toward him at his left, but the traffic light is yellow, so he continues through, because it is legal to continue through a yellow traffic light. He assumes Rae will apply her brakes because the light is still red in her direction. D. E.'s assumption is wrong, and Mae's car hits his. Discuss liability.

Answer to Problem III

Both parties are liable for negligence. By not slowing down as she approached a red traffic signal, Rae C. Driver imposed an unreasonable risk upon others. Her conduct was the cause-in-fact of the harm that she and D. E. Termind suffered; "but for" her negligence, the collision would not have occurred.

On the other hand, "but for" D. E. Termind's attempt to beat Driver's approaching car by proceeding through the intersection on a yellow light, the collision would not have occurred. D. E. Termind's conduct may therefore be considered to be the cause-in-fact of the accident.

His conduct will also be considered negligent because of the "last clear chance" rule. Seeing Driver approaching, he had the final opportunity to slow down and stop on the yellow light, thus averting the collision. Even if Termind is not held negligent for failing to take advantage of the last clear chance to avoid the accident, he will probably be barred from recovery because of contributory negligence or assumption of risk. His behavior contributed to the accident, and he chose to assume the risk of crossing the intersection in front of an oncoming car.

WRITING PROBLEMS, SET III

Assume that the following legal rules are in effect. Then write an essay answer to each question posed at the end of the hypothetical fact situation. Use only the rules provided; all of the rules may not be required for each question. These rules come from the Restatement (Second) of Torts, but they are not to be considered complete and should therefore not be relied upon to answer any but the problems presented here.

Legal Rules

I. A person is liable to another for battery if he acts intending to cause a harmful or offensive contact with another, or the apprehension of such contact, and harmful or offensive contact results.

   A. If a person intends a harmful or offensive contact with another, or intends to cause apprehension of a harmful or offensive contact with another, and harmful or offensive contact with a third person results instead, the one causing the harm or offense is liable to the third person.

   B. In order for a person to be harmed or offended, he need not himself be touched; anything so closely connected with his body as to be customarily regarded as part of his person is considered to be part of himself.

II. A person is liable to another for assault if he acts intending to cause a harmful or offensive contact or apprehension of an imminent contact to another person and he thereby causes the other person to be apprehensive of an imminent contact.

   A. Assault lies even though the person gives the other person the opportunity to avoid the result by obeying a command, unless the first person is privileged to enforce the command.

   B. Mere words do not constitute assault.

III. A person is not liable for otherwise actionable conduct in assault or battery if the receiver of the conduct has consented to it or if public interest in the conduct is great enough to justify the harm caused or threatened to the receiver.

   A. Anyone subjected to assault or battery has the privilege of using reasonable force to protect himself, but exceeding this privilege will make him the aggressor.

   B. Consent to conduct is terminated if the person to whom the consent was given exceeds the bounds of the consent.

Problem I

Alfred and Betty are friends who enjoy practical jokes and often play them on each other. Without any ill will and entirely as a joke, Alfred hangs a bucketful of cornmeal over a closed door in such a way that when Betty opens the door the cornmeal will fall on her. The trick works; Betty is covered with cornmeal. Being a good sport Betty laughs at first. Later, however, she develops an eye infection from the cornmeal and requires extensive medical treatment. Betty is now considering legal action. What likelihood has she of success?

Answer to Problem I

Betty (B) may have a cause of action against Alfred (A) in battery. A intended to place the cornmeal so that it would fall on B. The resulting contact may well be considered enough to constitute the "offensive contact" required for battery. That A did not intend to cause the eye infection that occurred does not reduce his liability for his action, since he did intend the conduct that resulted in the eye infection. The question is whether A intended an offensive or harmful contact. The facts state that A had no "ill will" and intended his prank "entirely as a joke." Without the intent to cause offense or harm, there can be no battery.

Also crucial in deciding A's liability for battery is whether B had consented to his conduct. If B's consent to their practical joking relationship is held to constitute her implicit consent to his cornmeal prank, A will not be held liable for battery, even if he did intend an offensive contact, unless the bounds of B's consent are judged to have been exceeded in this case.

A may argue that B, by her initial reaction of laughter following the incident, signified that she did not consider the bounds of her consent to have been exceeded. However, B's interest in pursuing a claim against A indicates that, at least after her initial laughter, she did consider her consent to their practical joking relationship to have been exceeded by A's conduct in this incident.

B's delay in taking action will not preclude her recovery of damages. There is no requirement that the victim of harmful or offensive conduct bring suit without delay. If the court is convinced that A intended an offensive or harmful contact that was not impliedly consented to by B, or if it believes A's conduct exceeded the bounds of B's consent, B will succeed in her action against A for battery.

Problem II

A. Player is playing tennis with a friend, B. Tsim, a much better player. A does not like to lose, and as the game progresses he becomes more and more irritable. Finally when B wins the set, A runs to the net brandishing his racquet and yells, "Duck, or I'll hit this ball right into your face!" He then hits the ball wildly. B ducks. A intended to miss B even if B did not duck, and the ball does not come close to B. However it does strike C. Knott, who is behind a bush out of A's vision, searching for a lost ball. C suffers a concussion. What is A liable for, if anything?

Answer to Problem II

Both B and C may bring suit against A. A is liable to B for assault. A drove the tennis ball toward B and intended to cause B apprehension of an imminent offensive or harmful contact. Although A provided B with an option by which B could escape harm, A is still liable, for A is not privileged to enforce his command ("Duck!"). Since B did duck, he clearly expected that otherwise the ball was likely to hit him, and feared injury as a result. Although "mere words" do not constitute assault, the words here were reinforced by conduct that is actionable.

Although A may argue that he was only joking and thus lacked the requisite intent to offend or harm B, the context indicates that this is not true. The further argument by A that B's consent to play tennis encompassed consent to A's final action will probably fail because A's conduct exceeds the bounds of what is normal in a game of tennis.

C has no claim against A in assault, for he did not see the tennis ball that A hit wildly toward C and therefore did not suffer apprehension of imminent contact. C does have a claim against A in battery although A did not intend to strike C with the ball and in fact was not even aware of C's presence behind the bush.

All of the elements requisite for C's claim of battery are present. A intended by his act to cause apprehension of imminent contact. That this apprehension occurred in B, not C, does not remove A's liability. A's liability extends to C, the injured third person. As to the argument that A struck C only by mistake, that fact does not eliminate A's liability to C. When intent to commit battery is present, and an unintended victim receives the action, the doer of the act is liable to that person just as if he were the intended victim. C therefore has a cause of action in battery against A.

In order to answer the next set of problems, you will need to add the following legal rules to those you have been using. Remember that all rules do not necessarily apply to all the problems.

Legal Rules

IV. If a person intends to confine another within fixed boundaries or if his action results in such a confinement and if the other person is conscious of or harmed by the confinement, the first person is liable for false imprisonment.

   A. If the person confining another person does not intend to do so, and

   B. If the confinement is transitory or otherwise harmless, the first person is not liable.

V. A person is privileged to retake property that another person has wrongfully taken from him, after first asking the taker to return it. If the first person is mistaken in his belief that the property was taken, the privilege is nullified.

VI. A person who recklessly or intentionally causes severe emotional distress to another is subject to liability for that distress and, if bodily harm results to the second person, is liable for that harm as well.

    A. In order for language to be reckless it must be so outrageous as to exceed the bounds of decency.

    B. A person is liable to a third person for emotional distress for conduct described in V (above) if that person is a member of the immediate family of the person at whom the conduct was directed, whether or not the third person suffers bodily harm, and to any other person present who suffers bodily harm from the conduct of the actor.

Problem III

While shopping at a grocery store, Ms. K. Smart (K) saw a five-pound bag of sugar with one price sticker placed over another. The top sticker read "$3.00," but K peeled it off and found another reading "$2.50." When she attempted to pay for the sugar at the checkout counter, the Checker (C) noticed that the top sticker had been removed and said to K, "What a cheat! What a gyp! It's cheats like you that make food prices go up!" K had already placed $2.50 on the counter, and, very upset at C's words, she picked up the sugar and headed for the door.

The store manager (M), hearing the checker's words, assumed that K had not paid for the sugar, and he stopped in front of K as she was about to leave the store. K pushed M to one side in order to get to the door, saying, "Get out of my way, you Jerk!" M attempted to take the sugar out of K's hand, but instead knocked her pocketbook to the floor, causing it to open and the contents to spill out. M then stepped aside, and K picked up her belongings and left the store, carrying the sugar. What liability, if any arises from this incident?

Answer to Problem III

K has no claim in assault against C because "mere words" do not suffice for an action in assault. As to a claim of intentional infliction of emotional distress by K against C, two elements of the tort are present: (1) C's words were uttered intentionally and (2) for the purpose of causing K distress. However, mere insults are not enough to activate this tort and C's words, though unfair and unkind, fall within the description of mere insults. To be actionable, the language would have to be describable as "outrageous" by a reasonable person.

M, in attempting to bar K's exit, may be liable for false imprisonment. His act seems intended to keep K inside the store. She was aware of her confinement, as evidenced by her pushing M aside in order to depart.

However, the fact that she was able to push him out of her way will probably nullify her claim of false confinement.

With regard to K's liability to M in battery, this action will also probably fail. Although K's words were accompanied by an action offensive to M (pushing him) she is privileged to free herself from her confinement, and her effort to do so does not seem excessive.

M's conduct, in trying to grab the sugar from K, is unprivileged whether he was reacting to K's shove or attempting to regain possession of merchandise he believed had not been paid for. He is privileged to use reasonable force in protecting himself against K's shove, but his grabbing of the sugar was not in self-protection, but an attempt to regain possession of the sugar. His effort in this respect is not privileged, for (1) he must request that K give him the sugar before trying to re-take it, and (2) the privilege to regain possession is nullified because he is mistaken in his belief that K has not paid for it. (Even if K owes an additional 50 cents for the sugar, the first reason nullifies any privilege of M.)

Whether M is liable for battery against K for knocking her pocketbook to the floor will depend upon whether his offensive intent was directed at some item closely related to K's person. If he had intended contact with K's pocketbook, he would be probably liable for battery, because a woman's pocketbook is so closely associated with her body as to be considered a part of her person. But although M's offensive contact was with K's pocketbook, he intended contact with the sugar. Unless the bag of sugar is considered so closely associated with K that an intended offensive contact with it is equivalent to an intended offensive contact with K herself, M will not be liable for battery.

The likelihood is therefore that none of the behavior described in the fact situation is actionable in torts: neither C's conduct toward K, nor K's conduct toward M, nor M's conduct toward K.

Problem IV

Two 12-year-old boys, Cain (C) and Abel (A), are playing a game of throwing stones at each other on the sidewalk in front of their house. A stone thrown by A hits C on the head, causing C considerable pain. In retaliation, C hurls a stone at A, which misses A and knocks off the hat of a pedestrian (P) who is walking past.

Thinking that A had thrown the stone, P angrily grabs A and shakes him, saying, "I'm going to knock your block off." A kicks and hits P until P frees A and leaves, threatening to have A arrested. Discuss tort liability.

Answer to Problem IV

Regarding A's liability to C: C was harmed by a stone that A threw at him intentionally. In order to satisfy the requirements of battery, A must have intended to cause the harmful or offensive contact. The element of assault may be present if C saw the stone approaching and was apprehensive of imminent, offensive contact.

However, A will probably not be held liable to C because C has consented to A's conduct by agreeing to play the game—and in fact was also engaging in throwing stones. C's consent will eliminate liability for an act for which A would otherwise be liable.

Regarding C's liability to P: C is liable to P for battery because C acted intending to cause a harmful or offensive contact (throwing the stone) and did so when the stone struck P's hat. The hat that was knocked from P's head is so closely connected with P that it will probably be considered part of P's person. If P saw the stone before it reached him, C may also be liable to P in assault, for placing P in apprehension of an imminent contact. However, since P did not know who had thrown the stone, he may not have seen it before he was struck, removing C's assault liability.

If A was placed in reasonable apprehension of imminent physical harm by P's threat, accompanied by P's act of shaking A, P is liable for assault. Whether P actually intended to "knock [A's] block off" is not relevant if A was apprehensive that P would do so. Even if P did not harm A by shaking him, if A was offended by that act, P is liable to A for battery since P's behavior was intentional and without privilege.

P may also be liable to A for false imprisonment. By holding his arm, P briefly prevented A from getting away. A was aware that he was confined, as indicated by his struggle to free himself. However, P may argue that he did not intend to confine A, only to retaliate for A's supposed act of striking P's hat with a stone. Since A's confinement was only transitory and since A was not harmed by it, P's defense against the charge of false imprisonment may succeed.

Finally, regarding A's kicking and hitting of P: Since A acted in order to escape from P, who had mistakenly confined A, A will probably not be held liable to P for battery. One is permitted to defend himself against another unless one's reaction is excessive, which it does not seem to have been in this case.

Problem V

Ima Customer went to A. Dolt's jewelry store with her six-year-old daughter Jean and Monte, another child the same age. Ima intended to buy a watch for Jean's birthday, but after Jean had chosen the watch and tried it on, Ima discovered she did not have enough money to pay for the watch. She therefore asked A to allow her to charge the watch, although she had no charge account with the store. A responded that Ima could instead pay for the watch by sexual favors to him.

When Ima indignantly refused, A yelled at her: "Don't be so high and mighty; I know you are a whore!" He then reached across the counter as if to grab Ima, but did not do so.

By this time Ima had removed the watch from Jean's wrist and the three persons left the store, Ima yelling, "You'll be sorry for this!" Both Jean and her little friend Monte have had frequent nightmares as a result of this incident. Ima would like to bring suit against A. Dolt. What are her chances of success?

Answer to Problem V

Because of A. Dolt's conduct, Ima may have a cause of action for assault against him on her own behalf and for the intentional infliction of emotional distress on behalf of herself and Jean.

When A reached across the counter to grab Ima, he intended to cause an offensive contact with her. If she was indeed offended by his act, as seems certain by her interest in taking legal action, the only remaining issue is whether Ima was apprehensive of *imminent* contact. If A's proximity was such that a reasonable person could apprehend immediate contact by his reaching across the counter, or if he were close enought to come quickly around the counter to make contact with Ima, all elements of assault exist and A will be held liable to Ima for assault.

In order for A to be liable for the intentional infliction of emotional distress, the words he used must have been beyond the bounds of decency, such that a reasonable person would, on hearing them, exclaim, "Outrageous!" If Ima is not a prostitute, A's words may certainly meet this criterion. If, as well, Ima can prove that she has suffered mental or physical distress resulting from his language, A will be liable to Ima for this tort. The facts do not indicate that she suffered such distress, although she was angry enough to consider legal action.

Ima's daughter Jean has suffered demonstrable mental distress resulting from A's conduct toward her mother. Her nightmares are traceable to this incident. That A did not address his comments to the child, and may even have been unaware of her presence is no defense. Jean's presence and her status of close relationship with her mother make A liable to her for any emotional distress she suffers from the incident.

This close relationship does not exist between Ima and Jean's little friend Monte. A therefore will not be liable to Monte for the emotional distress (nightmares) he suffered from the encounter. But if Monte suffers "bodily harm," such as loss of weight or other physical effects resulting from A's conduct toward Ima, A will also be liable to Monte for the intentional infliction of emotional distress.

Problem VI

Arline (A) is a telephone operator in a small town. Bainsby (B) asks her help in finding the address of a client in another town. A refuses to give B the information he wants, but does not explain why she will not give him the information. (In fact, the telephone company prohibits such information to callers.)

B is irritated. He tells A that he is a very important executive in B's Automotive Agency, and he demands to speak to A's employer. A refuses to connect B. B then calls A a worthless critter, a loser, and a god-damned female. He further states that he will teach her a lesson the next time he sees her.

Late that night as she is leaving work A sees B, about ten yards away, leaning against the lamppost at the corner of the street, with his hands in his pockets. Much upset, A nevertheless walks past B, who does not change his position, but stares at A, unblinkingly. A suffers from nervousness and sleeplessness for several weeks afterwards. What liability?

Answer to Problem VI

B's language on the telephone to A is rude and insulting, but will probably not meet the standard of "outrageousness" required for the intentional infliction of emotional distress. His telephone threat to teach her a lesson the next time he sees her is offensive and places A in fear of attack, but two elements of assault are lacking: words alone do not constitute assault, and B did not threaten immediate contact. Nor is B liable for assault when A sees him staring at her as she leaves work, since he makes no attempt at a harmful or offensive contact at that time.

B may, however, be liable to A for the infliction of emotional distress because by the combination of threatening language (by telephone) and his subsequent appearance, seemingly to carry out his threat, he has caused A emotional and physical distress. B's defense against this charge may be that he did not intend his presence to cause A emotional distress and that his position at the lamppost as B approached was entirely coincidental. If the jury believes him, B will not be found liable to A. The key issue is whether B's action is outrageous and beyond the bounds of reasonable behavior. If so, B will be liable to A.

Problem VII

Aikins (A) and Baldy (B) are clients of a large private gymnasium. After working out with barbells and other weights, A and B, as is their custom, undress and enjoy a long soak in the gym's Turkish bath.

While they are soaking, through an error, the gymnasium owner locks the door leading from the bath to the room where they have left their clothes. When they attempt to leave the room they discover that the only exit from the bath is through a large room, lined with mirrors, in which about 50 teenaged girls are practising ballet.

They discuss their dilemma and A decides to leave. Wrapping his towel around himself he traverses the room, ignoring as well as he can the stares of the ballet dancers. A subsequently informs the owner about B's plight and the owner unlocks the door to the room holding B's clothes. B contracts a heavy cold from his long stay in the Turkish bath, and the cold turns into pneumonia. What liability results?

Answer to Problem VII

The confinement of both A and B by the gymnasium owner was unintentional. Therefore if the confinement was transitory or otherwise harmless, the owner will not be liable. The men were both aware of and annoyed by their confinement. A, however, was confined for only a brief time and was not harmed in any other way by it. A therefore has no claim against the owner.

The question to be decided before the owner's liability to B can be determined is whether the only means of exit that was available was one that a reasonable person would choose over confinement. A did choose that exit and suffered only minor embarrassment and no physical harm, but A's sensitivity to indignity might be less than that of a normal reasonable person. If the court decides that B was justified in remaining in the Turkish bath rather than exiting in front of the ballerinas, the gymnasium owner will be liable to B for false confinement, since B's subsequent illness satisfies the requisite harmful result.

WRITING PROBLEMS, SET IV

Only the legal rules given below are to be used in answering the problems that follow. All rules may not be applicable to each problem, and the usual caution applies: the rules are not complete and should not be relied upon in answering problems other than those posed here.

Legal Rules

(Possession of Personal Property) [1]

I. Possession of property consists of physical possession plus the intent to possess and exclude others from possession.

II. Possession is a basic property interest carrying certain rights such as:

   A. the right to continue peaceful possession against everyone except those who have a better right;

   B. the right to recover possession when the property is wrongfully taken.

III. The finder of property has certain rights:

   A. the finder of lost property on the land of another acquires title against all but the true owner, especially when the finder is not a trespasser;

   B. the finder of "treasure trove"—coins or money secreted by an unknown owner—has the same rights as the finder of lost property;

   C. the finder of abandoned property (property voluntarily relinquished by its owner) is entitled to possession and title of the property;

   D. the finder of misplaced property, however, does not obtain title, but the owner of the property on which it was found is considered to be the holder of the goods for the true owner.

Problem I

One A. Hunter was engaged, with his hounds, in the hot pursuit of a fox in a wild, unpossessed area. N. Termeddler, happening upon the scene and

1. From C. H. Smith and R. E. Boyer, *Survey of the Law of Property*, 2nd Ed., 1971, pp. 456–457.

seeing that the fox was tiring, killed the fox and carried it away. A. Hunter sued for the value of the fox and received a judgment in his favor; N. Termeddler now appeals. You are a judge in the court of appeals; write an opinion for the court.[2]

Answer to Problem I

Wild animals living in their natural state are owned by no one. Therefore he who (1) has the intent to possess the animal and exclude others from possession and (2) gains physical possession of the animal is the rightful owner.

A. Hunter (A) intended to possess the fox and was engaged in the effort to capture it. However he had not yet mortally wounded the fox or in any other way brought it under certain control. Mere pursuit of a wild animal, although accompanied by the intent to capture it, does not convey the right of possession.

N. Termeddler's (N's) interception of A's pursuit of the fox and his subsequent gaining of physical possession of the animal satisfied the two requirements of possession: intent to possess exclusively and physical possession. N's conduct may have been unkind and discourteous, but A has no legal remedy available to him. Therefore the judgment of the court in awarding ownership of the fox to A was erroneous and should be reversed. This court finds in favor of the plaintiff, N. Termeddler.

Problem II

A group of four boys were playing, as was their custom, in a vacant lot. One of the boys found what looked like a large ball of used twine that had been re-wound for later use and then either lost or thrown away. The boys played with the ball of twine for some time, throwing it from one to the other until it finally began to unravel, revealing that the center was composed of old paper currency in the amount of $10,000. The boy who found the ball now claims the money. Is his claim likely to be upheld by a court?

Answer to Problem II

The boy's entitlement to the money inside the ball of twine depends first of all upon whether it was lost, abandoned, or misplaced. If the ball of twine was abandoned the finder has title superior to that of any other person. If the twine was lost, or is classified as treasure trove, the finder has rights superior to all but the right of the true owner. If the twine is classified as misplaced, the lot owner may hold it for its true owner.

In this fact situation the true owner of the twine is making no claim for it and is, in fact, unknown. The twine may well be considered to be lost property. Then the only claim to the money other than that of the finder would be that of the owner of the vacant lot, if the boys were trespassers upon the lot when they found the twine. Since they were in the habit of playing on

---

2. These facts are adapted from a famous early legal decision which you may wish to read. See *Pierson v. Post,* 3 Caines 175 (Supreme Court of N. Y. 1805).

the lot, they will probably not be considered trespassers. If they are not trespassers, the boy who found the twine may be held to be the rightful owner.

The question now becomes whether the boy who found the twine can be said to have found the money enclosed within the ball of twine. It is arguable that he did not, but that the money was not found until it was revealed by the unravelling twine. If so, then all the boys, by their tossing the ball of twine back and forth, participated in "finding" the money and all will be considered co-finders and entitled to a pro rata share of the money.

If the true owner of the money should appear and demand the money back, his claim will prevail unless the boys were able to prove that the ball of twine had been abandoned by the true owner.

Problem III

A maid in a motel, while cleaning the room of a departed guest, found a bundle of dollars, secured by a rubber band, between the mattress and box springs of the bed. She took the money to the motel owner and gave it to him for keeping until the original owner claimed it. She made the provision, however, that should the original owner not claim the money within a year, she would return for it. The motel owner attempted to locate the owner of the bills, but did not succeed. At the end of the year, the maid returned and demanded that the money be turned over to her. Does she have the right to it?

Answer to Problem III

The maid's right to the money, if she has the right, is only against all others except the rightful owner. The question of whether she has even that right depends upon whether the money is considered to have been lost, abandoned, or misplaced.

In this situation, the final category seems to be the appropriate one. The money was probably not abandoned, since it was carefully secured by a rubber band and placed in a spot from which the owner intended to remove it. For the same reason, it will probably not be classified as lost. The owner probably knew where it was; he merely forgot to retrieve it when he left the motel.

If the money was misplaced by the owner, the owner of the property where the money was left is entitled to retain possession of it, as against the right of the maid, for two reasons: (1) the original owner may still remember where he left the money and return to claim it; and (2) the duty of the maid is to turn over to her employer any property left in the rooms and found in the course of her employment.

The maid therefore has no legal right to enforce her provision that the money be turned over to her by the motel owner at the expiration of a year unless the original owner was found. The motel owner will continue to hold the money for the true owner.

Problem IV

A. Bird is a birdwatcher who enjoys early morning walks in the country. One weekend, intent on such a walk, she parked her car on the highway adjacent to property that Farmer Clark owns but does not cultivate and that is not visible from his farmhouse. Bird went onto Clark's property looking for birds, and while walking along discovered a mound of dirt. Curious, she dug into the dirt and found a rusty tin box, which, when opened, revealed numerous gold coins.

Bird carried the box to her car and placed it in the trunk, then headed home. En route she had a flat tire. A passing motorist, B. Helpful, stopped to aid her in changing the tire, and Bird told him of her find and showed him the coins. Aware that they were very valuable, Helpful helped himself to as many coins as he could stuff into his pockets while Bird was not watching.

Helpful has now come to you to find out what rights he, Bird, and Clark have with regard to the coins. Answer his question, using only the rules provided for this group of problems.

Answer to Problem IV

Since the coins were on the property of Farmer Clark, he had physical possession of them. However, if he was unaware of their presence on his property, he cannot be said to have the intent to possess them or to exclude others from possessing them. In order to decide whether Clark has a right to the coins, therefore, the first question to be answered is whether he knew of the presence of the coins on his property.

If Clark himself placed the coins where A. Bird found them, he is their rightful owner, having met the two requirements for possession: physical possession and the intent to possess and to exclude others from possession. Clark then has the right to peaceful possession against all other persons and to recover possession of the coins if they were wrongfully taken.

It seems unlikely, however, that Clark had placed the coins in the place where Bird found them. If he had had the intent to exclude others from possession, he would probably not have buried the coins so near the highway and so far from his home as not to be visible from there.

If Clark had not placed the coins where Bird found them, but knew they were there, he may still have the requisite intent to possess them, and would then have the right to maintain peaceful possession against all except the true owner of the coins. However, this also seems unlikely. If Clark had found the coins, he would probably have moved them to a spot where he could better maintain exclusive possession of them. Thus his intent to possess the coins may be negated by his failure to move them, even if he claims awareness of their presence.

If the coins are defined as misplaced property, Clark would still retain possession of them, as against both Bird and Helpful, despite his unawareness of their existence. With respect to misplaced property (goods left by error), the owner of the property on which it is found retains it until the return of the true owner. Thus, although Bird found the coins, Clark's right to them would be superior to hers.

That the coins will be designated as misplaced property, however, seems unlikely. They have more the characteristics of "treasure trove" (valuable coins secreted in the earth by an unknown owner). Since whoever left them covered them with a mound of dirt, they do not seem to have been left inadvertently.

As finder of treasure trove, Bird has the same rights as the finder of lost property. Generally the finder of lost property acquires title to it against all except the true owner (in this case the unknown person who buried it). But to clarify Bird's rights, her status on Clark's property must be decided. She may have permission to walk on Clark's farm. If so, she is not a trespasser and had rights to the coins superior to Clark's. But if, as the facts suggest, Bird has come onto Clark's land without his knowledge, she may be classified as a trespasser. Her rights to the coins are then less certain and may be a question for the court to decide, since the legal rule is not clear on this point.

Less questionable is Helpful's status with regard to the coins. In removing the coins from Bird's car trunk without her permission, Helpful is a wrongdoer and, although he has the intent to possess the coins as well as physical possession of them, both Bird and Clark have a better right to the coins than Helpful and may recover peaceful possession of them from him.

Problem V [3]

N. Owner bought an unoccupied house in 1938, which he never lived in. About two years later, during World War II, the house was requisitioned by the armed forces, and soldiers were stationed there. During this period, A. Soldier lived in the house.

One day, while he was in the bedroom that was used as sick bay, Soldier found a brooch wedged into the upper frame of a window of the room. The brooch was covered with cobwebs and dust, as if it had been there for years. Soldier took it home to his wife during his next leave, and she told him that it looked very valuable. He then consulted his commissioned officer, who advised him to take it to the police, which he did. The police gave Soldier a receipt for the brooch and held it for two years. When no one claimed it, the police turned the brooch over to Owner, who sold it. Owner offered Soldier a reward for finding the brooch, but Soldier refused, claiming that he, not Owner, was the rightful owner.

In 1945, Soldier sued Owner for the value of the brooch. What would you believe the reasoning of the Court will be and what the decision?

Answer to Problem V

First to be decided is how the brooch is to be classified. It will probably not be considered abandoned property because a person intending to abandon property would probably not take the trouble to place it carefully into a crevice

---

3. This problem is an adaptation of a famous English case which you may wish to read. See *Hannah v. Peel*, 1 K.B. (1945).

out of sight of the average observer. The brooch will therefore probably be considered either misplaced or lost property.

The owner of the brooch may (like the owner of the billfold found under the mattress in a motel) have removed the brooch and put it into the crevice for safekeeping, then forgotten it was there. If so, the brooch would be considered misplaced property. Or the owner, while cleaning the window, may have lost the brooch. It may have dropped into the crevice without the owner's knowledge and remained there despite a search for it. If so, the brooch would be classified as lost property.

If the brooch is considered misplaced, Owner will have rights to it superior to the right of Soldier, presumably because the true owner of the brooch would be more likely to return for the brooch to the house where it was lost. But this reasoning does not really apply to the present facts because the house was never occupied by Owner, and at least 7 years have passed since he purchased the house, which was then already vacant. The brooch almost certainly was left in the crevice during the occupancy of previous owners. Owner never knew of its existence and therefore had no intent to possess it until it was given to him by the police, some two years after Soldier found it.

If, on the other hand, the brooch is classified as lost, Soldier will have title to the brooch superior to all others except that of the true owner. Since Soldier was living in the house in which he found the brooch, Soldier was not a trespasser. Soldier did not find the brooch in the process of carrying out his duties as an employee of Owner (as did the maid in the motel who found the money under the mattress while changing the bed).

Soldier's conduct, with regard to the brooch was exemplary. Though he might have kept the brooch for himself without being discovered, he turned it over to the police and waited for the true owner to appear. Equity seems to require that the brooch be designated as lost rather than misplaced, since Soldier, by the facts, seems to have a superior right to possession of the brooch, or the value thereof, than Owner.

The Court will therefore probably find that the brooch was lost and that Soldier is entitled to recover its full value.

WRITING PROBLEMS, SET V

The following set of problems deals with contracts. The same caveats apply here as to the previous problems. The rules provided are not necessarily in effect in your jurisdiction and are certainly not complete. They should be used only in the problems provided here. All of the rules are not applicable to every problem, but you will need no other rules to deal with the problems. Allow about one hour to read and answer each question.

Legal Rules

I. Parties are free to make whatever contracts they please as long as the contracts involve no fraud or illegality.

II. Minors (persons under 21) and mentally incompetent persons have no legal capacity to incur contractual duties.

   A. Thus contracts entered into by minors are voidable by them.

   B. But contracts entered into by minors for the necessities of life are not voidable.

   C. If a minor represents himself as an adult and thereby receives and retains benefits from a contract, he can not avoid the contract by pleading his minority.

III. The mental illness or defect of one party to a contract makes the contract voidable by that party or his successor in interest, unless the party's mental disability has not affected the making of the contract.

IV. Courts will not permit the enforcement of shockingly unfair (unconscionable) contracts.

Problem I [4]

A, a public school teacher for more than 40 years, became mentally ill at age 60 and took a one-year leave of absence from her teaching. Her psychiatrist subsequently diagnosed her illness as involutional psychosis, complicated by cerebral arteriosclerosis.

Some years before her illness, she had elected Option One of the Teachers Retirement System in which she was enrolled, this option allotting small periodic money payments to her after her retirement, with her husband as beneficiary of the unexhausted reserve after her death. However, when her leave of absence expired at the end of the year, and while she was still under psychiatric treatment, A executed an application of retirement revoking her previous assignment of her husband as beneficiary and requested instead the maximum payment of benefits during her lifetime, with nothing payable after death. At the same time she borrowed $8760, the maximum cash withdrawal possible, from the retirement system.

Three days before she changed her retirement option she had written the Retirement Board a lucid letter stating her intention to retire and requesting the answers to eight specific questions about the various alternatives available to her. The chief clerk of the Board testified that he responded to A's questions both in writing, and orally when she appeared before him. She did not receive the written statement, however, until after she had changed her retirement plan during her personal visit. Two months after retiring, A died.

A and her husband, B, had been married happily for 38 years at the time of her death. After she took leave of absence from her teaching, B quit his job to care for her, because she had, according to both B and the psychiatrist, become very depressed. The couple were in very modest circumstances. On the day she changed her retirement plan, B drove her to the Retirement

---

4. These facts are similar to those of a famous case, *Ortelere v. Teachers Retirement Bd.*, 25 N.Y.2d 196, 303 N.Y.S.2d 362, 250 N.E.2d 460 (1969). You may wish to read the actual decision and dissent.

Board, but he said that he did not know why she was going and did not ask for fear she would "begin crying hysterically."

B now brings suit against the Retirement Board to revoke his deceased wife's actions in changing her retirement benefits so as to exclude him from benefits as her beneficiary. What result?

Answer to Problem I

Since there was no evidence of fraud or illegality in the final contract between A and the retirement system only two issues must be considered in deciding whether contract signed by her is voidable.

The first issue is whether A was mentally ill and thus without legal capacity to incur contractual duties. Since A had been diagnosed as mentally ill by the psychiatrist who took care of her, and had been forced by that illness to take a leave of absence from her teaching, there seems no doubt that she comes under this classification. Furthermore, her very action of changing her retirement plan two months before her death so as to cut her husband, B, off from benefits as her beneficiary may be considered additional proof of her mental illness. She and her husband had been happily married for many years, he had quit his own job so as to care for her during her final illness, and she was well aware of their "modest" financial condition. The conclusion may therefore be that had she been mentally competent, she would hardly have elected to change her retirement plan so as to greatly reduce the amount paid from the funds she had contributed to for 40 years and at the same time deprive her husband of all beneficiary rights on her death. If A is found to have been mentally ill when she signed the final contract with the retirement system, the contract will be held void and her earlier option will prevail, reinstating her husband as beneficiary.

But it is at least arguable that despite the diagnosis of involutional psychosis, A was mentally competent at the time she entered into her final transaction with the board. One indication that she was mentally competent is that at the same time she wrote a letter to the board, lucidly listing eight specific questions about alternatives available to her. Her letter reflected substantial understanding of the retirement system.

A second indication that A was mentally competent during her final transaction with the board is that her choice of the new option is rationally explicable in view of the new circumstances in which A found herself. Her decision to receive the maximum payments seems reasonable, based upon the greater needs of support for herself and her husband, since he had quit his job to take care of her. There is no evidence in the facts that A had any premonition of impending death, so her election of the maximum retirement benefits may well have been made to provide the greatest possible returns during her lifetime. Her borrowing of the maximum amount from the retirement fund ($8760) also seems reasonable in this context.

If the court finds that A's acts in her final transaction with the retirement system were unaffected by her mental illness, despite her physician's diagnosis of involutional psychosis, the final contract will be held enforceable and B's claim that A's previous contract be enforced instead will probably be denied.

There is, however, one other issue that may result in a decision favorable to B. If the transaction between A and the retirement board two months before A's death resulted in an unconscionable contract, the court may refuse to enforce it. The court may consider it unconscionable to enforce a contract made by a person mentally ill, two months before her death, effectively nullifying 40 years of participation in a system established for the protection of its participating teachers and their heirs.

Problem II [5]

A married couple, who were Spanish immigrants and spoke no English, visited an appliance store in New York City. While they were looking at a refrigerator-freezer, they were approached by a Spanish-speaking salesman, who attempted to sell them the appliance. The husband explained that they could not buy the refrigerator-freezer because he was about to lose his job the following week. In response, the salesman explained that the appliance would actually be free; they would be paid $25.00 in commission for each similar appliance that they sold friends and neighbors.

Following this salestalk, the husband signed a contract, written in English, for $1,145.88: $900.00, the cash price of the refrigerator-freezer, and $245.88 in credit charges. The cost of the refrigerator-freezer to the dealer was $348.00.

The refrigerator-freezer is now in the possession of the purchasers. The only payment made by them was in the amount of $32.00. The appliance store owner (plaintiff) brings action for a total of $1,364.10: $1,145.88, for the original purchase price; $227.35 for attorney fees; and $22.87 for late charges. What result?

Answer to Problem II

In order to determine the probable result, two issues need to be resolved: (1) whether the contract between the seller and the purchaser was fraudulent; and (2) if not, whether the contract was unconscionable. An affirmative answer to either question would make the contract voidable.

With regard to possible fraud on the seller's part, since the buyers could understand no English, they were completely dependent upon the Spanish-speaking salesman, who seems to have improperly influenced them by convincing them that they would not need to pay for the appliance. Since their "friends and neighbors" were poor like themselves, there was almost no possibility that the purchasers could sell enough similar appliances to avoid paying for the appliance they purchased. If the salesman knew that such a possibility was so remote as hardly to exist, the seller may be deemed to have committed fraud.

5. This is a paraphrase of an actual court case. For the decision, see *Frosti-* *fresh Corp. v. Reynoso,* N.Y.Dist.Ct., 52 Misc.2d 26, 274 N.Y.S.2d 757 (1966).

Fraud might also have existed in the signing of the sales contract. Had the contract been written in Spanish, the defendants might have detected the exorbitant credit cost of the purchase. Since it was not, and the plaintiffs knew the defendants understood no English, fraud by the seller may be suggested. If the court finds that the defendant was fraudulently induced to sign the contract, it will refuse to enforce it.

If the court finds no fraud, however, it may still consider the contract unconscionable. The credit charge of $245.88 was almost equal to the plaintiff's cost of the appliance. There is no indication that defendants were told of these exorbitant credit costs, and they were unable to discover this fact for themselves because the contract was printed in a language they could not read. If the court finds that the contract was unconscionable, it may refuse to enforce it and to elect one of the following options: (1) Defendant might be required to reimburse plaintiff only for plaintiff's cost of the appliance ($348.00); (2) defendant might be required to pay for plaintiff's cost of the appliance, plus a reasonable markup and installment cost; or (3) defendant may be offered the alternative of returning the appliance to the seller at no cost to plaintiff or at a charge covering the amount of use he has had of the appliance.

Problem III [6]

A, who is sixteen years old, purchased from B, an automobile dealer, a used car. B was aware that A was a minor. A at first put $50.00 down toward the price of the car, then returned two days later accompanied by his grandmother and aunt. During this second visit, A's aunt drove the car around the lot several times. Then A paid the remaining $90.00 due on the car, with money his aunt had lent him for this purpose. The dealer gave A a receipt, naming A as the purchaser.

A kept the car for a week. The car then broke down and he took it back to the dealer and was told by the dealer's mechanic that the main bearing was burned out and repairs would cost from $45.00 to $95.00. He refused to pay this amount and left the car on the dealer's lot. Then he wrote a letter to the dealer disaffirming the sales contract and demanding the return of his purchase price.

The dealer states that he "understood" that A needed the car for transportation to and from his summer job at a restaurant eight miles from his home. A said, however, that he never drove it to work, and used it only for recreational purposes. A stated that his usual method of getting to work was with the restaurant cook, and that sometimes he "bummed" rides. The dealer further stated that an inference could be drawn from the evidence that the burned-out bearing was caused by A's operation of the car without putting oil in the crankcase.

Is A legally entitled to a refund?

6. These facts are substantially the same as those of *Bowling v. Sperry*, 133 Ind.App. 692, 184 N.E.2d 901 (1962). You may wish to read the decision of the court in its entirety.

Answer to Problem III

Since A paid for the car in cash and received a receipt from B, the dealer, and since there seems no evidence of fraud or other illegality in the sale, a legal sales contract exists. It is not relevant that A borrowed money from his aunt for part of the purchase price of the car or that his aunt apparently approved the purchase after driving the car around the dealer's lot. The contract, signed by the dealer, contained A's name as purchaser.

As a minor, however, A has no legal capacity to incur contractual duties, and he may therefore choose to disaffirm any contract signed by himself unless the article purchased was for a necessity of life. The dealer says he understood that A needed the car to drive back and forth to his employment. Even if A did make such a statement, the car was in fact not used for that purpose, but only for recreational purposes, during the week that A owned it. Thus, although to a teenager, a car might seem a necessity, the dealer has no ground for claiming "necessity" as a means of holding A to the contract.

The question of whether the burned-out bearing was due to an inherent defect in the car or to A's failure to put oil in the crankcase need not be considered. Whichever the case, A is legally within his rights as a minor to disaffirm the contract.

The court will probably force the dealer to refund A's purchase price of $140.00, minus a charge to A for whatever benefit he received from the use of the car for one week.

Problem IV

A, a student at Podunk University law school, is 20 years old, but looks older. Because his handwriting is almost illegible, he buys an electric typewriter costing $1,000.00 from B, owner of a local office supply company. A pays cash for the typewriter and receives a receipt from B. At the bottom of the receipt is printed the following statement: "The buyer hereby warrants that he is 21 years old or older." A line follows the statement, and at B's suggestion, A signs his name on the line without reading the statement.

A uses the typewriter for a few months, but then he decides that law school requires too much effort and time. He also discovers that his use of the typewriter has not brought him success in his final examinations. Therefore, one month after his twenty-first birthday, he returns to the office supply store, places the typewriter on the counter, and informs B that he no longer has any use for the typewriter and wants his $1,000.00 back. B promises to think about A's request and give him an answer in a few days.

B now consults you, knowing that you are in law school. He explains that he cannot sell the used typewriter at anything like its "new" price. For one thing, the machine, while not abused, has had considerable use, and for another, the new models have just come out, reducing the value of this earlier model. Advise B of his probable rights.

Answer to Problem IV

The sales contract entered into by A and B seems valid, involving no fraud or illegality. B had no reason to doubt that he was dealing with an adult, and cannot be said to have used fraud to persuade A to sign the contract. Nor does there seem to have been any fraudulent intent on A's part in signing the contract signifying that he was an adult.

Since A was in fact a minor when he bought the typewriter, he would ordinarily not be held to a contract he wished to disaffirm. In this case, however, A represented himself as an adult and received certain benefits from the contract, namely the use of the typewriter for several months. On the other hand, A's return of the typewriter is evidence that he no longer wishes to retain these benefits. The legal rule states that in order for A to be held to a contract he signed while a minor, claiming to be an adult, he must both *receive* and *retain* the benefits of the contract. The court must decide whether A has done so.

If the court decides he has, A will not be aided by the defense that he erred in signing the statement that he was at least 21 years old. Courts generally consider that persons should be held to promises made in writing and not be permitted to waive such promises on the ground that they did not read what they signed.

If the court decides that A's return of the typewriter permits him to avoid the contract, B may argue that A should nevertheless be held to it because the typewriter was a necessity, and minors cannot void contracts for necessities. This argument is likely to fail. Courts generally consider that only items like food, clothing, and shelter, are definable as necessities. An electric typewriter for a law student would not come under this classification.

The court may choose a middle path between holding A to his contract and permitting him to avoid it. It may instead require B to accept the returned typewriter and refund to A the amount of money it can be sold for in its used condition.

APPENDIX

Everyone knows that a good way to learn a subject is to teach it. This applies to almost any skill, from chess to tennis, and it is the reason for this Appendix. Now that you have studied important writing techniques, you can apply them, as you correct the writing errors of other persons like yourself.

All of the writing problems that appear in the sentences and paragraphs in this Appendix are taken from actual legal writing, most of them from the writing of law students, but some from newspapers and journals, and a few from appellate court opinions. Following each exercise are corrected answers. You can teach yourself by revising the incorrect examples and then comparing your revisions with the answers provided.

Two caveats: First, when you correct the writing errors, change the badly written sentences as little as possible, instead of revising them so as to avoid the problem altogether. For example, in the exercise dealing with the punctuation of restrictive and non-restrictive relative clauses (Chapter One, Section 7), you can sidestep the problem by changing the sentence structure to delete the relative clauses. But instead punctuate the relative clauses correctly. You will need to use relative clauses in your legal writing, and this is the time to learn how to punctuate them.

Second, when you revise the incorrectly written sentences, retain their original meaning. Even though the writer's meaning may be fuzzy because of her incorrect grammar or style, your job is to ascertain and retain her meaning so that what you write will express what she intended—grammatically, clearly, and succinctly.

This Appendix will help you understand the material discussed in the chapters that precede it, for the Appendix provides additional examples of the problems discussed there, along with correct revisions. The changes suggested in the answer sections of the Appendix are not, of course, the only correct changes you might make. If your answer differs from the answer in the Appendix, look back over the sections of the book that discuss the problem involved for alternate constructions. Discuss your answer with your legal writing instructor or with fellow students. Variety in sentence structure and style helps make writing interesting.

Even if you think you do not need the practice that these exercises provide, look through the Appendix until you find some subjects you need to review. Practice in good usage and style, like practice in any other skill, improves performance.

Exercise to Accompany Chapter One, Sections 2, 3, and 4

(When to Use a Comma; when to Use a Semi-colon; when to use a Colon)

Directions: Add the correct form of punctuation to the following unpunctuated sentences.

1. The committee gave as its reason for delaying action the absence of many of its members during the summer recess but it failed to take action on their return.

2. The witness for the defense failed to appear however the trial continued.

3. Three reasons were given for the cost overrun the general inflation the addition of features to the original plan and the delay in construction due to bad weather.

4. During the recession the national debt increased the interest rose and the people lost buying power.

5. Banks are like siblings the more there are of them the more they compete.

6. All other factors being equal the defendant's remorseful attitude may make a difference in the verdict.

7. The district attorney withdrew the charges several months later after a long and exhaustive investigation into the activities of the accused.

8. The Honorable John Jones former Secretary of the Interior was seated in the audience.

9. The noise of construction in the nearby building was deafening nevertheless classes continued inside the law school.

10. Although the appropriated funds were not released by the administration the school lunch program remained in effect.

Answers to the Exercise to Accompany Chapter One, Sections 2, 3, and 4

1. The committee gave as its reason for delaying action the absence of many of its members during the summer recess, but it failed to take action on their return.

2. The witness for the defense failed to appear; however the trial continued.

3. Three reasons were given for the cost overrun: the general inflation; the addition of features to the original plan; and the delay in construction due to bad weather.

4. During the recession the national debt increased, the interest rose, and the people lost buying power. (It is correct, also, to omit the final comma in this sentence.)

5. Banks are like siblings: the more there are of them the more they compete.

6. All other factors being equal, the defendant's remorseful attitude may make a difference in the verdict.

7. The district attorney withdrew the charges several months later, after a long and exhaustive investigation into the activities of the accused.

8. The Honorable John Jones, former Secretary of the Interior, was seated in the audience.

9. The noise of construction in the nearby building was deafening; nevertheless, classes continued inside the law school.

10. Although the appropriated funds were not released by the administration, the school lunch program remained in effect.

Exercise to Accompany Chapter One, Sections 5 and 6

(How to Avoid Sentence Fragments and Run-On Sentences)

Directions: Re-write the sentences that follow so that they are complete sentences. (Some sentences are already correct.)

1. A response arriving in the mail replying to the newspaper advertisement.

2. The depression in the ground was not apparent, the defendant did not act negligently since a reasonably prudent person might not have seen it.

3. Both defendants are liable for assault since they acted together. Although both will argue that they had no intent to harm the plaintiff.

4. Several important circuit court cases that follow the Supreme Court's reasoning.

5. Defendants were stopped by an inspector; he told them that if they would open the rear of the truck they could proceed.

6. The defendants had a duty under state law to have their truck inspected, by not stopping they violated the law.

7. Whether the defendant touched the person of the plaintiff. There seems no indication that he intended to do so.

8. Petitioner claims he was denied equal protection of the law due to the affirmative action quota system, petitioner argues that classifications based on race are invidiously discriminatory.

9. The essential role of the fact finder in determining the amount of contribution for which each party will be held accountable.

10. After the *Hoffman* decision, Florida becoming a comparative negligence state and thus plaintiff no longer being denied recovery when both plaintiff and defendant are negligent.

Answers to the Exercise to Accompany Chapter One, Sections 5 and 6

1. A response arrived in the mail replying to the newspaper advertisement.

2. Because the depression in the ground was not apparent, the defendant did not act negligently since a reasonably prudent person might not have seen it.

3. Both defendants are liable for assault since they acted together, although both will argue that they had no intent to harm the plaintiff.

4. Several important circuit court cases follow the Supreme Court's reasoning.

5. Defendants were stopped by an inspector; he told them that if they would open the rear of the truck, they could proceed.

6. The defendants had a duty under state law to have their truck inspected. By not stopping they violated the law.

7. Whether the defendant touched the person of the plaintiff is not known; there seems no indication that he intended to do so.

8. Petitioner claims he was denied equal protection of the law due to the affirmative action quota system and that classifications based on race are invidiously discriminatory.

9. The essential role of the fact finder is to determine the amount of contribution for which each party will be held accountable.

10. After the *Hoffman* decision, Florida became a comparative negligence state and thus plaintiff no longer is denied recovery when both plaintiff and defendant are negligent.

Exercise to Accompany Chapter One, Section 7

(How to Punctuate Restrictive and Non-Restrictive Relative Clauses)

Directions: Add commas, when necessary, to the following relative clauses.

1. *Maria and three other girls are in a room:* Maria spoke to the girl who was washing grapes.

2. *Maria, one girl, and three boys are in the room:* Maria spoke to the girl who was washing grapes.

3. *There are three dogs in a yard:* The dog which had been barking ran toward us.

4. *There is one dog and three cats in the yard:* The dog which had been barking ran toward us.

5. *There are three dogs and a cat in the yard:* The cat which had been sitting in the tree jumped onto Joe's shoulder.

6. *There is just one river in the vicinity:* The river which was still and deep bordered our land.

7. *There are several houses on the block:* Gordon bought the house which had green shutters.

8. *A pear, an apple, an orange, and a banana are in a bowl:* Mack chose the fruit which was ripest.

9. *A pear, an apple, an orange, and a banana are in a bowl:* Mack chose the apple which was ripest.

10. *The restaurant had only one waiter:* The diner questioned the waiter who was conciliatory.

11. *There are three dentists in town:* Mrs. Brown goes to the dentist who uses laughing gas.

12. *There is only one dentist in town:* Mrs. Brown goes to the dentist who uses laughing gas.

13. People who crossed the country in those days suffered many hardships.

14. Al Wilson who used to coach football coached the boys' team.

15. Our new car which we were so proud of was badly dented in the collision.

16. He talked to anyone who would listen.

17. The moon which was at the full gave enough light to read by.

18. Walker River which flowed by our house was too cold to swim in.

General Rules for the Use of Commas in Restrictive and Non-Restrictive Relative Clauses:

> When a relative clause identifies the noun it modifies, it is called "restrictive"; no commas are used to separate it from the rest of the sentence.

> When a relative clause is not needed to identify the noun it modifies, it is called "non-restrictive" and must be separated from the remainder of the sentences by commas.

> "Who" and "which" may introduce either restrictive or non-restrictive clauses, but "that" introduces only restrictive clauses. In sentences 3, 7, and 8, "that" would be used more frequently than "which" (the noun modified being a "non-person"), but either "that" or "which" is correct.

Answers to the Exercise to Accompany Chapter One, Section 7

1. Maria spoke to the girl who was washing grapes.

2. Maria spoke to the girl, who was washing grapes.

3. The dog which had been barking ran toward us.

4. The dog, which had been barking, ran toward us.

5. The cat, which had been sitting in the tree, jumped onto Joe's shoulder.

6. The river, which was still and deep, bordered our land.

7. Gordon bought the house which had green shutters.

8. Mack chose the fruit which was ripest.

9. Mack chose the apple, which was ripest.

10. The diner questioned the waiter, who was conciliatory.

11. Mrs. Brown goes to the dentist who uses laughing gas.

12. Mrs. Brown goes to the dentist, who uses laughing gas.

13. People who crossed the country in those days suffered many hardships.

14. Al Wilson, who used to coach football, coached the boys' team.

15. Our new car, which we were so proud of, was badly dented in the collision.

16. He talked to anyone who would listen.

17. The moon, which was at the full, gave enough light to read by.

18. Walker River, which flowed by our house, was too cold to swim in.

Exercise to Accompany Chapter One, Section 8

(How to Decide Whether to Use "Who" or "Whom")

Directions: Correct the following sentences if necessary

1. Who did you go out with last night?
2. Who did the coach choose to play first base?
3. Whom are you talking to?
4. If you can't trust John, who can you trust?
5. Now I know whom he laughed at.
6. He became enraged at whomever opposed him.
7. The man who they saw emerge from the car fired two shots.
8. The man who they say emerged from the car fired two shots.
9. The voters clearly indicated whom they wanted for mayor.
10. A suspect who the police said was John Jones was arrested.
11. A suspect who the police identified as John Jones was arrested.
12. I did not realize to who I was talking.
13. Whoever lived in the house opened the door.
14. A girl whom I knew last year returned to Gainesville to see me.
15. Whom was at the door?
16. I will go out with whoever I want.
17. I will borrow a pen from whomever has one.
18. Whoever is finished should leave.

Answers to the Exercise to Accompany Chapter One, Section 8

1. Whom did you go out with last night?
2. Whom did the coach choose to play first base?
3. Whom are you talking to?

4. If you can't trust John, whom can you trust?

5. Now I know whom he laughed at.

6. He became enraged at whoever opposed him.

7. The man whom they saw emerge from the car fired two shots.

8. The man who they say emerged from the car fired two shots.

9. The voters clearly indicated whom they wanted for mayor.

10. A suspect who the police said was John Jones was arrested.

11. A suspect whom the police identified as John Jones was arrested.

12. I did not realize to whom I was talking.

13. Whoever lived in the house opened the door.

14. A girl whom I knew last year returned to Gainesville to see me.

15. Who was at the door?

16. I will go out with whomever I want.

17. I will borrow a pen from whoever has one.

18. Whoever is finished should leave.

Exercise to Accompany Chapter One, Section 9
(Case of Personal Pronouns)

Directions: Choose the correct form of the personal pronoun

1. (We/us) women are still being discriminated against in some graduate programs.

2. Between you and (I/me) I am convinced the defendant is guilty as charged.

3. It is useless for John and (he/him) and for others with as little political clout as (they/them) to effect the changes they desire.

4. Professors call on (we/us) students who are unprepared.

5. It is not for (we/us) to decide the legality of the act.

6. Uninhabited areas still exist where nature lovers like (we/us) can enjoy visiting.

7. The speaker's attitude surprised both (he/him) and (we/us).

8. John likes Ruth and Joan better than (we/us). [That is, John prefers Ruth and Joan.]

9. John likes Ruth and Joan better than (we/us). [That is, we do not like Ruth and Joan as well as John does.]

10. Neither (he/him) nor (she/her) has any writing problems.

11. After her attorney and (she/her) left, the office was closed.

12. The door closed after her attorney and (she/her).

Answers to the Exercise to Accompany Chapter One, Section 9

1.	we		7.	him . . . us	
2.	me		8.	us	
3.	him . . . they		9.	we	
4.	us		10.	he . . . she	
5.	us		11.	she	
6.	us		12.	her	

Exercise to Accompany Chapter One, Section 10

(The Dangling Participle)

Directions: Re-write the sentences to avoid the dangling participles

1. In discussing the suits that may arise from the car-truck collision, the first possible suit is battery.

2. Having committed a heinous crime, the judge gave the defendant the maximum sentence.

3. Couched in ungrammatical English, the writer risks his good legal reasoning being underestimated.

4. Damaged by lightning, the insurance policy did not cover the cost of the repairs to the house.

5. Construing the statute, the evidence fails to establish the charge.

6. By keeping the prisoners in jail, they are unable to function when their sentence is finished.

7. Having failed to establish a cause of action, the court refused to hear the complaint.

8. Arriving in the mail, the student received a response to his law school application.

9. Committed to a legal career, the rejection letter was disheartening to the student.

10. After studying hard all semester, the final examination seemed relatively easy.

Answers to the Exercise to Accompany Chapter One, Section 10

1. The first suit to discuss, of those that may arise from the car-truck collision, is the suit for battery.

2. The defendant having committed a heinous crime, the judge gave him the maximum sentence.

3. If the writer couches his good legal reasoning in ungrammatical English, he risks its being underestimated.

4. The insurance policy did not cover the cost of the repairs to the house damaged by lightning.

5. The court, in construing the statute, found that the evidence failed to establish the charge.

6. Prisoners kept in jail are unable to function when their sentence is finished.

7. The plaintiff having failed to establish a cause of action, the court refused to hear its complaint.

8. The student received in the mail a response to his law school application.

9. The rejection letter disheartened the student, because he was committed to a legal career.

10. After studying hard all semester, she found the final examination relatively easy.

Exercise to Accompany Chapter One, Section 11

(Squinting Modifiers and Split Infinitives)

Directions: Re-write the incorrect or unclear sentences so that they are correct and clear.

1. The trial that was postponed twice apparently will take place next month.

2. She agreed to never, under any circumstances, to drink and drive.

3. The attorney agreed eventually to assist the plaintiff.

4. The judge agreed to hear the case on the fourteenth of April.

5. It is tempting to not do what one has agreed to do.

6. The defendant who was complaining noisily entered the courtroom.

7. He shot her fifteen times in the screen door she was trying to get out of the house through.

8. The judge decided to not call the witness immediately.

Answers to the Exercise to Accompany Chapter One, Section 11

1. The twice-postponed trial will apparently take place next month.

2. She agreed never to drink and drive, under any circumstances.

3. The attorney eventually agreed to assist the plaintiff.

4. On the fourteenth of April the judge agreed to hear the case.

5. It is tempting not to do what one has agreed to do.

6. The defendant who was noisily complaining entered the courtroom.

7. He shot her fifteen times as she was trying to get out of the house through the screen door.

8. The judge decided not to call the witness immediately.

Exercise to Accompany Chapter One, Section 12

(The Possessive Apostrophe)

Directions: Add the possessive apostrophe when it is necessary in the following sentences, and change construction to the periphrastic possessive or the possessive contraction when appropriate.

1. The professors assignments did not include the revenue codes exceptions.
2. The courses objectives did not appear in the syllabuses explanations.
3. The committee gave as its reason for delaying action the absence of its members.
4. Malcolm and Greta Browns will left everything to their children.
5. Ladies clubs have been known to be politically conservative.
6. Mr. Smiths and Mrs. Whites tax forms are in the desks file.
7. Office supplies belong to individuals; yours must be separated from theirs.

Answers to the Exercise to Accompany Chapter One, Section 12

1. The professor's (or professors') assignments did not include the exceptions to the revenue code.
2. The objectives of the course did not appear in the explanations in the syllabus.
3. (The sentence is correct as it stands.)
4. Malcolm and Greta Brown's will left everything to their children.
5. Ladies' clubs have been known to be politically conservative.
6. Mr. Smith's and Mrs. White's tax forms are in the file on the desk.
7. (The sentence is correct as it stands.)

Exercise to Accompany Chapter One, Section 13

(Number Errors)

Directions: Choose the proper form (in parentheses).

1. Mr. Jones is an outstanding (alumnus, alumna, alumni, alumnae) of the university.
2. Bretanie Women's College (alumnus, alumna, alumni, alumnae) of the class of 1944 were in attendance 75% strong at their 30th reunion.
3. The main (criterion/criteria) for high grades in law school (is/are) the ability to analyze and write effectively.
4. The broadcasting and newspaper (medium/media) (is/are) well represented, the former (medium/media) including both television and radio.

5. Included in the (dictum/dicta) of both the majority and minority opinions were the same legal points.

6. All of the (datum/data) collected by the research team (is/are) relevant to the case.

7. The plaintiff corporation changed (its/their) headquarters since instituting (its/their) suit.

8. The city of Dallas has added bicycle lanes to (its/their) road maps of the metropolitan area.

9. (Change the following sentence to avoid the masculine singular pronoun.) An attorney is expected to be on time for his appointments and to meet his deadlines.

10. (Change the following sentence to avoid the masculine singular pronoun.) When a person writes on legal subjects, he must seek to write accurately, clearly, and succinctly.

Answers to the Exercise to Accompany Chapter One, Section 13

1. alumnus

2. alumnae

3. criterion . . . is

4. media . . . are . . . medium

5. dicta

6. data . . . are

7. its . . . its

8. its

9. An attorney is expected to be on time for appointments and to meet deadlines.

(or)

Attorneys are expected to be on time for (their) appointments and to meet (their) deadlines.

10. A person who writes on legal subjects must seek to write accurately, clearly, and succinctly.

(or)

Persons writing on legal subjects must seek to write accurately, clearly, and succinctly.

Exercise to Accompany Chapter One, Section 14
(Redundancy and Improper Deletion)

Directions: Correct all errors.

1. The question is is whether the porch of the victim's apartment is a "dwelling," according to the definition in the statute.

2. I recognize the valid national security reasons it was done.

3. Security Builders has filed a cross claim for any amount it is held liable in the original action.

4. It can and has been argued that if this reasoning were applied, all distributions of appreciated property would be subject to tax.

5. If the plaintiff would have slowed down at the intersection, the defendant would have been able to avoid the accident.

6. The appropriate forum for the trial to take place is now being decided.

7. A contract which one party is a minor is avoidable.

8. The case would have been settled out of court if the defendant would have agreed to the settlement.

Answers to Exercise to Accompany Chapter One, Section 14

1. The question is whether the porch of the victim's apartment is a "dwelling," according to the definition in the statute.

2. I recognize the valid national security for which it was done.

3. Security Builders has filed a cross claim for any amount for which it is held liable in the original action. (Or, . . . for any amount it is held liable for . . .)

4. It can be and has been argued that if this reasoning were applied, all distributions of appreciated property would be subject to tax.

5. If the plaintiff had slowed down at the intersection, the defendant would have been able to avoid the accident.

6. The appropriate forum for the trial to take place in is now being decided.

7. A contract in which one party is a minor is avoidable.

8. The case would have been settled out of court if the defendant had agreed to the settlement.

Exercise to Accompany Chapter One, Section 15

Count and Non-Count Nouns

Directions: Fill each blank with the appropriate word from the list. Use each word at least once: amount, number.

much	less
many	fewer
little	amount
few	number

1. _____ money is being spent to insure the most complete athletic facility available.

2. _____ tickets are available by mail than at the door.

3. A large _____ of information is being provided by research.

4. A large _____ of sharks were sighted yesterday in the Gulf.

5. According to many nutritionists, Americans eat too _____ salt.

6. A large _____ of studies have been done on the relationship of exercise to heart attack incidence.

7. _____ mail is undeliverable because the sender has omitted the zip code.

8. _____ expense was spared to provide enough data.

9. _____ statistics are available, however.

10. There is not _____ evidence that agreement is imminent.

11. On the other hand, there are _____ indications that the controversy has broadened.

Answers to Exercise to Accompany Chapter One, Section 15

1. much,
2. fewer,
3. amount,
4. number,
5. much (or little),
6. number,
7. much (or little),
8. little,
9. few (or many),
10. much,
11. many (or few).

Exercise to Accompany Chapter Two(A), Section 1

(Write with Verbs.)

Directions: Change the following sentences by substituting verbs when possible.

1. Courts have given consideration to and provided interpretations of the Doctrine of Exclusion.

2. We encourage you to make a reapplication to law school next Summer.

3. The document you submitted in your application does not contain a complete enough evaluation of your arrest record.

4. Prior to our making the final status decision, there is a requirement that you do so.

5. You must use language that is understandable to all persons.

6. Plaintiff was injured by a sudden fall of ice and snow from the peaked roof of defendant's building onto the sidewalk where she was walking.

7. The Court said that the defendant's act was an improper use of his neighbor's land.

8. The Department of Revenue attempted to invoke construction of § 214.14, arguing that the statute's meaning was unclear.

9. The language of the donee's letter might show a benefit that he would derive from the donor's promise.

10. To ascertain Mr. Rich's chances of success requires a determination of the following issues.

Answers to the Exercise to Accompany
Chapter Two(A), Section 1

1. Courts have considered and interpreted the Doctrine of Exclusion.

2. We encourage you to reapply to law school next Summer.

3. In your application you do not completely document your arrest record.

4. Before we decide your final status, you must do so.

5. Use language that all persons can understand.

6. The plaintiff was injured when ice and snow suddenly fell from the peaked roof of defendant's building onto her as she walked on the sidewalk.

7. The Court said that the defendant improperly used his neighbor's land.

8. In construing § 214.14, the Department of Revenue argued that its meaning was unclear.

9. In his letter, the donee might indicate that he would benefit from the donor's promise.

10. Answers to the following issues will determine whether Mr. Rich will succeed.

Exercise to Accompany Chapter Two(A), Section 2

(Prefer Active Voice)

Directions: Change passive to active verbs when desirable.

1. Many points are still to be considered by the jury.

2. The broadcast media should be included under the first amendment. It can be argued that the TV station was seeking to gather news when the trial was televised by the station. Thus, the judge's order can be viewed as prior restraint.

3. From the facts and reasoning of the *Allen* case, it could be plausibly inferred that the institution of affirmative action programs is supported by public opinion.

4. It was then illustrated in *Zell,* that there is almost universal acceptance of the concept of extrinsic parol or any other extrinsic evidence being admitted if the written agreement of the parties lacks legal efficacy.

5. It was feared by defendants that without a jury trial they would be disadvantaged.

6. If a defendant made a substantial preliminary showing that a false statement was made intentionally by an affiant in his affidavit for a search warrant, the search warrant should be voided and the products of the search excluded.

7. In *Hugendorf,* defendant was convicted of knowingly receiving, concealing and storing stolen furpieces which had been transported by him in interstate commerce.

8. The taxi driver's actions could be considered outrageous and intentional and harm was suffered by the passenger from the incident.

9. Persons serving the public are held to higher standards of conduct than other persons; therefore a strong case can be made by the defendant in assault. As soon as her purse was grabbed, there was battery.

10. When one's possessions are being held by another for the purpose of not allowing a person to leave a place, there is also false imprisonment.

11. It is assumed that actual knowledge of his possessions is held by everyone; therefore even without actual knowledge, the defendant is held liable for all that which he possesses.

Answers to Exercise to Accompany
Chapter Two(A), Section 2

1. The jury still has to consider many points.

2. The first amendment should apply to the broadcast media. The TV station can argue that it was seeking to gather news when it televised the trial. The judge's order would thus be prior restraint.

3. The facts and reasoning of the *Allen* case imply that public opinion supports affirmative action programs.

4. *Zell* illustrates that extrinsic parol or any other extrinsic evidence is admissible if the written agreement of the parties lacks legal efficacy.

5. Defendants feared that they would be at a disadvantage without a jury trial.

6. If a defendant makes a substantial preliminary showing that an affiant intentionally made a false statement in his affidavit for a search warrant,

the search warrant should be voided and the products of the search excluded. *

7. In *Hugendorf,* defendant was convicted of knowingly receiving, concealing, and storing stolen furpieces which he had transported in interstate commerce.

8. The taxi driver's actions, which can be considered outrageous and intentional, caused his passenger harm. **

9. Persons who serve the public are held to higher standards of conduct than other persons; therefore the defendant has a strong case in assault, because when the waiter grabbed her purse, he committed battery.

10. A person holding the possessions of another so that the second person is unable to leave is liable for false imprisonment.

11. The assumption is that everyone has actual knowledge of his possessions; therefore even if he does not have such knowledge, the defendant is liable for all his possessions.

Exercise to Accompany Chapter Two(A), Section 3

(Use Expletives Sparingly.)

Directions: Delete Unnecessary Expletives

1. As soon as the purse was grabbed, there was battery. There was certainly no consent.[1]

2. When one's personal possessions are being held by another for the purpose of not allowing the person to leave a place, there is false imprisonment.[2]

3. There is a cause of action on behalf of the minor who, the evidence shows, suffered injury from the reckless action of the taxicab driver . . . . It is, in the public conscience, uncommon and outrageous for cab drivers to conduct themselves in the manner shown here.

4. There is a strong suspicion on the part of the police officers that a crime has taken place.

5. There is a presumption that a child born during wedlock is the offspring of the husband and wife.

6. There is almost universal acceptance of the concept of extrinsic parol being admitted as evidence.

---

* The last two passive forms are left intact because the doer of the action is not important.

** In the original sentence the causal relationship that seems to be an important factor was not expressed.

1. Note here also (1) hysteron-proteron and (2) lack of causality indication. (The consent would have had to occur before the grabbing; and because the victim has not consented, battery lies.)

2. In this sentence, note also the shift of viewpoint. In your rewrite, correct both the expletive and the shift of viewpoint.

7. It was the intention of the defendant to confine the plaintiff against his will.

8. It would seem that the petitioner does not have standing in this matter.

9. It is the parents' duty, according to the 2nd Restatement of Torts, to control his child's behavior under certain circumstances.

10. It is extremely likely that defendant was unaware that he had killed his victim.

11. It is a fact that children who have been abused grow up to abuse their own children.

12. There is a well-established rule in tort theory that a person rendering aid must not place the receiver of that aid in a worse situation than he was in when the person found him.

13. It is highly unlikely that the jury will accept the argument that the murderer acted in self-defense, since the victim was shot in the back.

14. It becomes obvious that relief will be granted to the party who brings suit if that party acted on reliance of the parol agreement.

Answers to the Exercise to Accompany Chapter Two(A), Section 3

1. Since the victim had not consented to the act, the grabbing of her purse constituted battery.

2. False imprisonment occurs when the personal possessions of one person are held by another so that the first person is prevented from leaving a place.

3. Action may be brought on behalf of the minor who suffered injury from the taxi driver's behavior, which can be characterized as so reckless and outrageous as to offend the public conscience.

4. Police officers strongly suspect that a crime has taken place.

5. A child born during wedlock is presumed to be the offspring of the husband and wife.

6. Extrinsic parol evidence is almost universally accepted.

7. The defendant intended to confine the plaintiff against his will.

8. The petitioner does not seem to have standing in this matter.

9. According to the 2nd Restatement of Torts, one duty of the parent is to control his child's behavior under certain circumstances.

10. The defendant was probably unaware that he had killed his victim.

11. Children who have been abused often grow up to abuse their own children.

12. A well-established rule in tort theory states that a person rendering aid must not place the receiver of that aid in a worse situation than he was in when the person found him.

13. The argument that the murderer acted in self-defense will doubtless be rejected by the jury since the victim was shot in the back.

14. If the party who brings suit acted in reliance of the parol agreement, he will obviously be granted relief.

Exercise to Acompany Chapter Two(A), Section 4

(Use Concrete Language.)

Directions: Clarify the following sentences by substituting concrete for abstract language.

1. The gravamen of this study is that it would appear from the relationship of the issues that all issues would be most expeditiously litigated in a single judicial proceeding.

2. While one can well appreciate an editorial policy which does not verify the contents of every letter to the editor or the identity of every signatory, it is clear that arguably scurrilous personal attacks ought not to be published anonymously with an editorial note explaining the exigency. (This sentence has an additional disadvantage of ambiguity because of the negative construction. Should such letters be published, then, *without* the editorial note explaining the exigency?)

3. When concepts are identified with the same cognomen, it is easy for the mind to slip into the assumption that the verbal identity is accompanied, in all its sequences, by identity of meaning.

4. There are a lot of loose ends to be finalized with the program, and its effectiveness will depend upon available personnel and the relationship developed between centers and various agencies.

5. A significant proportion of qualified persons are excluded from the judiciary because of the existing level of compensation.

6. This is in no way to be construed as a negative appraisal of the intellectual community nor of the current general condition of academia.

7. The peroration of a judicial tribunal must ultimately arrive at some point of finality.

8. In the interest of justice and elimination of continuous and protracted future litigation, it appears to be proper and dutiful to exercise the right of permutation in this matter even though it may tend to be hortative in the litigants involved.

9. The consumer affairs coordinator will have the following duties: to review existing mechanisms of consumer input, thruput and output, and seek ways of improving these linkages via the "consumer communications channel."

10. What I try to do is to orchestrate a series of people who put in inputs that eventually come out as a draft speech which I personally submit to the Secretary-General.

11. The remittance of sums paid by customers purchasing articles in or of this establishment is hereby guaranteed in the event that such articles, or one or more thereof, shall be hereafter deemed unsatisfactory to or by the said customers.

12. There is a problem of judicial discretion as to whether to take cognizance of this case.

13. The Lord is my external-internal mechanism . . . He positions me in a non-decisional situation. He maximizes my adjustment.

Answers to the Exercise to Accompany Chapter Two(A), Section 4

1. This study indicates that all issues are so closely related that they should be litigated in one judicial proceeding.

2. Although the editor understandably cannot verify either the identity of each letter writer or the contents of every letter, letters containing what might be considered scurrilous personal attacks should not be published, even with an editorial note of explanation.

3. Concepts with the same name are assumed to have the same meaning.

4. The program needs to be improved, and its effectiveness will depend upon how good its personnel is and how it gets along with other centers and agencies.

5. Present salaries are too low to attract qualified persons to the judiciary. (But what level of the judiciary does the writer mean?)

6. I am not criticizing the intellectual community nor the state of academics.

7. A judicial tribunal must eventually end its deliberations. (Since this was part of a written opinion, the word "peroration" is improper, and was probably an error.)

8. (This is only a guess, but the judge who wrote this opinion may have meant,) "In order to serve justice and eliminate litigation, this Court exercises its right to disagree with previous decisions, even though the present opinion is merely advisory."

9. (This sentence cannot be redrafted because it is couched so that there is no way to tell what the coordinator's actual duties are.)

10. I combine material written by staff experts into a draft speech for the [UN] Secretary-General.

11. Satisfaction or your money back.

12. The court must decide whether to hear this case.

13. (This is the 23rd Psalm, re-written by a bureaucrat.)

Exercise to Accompany Chapter Two(A), Section 5

(Use Connectors Carefully.)

Directions: Correct all errors:

1. When the plaintiff limps in, the jury will be inclined toward her favor because we must remember the old axiom that juries tend to be more favorable toward plaintiffs.

2. In this case, the depression was not readily apparent and it would be hard to prove the plaintiff was acting negligently, and if she was acting reasonably, as she claims she was, the same accident might have happened to anyone; it is possible a reasonable person might not have seen the depression.

3. The record discloses agreements between the attorneys and 170 of the parties owning land, and whose property was benefitted by the decree.

4. Four petitioners challenged their respective states' statutes as violative of *Furman* standards, and re-submitted the argument that the death penalty was unconstitutional, per se, in violation of the 8th and 14th amendment's prohibition of "cruel and unusual punishment."

5. If the instructors would put down a little pressure it could help, but it's hard for the instructor to stand in front of class and smoke and enforce this rule.

6. In the course of a busy life he built the Fitchburg Railroad, the Hoosac Tunnel, founded a great paper company, went to Congress and learned to write well.

7. There are fourteen programs working with old folks, underprivileged, handicapped, foreign students and many more.

8. The criteria for receiving a license calls for qualified faculty members, organization and curriculum structure.

9. In view of the ease that the draft could be evaded, something good can be said about those who openly resisted.

10. Since the operation was unconsented, the patient has a cause of action.

Answers to the Exercise to Accompany Chapter Two(A), Section 5

1. Because juries tend to favor plaintiffs, and particularly plaintiffs who have obviously been injured, the jury will no doubt favor this plaintiff when she limps in.

2. The plaintiff claims she was acting reasonably, and to prove that she acted negligently would be difficult since the depression into which she fell was not readily apparent and a similar accident might therefore have happened to any reasonable person.

3. The record discloses agreements between the attorneys and 170 of the landowners whose property was benefited by the decree.

4. In challenging their respective states' statutes for violating *Furman* standards, four petitioners re-submitted the argument that the death penalty was unconstitutional because it violated the 8th and 14th amendments' prohibition of "cruel and unusual punishment."

5. If the instructors made a real effort they could enforce the "no smoking" rule, but not if they themselves smoke while teaching.

6. In the course of a busy life he built the Fitchburg Railroad and the Hoosac Tunnel, founded a great paper company, served in Congress, and learned to write well.

7. There are fourteen programs: for old, underprivileged, and handicapped persons, and for foreign students. Many other programs exist in addition to these.

8. In order to receive a license, the school must provide qualified faculty members, adequate organization, and an appropriate curriculum.

9. In view of the ease with which the draft could be evaded, something good can be said for those who openly resisted it.

10. Since the patient did not consent to the operation, he has a cause of action.

Exercise to Accompany Chapter Two(A), Section 6

(Put Words in Their Best Order.)

Directions: Revise the sentences to provide the suggested emphasis.

1. It was expressly decided in *Humbert v. Trinity Church* that the original owner must still bring action even if the tenant obtained or continued possession of land by fraud or if the tenant's claim was unfounded, wrongful, and fraudulent in any respect. (Important idea: the original owner must bring action.)

2. It could plausibly be inferred that public policy supports the formulation and institution of affirmative action programs, from the facts and reasoning of the *Allen* case. (Important idea: affirmative action programs are supported by public policy).

3. The key point here is that even if unknown to him, since he is the operator of a business, the owner will be held liable for what he should know and certain portions of his premises used by the public should thus be reasonably safe. (Important idea: the owner is liable for maintaining safe premises).

4. The court, in a later case, held that a storekeeper need exercise only reasonable care to keep his premises in a safe condition, where plaintiff was denied recovery when he slipped and fell on waxy paper in front of

the storeowner's door, of uncertain origin.   (Important idea: storekeepers need exercise only reasonable care).

5. The problem is the amount of time the condition existed; in one recent case where a customer slipped on trash on the floor of a business, the court found no liability where there had been no inspection for 3 hours, but in another case where a substance was on the floor of a store for 15 minutes, the court found liability, although both of these cases occurred inside the stores. (Important idea: courts differ on how long a condition must exist before a storeowner is liable for injury to customers caused by the condition).

6. Back in 1943, there was a news story in the Times about a returning war veteran with his wife and baby boy who could not find a place to live because they had a child; I was that baby and now 35 years later, with a wife and baby, I have not changed. (Important idea: persons refuse to rent to couples with children).

7. The dental surgeon testified, however, that football players whose mouths are injured can often be repaired with modern dental surgical techniques. (Important idea: modern surgery repairs gridiron dental injuries).

8. Since the bus driver raved and ranted at both passengers he could be liable for intentional infliction of emotional distress. (Important idea: both passengers have a cause of action against the driver for the intentional infliction of emotional distress.)

———————

Answers to the Exercise to Accompany Chapter Two(A), Section 6

1. The court held, in *Humbert v. Trinity Church,* that even if (1) the tenant obtained the continued possession of land by fraud, or (2) the tenant's claim was unfounded, wrongful, or fraudulent, the original owner must still bring action to oust the tenant.

2. The holding of the *Allen* case implies that public policy supports the formulation and institution of affirmative action programs.

3. The owner must keep those portions of his premises used by the public reasonably safe since he will be held liable for all dangerous conditions about which he should have knowledge.

4. The plaintiff, in a later case, was denied recovery after he fell on waxy paper of uncertain origin in front of the storeowner's door, the court holding that the storeowner need exercise only reasonable care in maintaining safe premises.

5. Courts differ on how long a dangerous condition must exist inside a store before a storeowner is liable for customer injuries resulting from the condition. In one recent case in which a customer slipped on trash

on the floor of a business when there had been no inspection for three hours, the court found the owner not liable; but in another case, when a substance had been on the floor only 15 minutes, the owner was found liable.

6. Times have not changed in the 35 years since a war veteran returing in 1943 with his wife and baby boy could not find a place to live; now, I, that baby grown up, still am unable to rent a place to live in with my wife and baby because persons refuse to rent to couples with children.

7. The dental surgeon testified, however, that modern surgical techniques can often repair the mouths of football players with gridiron injuries.

8. Because the bus driver raved and ranted at them, both passengers have a cause of action against him for the intentional infliction of emotional distress.

Exercise to Accompany Chapter Two(A), Section 7

(Place Modifiers Next to the Words They Modify.)

Directions: Move the modifiers so as to convey the intended meaning.

1. [Sign in a restaurant window] Wanted: dishwasher to wash dishes and two waitresses.

2. Halley's comet will look like a star with a pair of binoculars.

3. The proposed site was deemed unsafe due to possible contamination by one of our leading university researchers.

4. The question is whether to sell land that is contaminated for building purposes.

5. Since 1965, the Jones family has buried six relatives in seven of the remaining cemetery plots.

6. The last World War II sailing ship was sunk in 1958 in the Pacific with a load of guano.

7. A bicycle service messenger made his rounds yesterday despite a winter storm that dumped nearly a foot of snow on the city which drifted in from Canada yesterday.

8. The closest man to the President is the Chief of Staff.

9. The hornbook is a useful product to the law student.

Answers to the Exercise to Accompany Chapter Two(A), Section 7

1. Wanted: Two waitresses and a dishwasher to wash dishes.

2. With a pair of binoculars, Halley's comet will look like a star.

3. Due to possible contamination, the proposed site was deemed unsafe by one of our leading university researchers.

4. The question is whether to sell contaminated land for building purposes.

5. Since 1965, the Jones family has buried relatives in six of the seven remaining cemetery plots.

6. The last World War II sailing ship, while carrying a load of guano, was sunk in 1958 in the Pacific.

7. A bicycle service messenger made his rounds yesterday despite a winter storm which drifted in from Canada, dumping nearly a foot of snow on the city.

8. The man closest to the President is the Chief of Staff.

9. The hornbook is a product useful to the law student.

Exercise to Accompany Chapter Two(A), Section 8

(Make Lists; Use Parallel Structure.)

Directions: Use lists and parallel structure to state the ideas in the following sentences.

1. For an incorrect statement to be material and thus vitiate a policy it must have been made by the insured in response to a question that he understood or could reasonably be expected to understand or be expected to have sufficient information to answer. (Important idea: the insured person must be able to understand the contract he signs.)

2. When choosing a forum for trial, one should weigh whether witnesses to the action can be brought to the forum, whether there will be great expense to bring the defendant to the forum, and whether the local nature of the controversy affects the jury's knowledge of it.

3. The contract neither complies with the statute nor is there agreement between the contracting parties as to its terms.

4. An individual can assert four principal claims: claim to possession of tangible property; freely laboring and contracting; having the right to promised advantages (e.g., performance); and no interference in relationships.

5. The *Barwick* decision is unfair because the wrongdoer may profit from his wrong, and injuring of the present possessor occurs.

6. Bailment is established by agreed upon transfer of property when there is mutual benefit and the involved parties agree upon a period of time.

7. In *Payne v. Payne,* the court defined impotency as not only non-procreation nor copulation but that it also must be incurable.

8. The owner reasonably has the responsibility to maintain the structure so that it is safe for the use of the lessee, that it is a sturdy structure, with proper wiring.

Answers to the Exercise to Accompany Chapter Two(A), Section 8

1. An insurance policy containing an incorrect answer by the insured person to a question asked on the policy will be vitiated unless the insured (1) understood the question, (2) could reasonably be expected to understand the question, or (3) could be expected to have sufficient information to answer the question.

2. In choosing a forum for trial, the following must be considered: (1) whether witnesses to the action can be brought to the forum; (2) what the cost of bringing the defendant to the forum will be; and (3) whether the local nature of the controversy will affect the jury's knowledge of it.

3. The contract does not comply with the statute, nor do the contracting parties agree on its terms.

4. An individual can assert four principal claims: (1) to possession of tangible property; (2) to freedom to labor and contract; (3) to the right to promised advantages (e.g., performance); and (4) to freedom from interference in relationships.

5. The *Barwick* decision is unfair because the present possessor may be injured and because the wrongdoer may profit from his wrong.

6. Bailment is established when property is transferred, if the involved parties mutually benefit and agree on a period of time.

7. In *Payne v. Payne,* the court defined impotence as not only non-procreation or non-copulation, but also as an incurable condition.

8. The owner is responsible for maintaining a sturdy structure, safe for the lessee and properly wired.

Exercise to Accompany Chapter Two(B), Section 1

(Don't Use Jargon.)

Directions: Re-write the sentences to eliminate jargon.

1. If she ought to have known that the floor was being repaired, her prior knowledge goes to the question of contributory negligence, but if her negligence did not go to the cause of her injury she may recover in full.

2. The plaintiff has a case of intentional infliction of emotional distress because she was enticed, induced, and inveigled by the defendant, and his trickery, deceit, and subterfuge caused her to suffer from a case of depression.

3. The defendant may raise consent, but that defense will probably not succeed since the plaintiff was not fully informed before the incident of what would occur.

4. The plaintiff in no shape, manner or form expected the harassment to which she was subjected, nor did she by any manner or means consent to it.

5. The common law relating to larceny is now null and void, but it was in full force and effect in 1900.

6. John Brown, during his lifetime, to wit, on the day of January 20, 1932, was possessed of two acres of land and a dwelling thereon, and whereas the said John Brown sold one acre of that land, to wit, on the day of January 20, 1932, to one James Smith . . . .

7. The deceased, in his last will and testament, did give, devise, and bequeath all rights, title and interest to all of his goods and chattel, free and clear, to his wife.

Answers to the Exercise to Accompany Chapter Two(B), Section 1

1. If she ought to have known that the floor was being repaired, she may be found contributorily negligent, but if her negligence did not contribute to her injury, she may recover in full.

2. Because the defendant enticed the plaintiff and caused her to suffer from depression by his trickery, the plaintiff has a cause of action for the intentional infliction of emotional distress against the defendant.

3. The defendant may argue that the plaintiff consented to his act, but he will probably fail in that plea since the plaintiff was not fully informed before the incident of what would occur.

4. The plaintiff neither expected nor consented to the harassment to which she was subjected.

5. The common law relating to larceny is now void, but it was in force in 1900.

6. John Brown, on January 20, 1932, possessed two acres of land and on that day sold one acre of it to James Smith . . . .

7. The deceased, in his will, gave all his possessions to his wife.

8. President Nixon's supporters insisted that the liberal press used Watergate as a political tool with which to defeat him.

9. The housing market, after years of prosperity, suffered in May its first decrease in real estate transactions, because of the excessive interest rate.

10. In this case, unlike the case of inter vivos gifts, the donee does not acquire full title to the property until the death of the donor.

Exercise to Accompany Chapter Two(B), Section 2

(Don't Use Vague Referents.)

Directions: Rewrite the sentences to eliminate Vague Referents.

1. We question the legality of the conviction for illegal possession of imported heroin; does this limit conviction to possession irregardless of

the importation issue? Or can we construe this statute on the grounds dealing solely with the knowledge of importation? This might be analogous to *Levy* in which Levy is to display the proper conduct of an officer, but one may well ask what this conduct is and how it is to be applied.

2. The doctor told both the plaintiff and the insurance agent that the plaintiff had only superficial cuts and bruises; this was a mutual mistake since neither would have made the contract had they known this is grounds to attack the agreement, nor would the plaintiff have signed a release form.

3. There was great disparity in bargaining power between the plaintiff and his insurer. Insurance companies are known to take advantage of potential claimants in this fashion and since this is the kind of release form that an experienced agent uses it should be torn down for unconscionability. This is a contract of adhesion which can be attacked on the grounds I have stated.

4. If one should summon one to court who was not guilty, who pays the court costs, the one who summons that one or the one who was summoned and that one was not guilty? This happened to my husband.

5. Because the defendant spoke harshly to the plaintiff does not mean that it was a gesture.

6. Since the damage to the crop was remote from the theft of the car, it would be a question of fact on which reasonable men could not differ, and defendant should be entitled to summary judgment.

7. The defendants might argue that if they had threatened to beat up plaintiff then and there, it might constitute assault.

8. In order for forced confinement to occur, it must include no consent to the confinement given by the one confined.

9. This tax is indirect, rather than direct, which would not be valid.

10. The examination resulted in a report by a psychiatrist that the accused was insane, which forces the court to hold a competency hearing.

———

Answers to the Exercise to Accompany Chapter Two(B), Section 2

1. The statute making possession of imported heroin illegal is overly vague because it does not state whether a person found guilty of such possession must have knowledge that the heroin he possesses is imported. The predicament of the heroin possessor is like that of the defendant in *Levy*, who was held to the standard of proper conduct as a police officer but had no knowledge what the standard was.

2. The doctor erroneously told both the plaintiff and the insurance agent that the plaintiff had only superficial cuts and bruises. The release form that the plaintiff then signed can be considered a mutual mistake since neither plaintiff nor agent would have signed it had they realized the doctor's statement was incorrect.

3. Since the plaintiff was at a bargaining disadvantage with relation to the insurance agent, the conduct of the agent was unconscionable when he took advantage of the plaintiff's ignorance to obtain from him a release agreement; and the agreement can be attacked as a contract of adhesion.

4. When a person is summoned to court on charges brought by another person and is subsequently found not guilty of the charges, should the person who brought the charges pay the court costs?

5. The defendant's harsh language to the plaintiff does not necessarily constitute a "gesture."

6. Reasonable men could not disagree that the damage to the crop was so remote from the theft of the car that the defendant is entitled to summary judgment.

7. The defendants might argue that their threat to beat up the plaintiff then and there would probably constitute assault.

8. One element of the tort of forced confinement is lack of consent to the confinement by the one confined.

9. A direct tax would not be valid; this tax is, however, an indirect tax.

10. The court must hold a competency hearing for the accused man because after psychiatric examination the psychiatrist reported that the man was insane.

Exercise to Accompany Chapter Two(B), Section 3

(Don't Use Negatives.)

Directions: Rewrite the following sentences so that they become clear, by eliminating as many negatives as possible.

1. All portions of your examination not written within the lined writing space will not be considered in evaluating your answer.

2. Appellant's counsel did not advise appellant competently of prospects for a successful defense, which were substantial because he [counsel] was not properly motivated.

3. They reported that people in Cuba do not revolt because of the repressive and powerful rule of Castro.

4. Counsel did not completely investigate the circumstances of the crime, did not request information in the prosecutor's file, and did not question the motives of the prosecutor in reducing the charge.

5. Whether the case of an intrusion by a stranger without title, on a peaceable possession, is not one to meet the exigencies of which the courts will recognize a still further qualification or explanation of the rule requiring the plaintiff to recover only on the strength of his own title, is a question which, I believe, has not as yet been decided by this court.

6. Couples do not elope for fear of parental disapproval.

7. He said the answer was not cutting budgets and hoping the problem will go away.

8. The state representative said that he would not honor the subpoena unless he decided the principle of legislative privilege was not worth going to jail for.

9. All mentally retarded persons shall not be sterilized without their consent.

10. I cannot say with great confidence, but I can say the data we do have do not suggest that this month's rise in prices will not be repeated next month.

Answers to Exercise to Accompany Chapter Two(B), Section 3

1. Only portions of your examination written within the lined writing space will be considered in the evaluation of your answer.

2. Appellant's counsel, lacking proper motivation, failed to advise appellant competently of prospects for a successful defense, which were substantial.

3. They reported that Castro's repressive and powerful rule prevents Cubans from revolting.

4. Counsel failed to (1) completely investigate the circumstances of the crime, (2) request information in the prosecutor's file, and (3) question the motives of the prosecutor in reducing the charge.

5. To my knowledge this court has not yet decided whether the intrusion of a stranger without title upon a peaceable possession will bring about a further qualification of the rule that requires an occupant of property to recover only on the strength of his own title. *

6. Fear of parental disapproval is not what makes couples elope.

7. Cutting budgets and hoping the problem will disappear is not the answer.

8. The state representative said that he would refuse to honor the subpoena unless he decided that the principle of legislative privilege was less important than a jail sentence.

---

* This re-draft of an excerpt from an actual court decision is only a guess. The negative in the second line of the original quotation seems to have been in error.

9. No mentally retarded persons shall be sterilized with out their consent.

10. I can say, with no great confidence, that the data we have indicate that this month's price rise will continue next month.

Exercise to Accompany Chapter Two(B), Section 4

(Don't Shift Point of View.)

Directions: Re-write to avoid confusing viewpoint shift.

1. In *Boring,* the Supreme Court indicated that a court of equity would not substitute its judgment for that of an administrative board when acting within the scope of its authority. [The administrative board's authority.]

2. The Florida supreme court decision in *Bray* established a duty on the part of landowners to keep canals and drains open. The court held that when the municipality undertook to maintain a drainage system it acted in a corporate capacity. It further held that if in the wrong it would be held to the same accountability as an individual. This action was one in tort complaining of injury caused by increased flow of water as a result of the drainage system.

3. The grabbing of the poster from the plaintiff's hand is battery under the rule of *Fisher,* where the grabbing of an object from one's hand was held to be an offensive invasion of one's person, and was intentional.

4. Defendants had a duty to let the inspector inspect the truck; not doing so was a direct violation of the statute.

5. Mr. D's guardian has given Mr. D's will to his doctor, saying it is senseless to postpone the death at the cost of $1000 per day in hospital expenses, arguing that the money could be used better to fund cancer research.

6. A Minnesota case also held that a surgeon, in performing an operation without the consent of the patient, constituted an assault and battery.

7. Possession of the home was not granted until majority.

8. The court decided that suspended public school students were entitled to due process protection by the 14th Amendment and that due process required notice of charges and opportunity to present a defense.

9. Does marking a whale establish ownership when whale escapes and is subsequently trapped?

10. Are an individual's due process rights denied when a contract is not renewed and there is no opportunity to air grievances?

11. A prima facie case of battery occurred when the woman store detective grabbed the customer's purse as she left, because under tort theory the purse is considered part of her body and thus an offensive contact.

Answers to Exercise to Accompany Chapter Two(B), Section 4

1. In *Boring,* the Supreme Court indicated that a court of equity would not substitute its own judgment for that of an administrative board which was acting within the scope of its authority.

2. In this action the plaintiff asserts that he suffered injury due to a defect in a drainage system owned by a municipality. The Florida supreme court held, in *Bray,* that if the municipality was in the wrong it would be held as accountable as if it were an individual landowner. The court further held that landowners have a duty to keep canals and drains open and that when the municipality undertook to maintain a drainage system it acted in a corporate capacity.

3. The intentional grabbing of the poster from the plaintiff's hand constitutes battery since, in *Fisher,* the intentional grabbing of an object from a person's hand was held to be an offensive invasion of that person's body.

4. Defendants violated the statute when they refused to allow the authorized inspection of their truck.

5. Mr. D's guardian has turned Mr. D's will over to Mr. D's doctor because, the guardian argues, the postponement of Mr. D's death at a cost of $1,000 a day in hospital expenses is senseless when that money might better be used for cancer research.

6. In a Minnesota case, the court held that a surgeon had committed assault and battery when he performed an operation without the consent of the patient.

7. The court held that the plaintiff be granted possession of the home when he reached majority.

8. The court held that suspended public school students were entitled to due process protection by the 14th amendment; this protection requires that they be provided notice of charges brought against them and an opportunity to present a defense. *

9. Does the marking of a whale by its possessor establish his ownership if the whale escapes and is subsequently trapped by another person?

10. Are an individual's due process rights denied when his contract is not renewed and he has no opportunity to air his grievances?

11. A prima facie case of battery occurred when the woman store detective grabbed the customer's purse as the customer left the store, because according to tort theory the purse is considered part of the body and the snatching of the purse is therefore an offensive contact to the woman's body.

* Faulty organization, added to shifts in viewpoint, make this sentence difficult to untangle. The restatement is an attempt to convey the intended sense.

Exercise to Accompany Chapter Two(B), Section 5

(Don't Make Impossible Comparisons.)

Directions: Re-write the following sentences to make the intended comparisons.

1. Unlike the above-mentioned cases, California, Texas, and Michigan rely on the rule of foreseeability in defining duty.
2. Man's brain is smaller than many animals.
3. The opinions of Alaska, like any other state, are only persuasive, not binding.
4. Compared with original purchase price, the property is now priced much lower.
5. In comparison with average salaries, the middle class resident today spends a lower percentage of her pay on food than she used to spend.
6. The taxes of Pennsylvania residents are higher than Missouri residents.
7. Florida's laws, like California, statutorily define first and second degree burglary.

Answers to the Exercise to Accompany Chapter Two(B), Section 5

1. The holdings of cases in California, Texas, and Michigan, unlike the holdings in the cases above, rely on the rule of foreseeability in defining duty.
2. Man's brain is smaller than the brains of many animals.
3. Alaska's opinions, like any other state's, are only persuasive, not binding.
4. Compared with its original purchase price, the price of the property is now much lower.
5. The middle class resident spends a lower percentage of her pay on food today than she used to spend, relative to her average salary.
6. The taxes of Pennsylvania residents are higher than those of Missouri residents.
7. Florida's laws, like California's, statutorily define first and second degree burglary.

Exercise to Accompany Chapter Two(B), Section 6

(Don't Mix or Mangle Metaphors.)

Directions: Re-phrase the following sentences to avoid the inept metaphors.

1. The battle must be bridged between the college of liberal arts and the college of business.

2. In my opinion, the student body president is dragging in this red herring to ferment dislike in the public's eye.

3. The candidate's speech left a bitter taste in my mind.

4. When you take the bull by the horns, you are apt to ruffle some feathers.

5. Our state department is not going to be left out in left field like a sore thumb.

6. Armed with the loophole in the tax code, many large corporations now pay no taxes legally.

7. The Justices have turned deaf ears, eyes, and pens to the practice of capital punishment.

Answers to the Exercise to Accompany Chapter Two(B), Section 6

1. The gap between the college of liberal arts and the college of business must be bridged. (OR, The battle must be ended . . ..)

2. (It is hard to know just what the writer's point was, but the following is a guess.) In my opinion, the student body president is causing a distraction in order to irritate the public.

3. The candidate's speech left a bitter taste in my mouth. (But it would be better to say specifically what you mean.)

4. When you take the bull by the horns, you are apt to annoy some people. (But better avoid the metaphor.)

5. Our state department is not going to be abandoned in left field. (But it would be better to explain how and why.)

6. Utilizing the tax code loophole, many large corporations legally avoid paying taxes.

7. The Justices have ignored the practice of capital punishment.

Exercise to Accompany Chapter Two(C), Section 1

(Problem Words)

Directions: Choose the correct word to fill in each blank.

1. Legislation to (affect/effect) the rights of Americans to free legal counsel has had the (affect/effect) of increasing the staffs of public defenders' offices.

2. The (principal/principle) plaintiff in this case said he had brought the case to trial as a matter of (principal/principle).

3. The visitor (lay/laid) his briefcase on the desk and (lay/laid) back in his chair.

4. To the alumni present, the laying of the cornerstone for the new law complex was a (unique/unusual) and (historic/historical) event.

5. (Further/farther) efforts to aid the injured person proved ineffective.

6. (Economic/economical) conditions being as they are, I looked for (economic/economical) quarters.

7. The widow of the convicted kidnapper of the (notorious/famous) Lindberg case is now attempting to clear her deceased husband's name.

8. (Healthy/healthful) foods and a (healthy/healthful) lifestyle help keep people (healthy/healthful).

9. The (enormousness/enormity) of the murder of the innocent American traveler shocked the conscience of the world.

10. The witness was (reluctant/reticent) to appear before the investigating committee.

Answers to the Exercise to Accompany Chapter Two(C), Section 1

1. affect; effect

2. principal; principle

3. laid; lay

4. unique; historic

5. further

6. economic; economical

7. notorious

8. healthful; healthful; healthy

9. enormity

10. reluctant

Exercise to Accompany Chapter Two(C), Sections 2 and 3

(Elegant Variation and Legerdemain With Two Senses)

Directions: Some of the sentences that follow contain elegant variation, some legerdemain with two senses. Re-write them to correct both errors.

1. Whether the construction material was steel or iron is not material to the decision.

2. The plaintiff in this case has an action against the defendant because the defendant's action was intentional, harmful, and offensive to the plaintiff.

3. Employees can utilize their own retirement system or participate in the program established by their employer; most employees choose the first plan.

4. The appellant's attorney requested a postponement, to which request the appellee's attorney agreed. Later, however, the respondent's attorney protested the delay.

5. Ending the battle in the mideast was only half the battle; the other half of the battle is maintaining the peace.

6. The missing desk was valuable because it was an antique; whether the hand-carved *objet d'art* was stolen or lost is not known.

Answers to the Exercise to Accompany Chapter 2(C), Sections 2 and 3

1. Whether the construction was of steel or iron is not important (crucial, germane, relevant) to the decision.

2. The plaintiff in this case has an action against the defendant because the defendant's conduct was intentional, harmful, and offensive to the plaintiff.

3. Employees can utilize their own retirement plans or participate in the one established by their employer; most employees choose their own retirement plans.

4. The appellant's attorney requested a postponement, to which request the appellee's attorney agreed. Later, however, the appellee's attorney protested the postponement.

5. Ending the fighting in the mideast solved only half of the problem; to solve the problem completely, we must maintain the peace.

6. The missing desk was valuable because it was an antique; whether the hand-carved desk, an *objet d'art*, was stolen or lost is not known.

Exercise to Accompany Chapter Two(C), Section 4
(Match Nouns and Verbs.)

Directions: Re-write the following sentences to express the intent of the writer.

1. Treat the rapist like a person; treating him with contempt may only irritate his dislike for women.

2. The Senate reported progress; progress is certainly on the move.

3. Expert testimony will establish the defective wheel of the tractor.

4. By pricing middle and low income students out of an education, we have lost the perspective of the concept of public education.

5. Double bogeys on the last two holes frustrated her momentum.

6. Hearings examining the California supreme court's judicial performance will add to the court's already damaged prestige.

7. Our distinguished panel will aid the staff by guiding and reacting to agendas and materials.

8. Many persons would rather look at hearsay than listen to evidence.

9. My fellow legislator rebuked the plan to reduce the price of license plates for small cars.

Answers to the Exercise to Accompany Chapter Two(C), Section 4

1. Treat the rapist like a person; treating him with contempt may only increase his dislike for women.

2. The Senate reported progress; the Senate is certainly on the move.

3. Expert testimony will establish that the wheel of the tractor is defective.

4. By pricing middle and low income students out of an education, we have lost the concept of public education.

5. Double bogeys on the last two holes frustrated her. (Or, slowed her momentum.)

6. Hearings examining the California supreme court's judicial performance will worsen the court's already damaged prestige.

7. Our distinguished panel will aid the staff by preparing and reacting to agendas and materials.

8. Many persons would rather listen to hearsay than examine evidence.

9. My fellow legislator rejected the plan to reduce the price of license plates for small cars.

Exercise to Accompany Chapter Three, Section B(2)(h)

Directions: Find in the enthymemes below the unstated premises; then decide whether they are valid and if not, why they are not.

1. Students who do well in law school get the best jobs; therefore, good law students make the best lawyers.

2. Since courts have held that policemen may shoot to stop a fleeing felon, police acted legally in shooting Jim Smith, a suspect in a recent holdup.

3. Since assault requires an intentional act, a blind man has no ground for an assault action against a person who verbally threatened him with attack.

4. The fact that women dent car fenders more frequently than men proves that more women than men are reckless drivers.

5. John Smith, a teenage, must be a careless driver because his car insurance rates are so high.

6. It is a fact that Supreme Court justices bicker about trivial matters; this is reported in a recent book written by two journalists about Supreme Court justices.

7. Colombian and Iranian students have similar political views; after all, they both held hostage citizens of other nations.

8. Law students learn more readily when their classes are interesting; therefore they learn most in those classes which have the most student discussion.

9. In Fairbanks, Alaska, women drive more safely than men because in 1979 women drivers there had only one-fifth as many motor accidents as men.

10. Since this is a democracy the state cannot force motorcyclists to wear helmets when they ride their motorcycles.

11. Jane Smith is a law student; she must be a supporter of E.R.A.

Answers to Appendix to Chapter Three, Section B(2)(h)

The unstated premises underlying the enthymemes in the Appendix are listed below. You can decide for yourself whether they are valid.

1. Students who get the best jobs make the best lawyers.

2. John Smith was a fleeing felon.

3. A verbal threat is not an intentional act.

4. Drivers who dent fenders are the only reckless drivers.

5. Auto insurance rates are based on the degree of carelessness of each driver.

6. The information contained in the two journalists' book is accurate.

7. The willingness of students to take hostages of other nations is the sole determinant of their political views.

8. Student discussion is the only factor that makes law classes interesting.

9. In Fairbanks, Alaska, the number of motor accidents people have is an accurate indication of how safely they drive.

10. A democratic government cannot pass laws requiring motorcyclists to wear helmets.

11. All female law students support E.R.A.

Exercise to Accompany Chapter Four, Sections B and C

(Analogizing and Synthesizing)

Below are the relevant facts of two cases, followed by a substandard discussion of the cases by one student, and a satisfactory discussion of the cases by another student. After reading the cases, write your own analysis/synthesis, then compare it with the two answers provided here. Note how, in the second analysis, the superior organization of ideas and proper transition improve the written product. Here are the pertinent facts of each case:

State v. McTigue

Court of Appeals of Florida, 1980.
387 So.2d 454.

This is an appeal . . . from a final order entered by a hearing officer, Division of Administrative Services, holding that Rule 10D–36.21(2), Florida Administrative Code, is an invalid exercise of delegated legislative authority. . . . We affirm the invalidation of the Rule, requiring a lay midwife license applicant to furnish a written statement from a licensed Florida physician, as an unlawful exercise of delegated legislative authority. . . .

An applicant for a license to practice midwifery must possess qualifications, under Section 485.031(4)(b), Florida Statutes (1977), including the requirement that the applicant

(b) Have attended under the supervision of a duly licensed and registered physician not less than 15 cases of labor and have had the care of at least 15 mothers and newborn infants during lying-in period of at least 10 days each; and shall possess a written statement from said physician that she has attended such cases in said 15 cases, with the date engaged and address of each; and she is reasonably skilled and competent. . . .

To implement the above statute, the Department [defined] "physician" as a "person who shall have been duly licensed in Florida to practice medicine or osteopathy." Appellee McTigue, who attended a two-year training program for physician's assistant in the State University of New York . . ., was unable to furnish a written statement from a [Florida] physician because [she had trained] in New York under the supervision of a New York physician. In support of her application, she furnished a statement [by the New York physician] certifying her compliance with the experience requirement of the statute.

We adopt the cogent reasoning and the law as applied by the hearing officer. The word "physician," as used in the statute, has a plain and ordinary meaning usually denoting a practitioner of medicine, a person duly authorized or licensed to treat diseases. . . . Applying the rule of statutory construction that words are to be given their plain and ordinary meaning, it is obvious that a "physician," unless the wording of the statute or the context requires otherwise, could be a physician duly licensed under the laws of any state, not just Florida. By adding the requirement that the physician be a Florida physician, the rule is an invalid exercise of delegated legislative authority because it modifies the statute by adding an additional criterion to be met by the applicant.* We find no indication from the statute that the supervising physician furnishing the written statement must be licensed in Florida. This requirement could easily have been imposed by simply adding the word "Florida" had the legislature so intended. . . .

* Citations omitted.

State Department of Health v. Framat Realty, Inc.

Court of Appeals of Florida, 1981.
407 So.2d 238.

The Department of Health and Rehabilitative Services appeals an order by a hearing officer of the Division of Administrative Hearings declaring invalid the Department's 1979 rule governing septic tank use in residential subdivisions. . . . The hearing officer concluded that in promulgating the rule the Department both exceeded its statutory authority and failed to prepare an adequate statement of the economic impact of the rule. We hold the rule was valid as against appellees' claim that it exceeds the scope of the substantive statute the rule elucidates; this interpretative rule is valid because it represents a permissible interpretation that has been validated by public rulemaking processes that are designed to test and refine the agency's policy. . . .

The statute in question, section 381.272(7), Fla.Stat. (1979), authorizes use of septic tanks as follows:

> Notwithstanding any other provisions of this chapter, residential subdivisions with a public water system may utilize individual sewage disposal facilities, *provided there are no more than four lots per acre,* and that all distance and setback, soil condition, water table elevation, and other related requirements which are generally applicable to the use of individual sewage disposal systems are met. (Emphasis in original.)

To gather views on implementing the 1977 statute, the Department held a workshop in February 1979, receiving recommendations from the Florida Home Builders Association, the Florida Septic Tank Association and the Department of Environmental Regulation. . . .

Eventually, with the benefit of this input, the Department adopted the rule under challenge, providing that . . . "residential subdivisions with a public water system may utilize individual sewage disposal facilities provided there are not more than four (4) lots per acre. . . ."

In practice, according to the Department's environmental health administrator, the rule requires a developer to show, as a condition to installing septic tanks on a platted lot or lots, that the subject lot and any three contiguous lots, excluding the specified common areas platted by the developer, make up at least an acre. An individual lot owner seeking a septic tank permit without regard to the size of the lots around him must have a lot containing at least one-quarter acre. This "four per acre" test, in the words of this administrator, is designed to get "the sewage spread homogenously [sic], if possible, throughout that subdivision."

The Department urges that its use of a "net acre" concept in defining the statutory "four lots per acre" is in keeping with its statutory duty to protect the public health through safe disposal of sewage. . . . Appellees, on the other hand, contend the statute permits septic tanks on every lot of a subdivision if the total acreage in the development, divided by the number of lots, yields an average density of less than four lots per acre. . . . The Department counters that this interpretation is absurd from a public health standpoint, because it would allow a developer to install large numbers of septic tanks densely in a very small section of his subdivision as long as acreage elsewhere in the subdivision . . . reduces the overall average sufficiently.

We reverse the hearing officer's order invalidating the rule as beyond the Department's statutory authority. Whether the Department's interpretation is the only possible interpretation of the statute, or the most desirable one, we need not say. It is within the range of permissible interpretations of the statute, and that interpretation has acquired legitimacy through rulemaking processes in which those challenging the rule fully participated or had an opportunity to participate. We must remember here one prime goal of the 1974 Administrative Procedure Act: to encourage agencies of the executive branch to interpret statutes in their regulatory care . . . that is, to interpret their statutes by rulemaking. . . .

When as here an agency has responded to rulemaking incentives and has allowed affected parties to help shape the rules they know will regulate them in the future, the judiciary must not, and we shall not, overly restrict the range of an agency's interpretative powers. Permissible interpretations of a statute must and will be sustained, though other interpretations are possible and may even seem preferable according to some views.

The following analysis of the *McTigue* and *Framat* cases is inadequate. Read it, list its shortcomings, and then write your own analysis of the cases. Then compare your analysis with the much-improved analysis that follows. When you read the second analysis, note which shortcomings that appear in the first analysis have been eliminated.

(1) Poor Analysis of *McTigue* and *Framat*

In *McTigue,* the issue was whether the statutory term "physicians" referred to all physicians or only Florida physicians. The Department of Health required a person to be under the supervision of a Florida physician before applying for a license to practice midwifery. The statute read only "physician." The court looked to legislative intent. The term "physician" has a plain and ordinary meaning. The Legislature could have added the word "Florida" had they intended. When the Department of Health added the requirement that the physician be a Florida physician, then the interpretation became invalid. The statute was modified by the addition of a new criterion.

The decision in *Framat* was in direct contradiction to *McTigue.* In *Framat,* a dispute arose over statutory construction of the word "acre." The developers proposed an interpretation permitting more septic tanks per acre. The Department of Health wished to limit the number for safety reasons. A hearing officer for the Division of Administrative Hearings ruled the Department of Health exceeded agency authority of statutory interpretation. The court overruled the hearing officer. The judiciary must not overly restrict the range of an agency's interpretive powers. Permissible interpretations of statutes must and will be sustained. Other interpretations may be possible and even preferable.

Listed below are some of the most damaging shortcomings of the above analysis of *McTigue* and *Framat:*

(1) The writer provides no orientation for the reader. Missing is a short statement saying what the analysis will deal with.

(2) Although the writer states the issue, she omits the facts of the case and the court's holding.

(3) The final sentence is written in passive voice, with the subject missing, so that the reader would have to be familiar with the facts to know who did what to whom.

(4) The issue is never resolved, nor is any rule stated, nor is the court's reasoning attributed or adequately explained.

(5) The organization is poor and little transitional language is present. Thus the writing is choppy and the ideas are undeveloped and disjointed.

(6) The writer does not compare and contrast the cases adequately.

You can no doubt find other defects in the first analysis of these two cases. Now read the second analysis to see how they have been eliminated. Then write your own analysis, which may be even better.

(2) Improved Analysis of *McTigue* and *Framat*

Two Florida cases deal with the degree of statutory interpretation that an agency of the executive branch of the state government is permitted to make in its rulemaking.

In *McTigue,* the 1980 case, the District Court of Appeal held that the State Department of Health and Related Services (HRS) had exceeded its authority when it interpreted the word "physician" in a state statute to mean "Florida Physician." In *McTigue,* an applicant to practice midwifery in Florida had attended a two-year training course for physician's assistant in New York state, under the supervision of a New York physician. The Florida Department of HRS refused to certify the applicant, although she otherwise held the proper credentials to practice midwifery, since she had not been supervised by a *Florida* physician.

In denying her application, HRS defined the language of the Florida statute, "duly licensed and registered physician," to mean a physician "who shall have been duly licensed *in Florida.*" The court said, however, that because a rule of statutory construction requires that words be given their plain and ordinary meaning, and because "physician" means any physician duly licensed under the laws of any state, the HRS requirement that the physician be a Florida physician was an "invalid exercise of delegated legislative authority" because it added a criterion to be met by the applicant.

However, a year later, in *Framat,* the same court held that HRS did not exceed its statutory authority when it interpreted another Florida statute, permitting residential subdivisions with a public water system to utilize individual sewage disposal facilities, provided there were no more than four lots per acre [plus other conditions].

In *Framat,* the appellee-developers contended that the statute permitted septic tanks on every lot of a subdivision if the total acreage in the development, divided by the number of lots, yielded an average density of less than four lots per acre. The appellant-Department contended that this interpretation was absurd from a public health standpoint, permitting developers to install septic tanks densely in a small section of the subdivision.

The court accepted the reasoning of the appellant and reversed the hearing officer's order, which had invalidated the rule as beyond the Department's statutory authority. The court noted that whether or not the Department's interpretation was the only possible one, or even the most desirable one, it had acquired legitimacy through the rulemaking process in which the appellees had participated, or had had the opportunity to participate. The court added that the 1974 Administrative Procedure Act had as its purpose encouraging executive branch agencies to interpret statutes by rulemaking, "after consideration of comments from the general public and affected parties," and the judiciary would not overly restrict these rulemaking powers.

Despite their different outcomes, *McTigue* and *Framat* do not represent contradictory opinions, for each opinion is based upon the intent of the legislature in the statute under consideration. The intent of the legislature, in *McTigue,* was to include all physicians, in its use of the term, because, had it intended to limit the term, it could have added the limiting language. However, the legislative intent, in *Framat,* was to encourage administrative agencies to interpret the statute in their rulemaking, after appropriate input from the affected parties. Thus, in *Framat,* the court held that the rulemaking of the administrative agency was a valid exercise of the agency's interpretative authority, while the plain language of the *McTigue* statute precluded administrative interpretation.

Exercise Two to Accompany Chapter Four,
Sections B and C

(Analogizing and Synthesizing)

Directions: You have answered Problem II in Chapter Six. Now, to practice your analytical and writing skills, apply the facts of the two court opinions excerpted below and a Restatement 2d rule to answer the same problem. Assume that the two opinions below are binding in your jurisdiction. Below are reproduced the facts of Problem II, Chapter Six, with additional instructions.

Facts

A. Player (A) is playing tennis with a friend, B. Tsim (B), a much better player. A does not like to lose, and as the game progresses he becomes more and more irritable. Finally, when B wins the set, A runs to the net brandishing his racquet and yelling, "Duck, or I'll hit this ball right into your face!" He then hits the ball wildly. B ducks. A intended to miss B even if B did not duck, and the ball does not come close to B. However it does strike C. Knott (C), who is behind a bush out of A's vision, searching for a lost ball. C suffers a concussion.

To whom, and for what is A liable? In answering, use as precedent the summarized facts of the two court opinions that follow, as well as the following Restatement Second (Torts) definition.

Talmage v. Smith

101 Mich. 370, 59 N.W. 656.

Supreme Court of Michigan, 1894.

[Action for personal injuries; judgment for plaintiff and defendant appeals, charging error in instructions of trial judge.]

Defendant threw a stick at two boys who were trespassing upon defendant's property. The boys were on the roof of defendant's shed, and were in the process of getting down from the roof after he had ordered them to do so, when he threw a stick, which did not hit either boy, but did hit a third boy (the plaintiff), who was also a trespasser. The stick hit the plaintiff above the eye so forcefully that he lost the sight of the eye. The defendant claims that he did not intend to hit any one, but merely was intending to frighten the two boys that he saw, not the boy who was hit, whom the defendant says he did not see. The defendant also argues that because the plaintiff was a trespasser, he was barred from recovering.

We think the charge a very fair statement of the law of the case. The fact that the plaintiff was a trespasser did not bar his recovery, as he did not anticipate the throwing of the stick. The right of the plaintiff to recover [depends] upon an intention on the part of the defendant to hit somebody, and to inflict an unwarranted injury upon someone. The fact that the injury resulted to another than was intended does not relieve the defendant from responsibility.

Allen v. Hannaford

138 Wash. 423, 244 P. 700.

Supreme Court of Washington, 1926.

[Action for damages for assault. Appeal from a jury verdict in favor of the plaintiff for $750 in damages.]

The appellant owned and operated an apartment in which respondent was a tenant. The respondent was attempting to transfer her furniture for a move to another apartment when the appellant appeared with a pistol in her hand and threatened to shoot the moving men if they moved "a single article" belonging to the respondent. She then pointed the pistol at the respondent's face and threatened to shoot her. The appellant admitted that she had a pistol in her hand, but denied that she pointed it at the respondent and threatened to shoot.

From the evidence as above indicated, the jury had a right to find that the appellant pointed the pistol at the respondent and threatened to shoot. So far as the respondent was concerned, the appellant had the apparent ability to make her threat good. . . .

Whether there is an assault in a given case depends more upon the apprehensions created in the mind of the person assaulted than upon what may be the secret intentions of the person committing the assault. . . . If the appellant pointed the pistol at the respondent, and threatened to shoot, this would constitute an assault, even though the respondent may not have known whether it was loaded. . . .

In the case now before us there was evidence as to the immediate effect upon the respondent of the pointing of the pistol at her with the threat to shoot and her nervous condition thereafter as a result thereof. The judgment will be affirmed.

Restatement (Second) of Torts § 18

BATTERY: OFFENSIVE CONTACT

(1) An actor is subject to liability to another for battery if

  (a) he acts intending to cause a harmful or offensive, contact with the person of the other or a third person, or an imminent apprehension of such a contact, and

  (b) an offensive contact with the person of the other directly or indirectly results.

(2) An act which is not done with the intention stated in Subsection (1,a) does not make the actor liable to the other for a mere offensive contact with the other's person although the act involves an unreasonable risk of inflicting it and therefore would be negligent or reckless if the risk threatened bodily harm.

Sample Answer to Problem II

A may be liable to B for assault and to C for battery. With regard to B's assault action, in a case with similar facts (*Allen v. Hannaford*), an apartment owner who pointed an unloaded pistol at a tenant while threatening to shoot her was held liable for assault. The court stated that society members have the right to live without fear of harm, and because the person at whom the apartment owner pointed the gun was apprehensive that she would be shot, the apartment owner was liable even though her pistol was not loaded. The court added that liability depends upon the apprehension of the person assaulted, not on the "secret intentions" of the assaulter.

According to the instant facts, B was reasonably apprehensive of immediate harm when A ran to the net after the tennis game, yelling that he was going to hit him in the face with the ball. Although A says he did not intend to do so and A actually hit the ball far from B, A is liable under *Allen* just as the apartment owner was liable despite her unloaded gun. The tenant in *Allen* was reasonably apprehensive that she would be shot; B was reasonably apprehensive that he would be hit in the face with the ball, since he ducked to avoid being hit. His assault action against A should therefore succeed.

C may succeed in an action against A in battery, based upon the Restatement 2d § 18 definition of battery, because A intended by his action to cause apprehension of harmful contact to B and an offensive contact to C resulted (§ 18(1)(a) and (b)). When B ducked, he showed that he was apprehensive of harmful contact, and the ball instead hit C.

However, in *Talmage v. Smith,* an action for personal injuries to a third person, the court stated that the right of the plaintiff to recover depended upon the defendant's intention "to hit somebody." In *Talmage,* the defendant threw a stick in the direction of one boy, but hit the plaintiff, causing the loss of his eye. The defendant argued that he did not even see the defendant, much less intend to hit him.

The jury found, however, that the defendant did intend to hit the other boy, and the appellate court affirmed because the defendant intended to "hit somebody." The defendant here claims he intended to hit no one, when he hit the tennis ball. If the jury believes him, C's claim of battery would fail, under *Talmage.*

Chapter Five, Section B

Directions: Identify the logical fallacies in the following sentences:

1. Jane Smith is a capable woman, but this great State needs a man to represent it forcefully.

2. Since radiation is a natural phenomenon, fears about the safety of nuclear energy are obviously unfounded.

3. One can see by the large quantities of land being bought by Middle Eastern Arabs in the U. S. that Arabs are extremely wealthy.

4. Even on one-way streets, all cars should keep to the right because in this country motor vehicles are supposed to drive on the right side of the road.

5. You should not believe any promises that an avowed atheist makes.

6. The professor told the class he did not consider absences in grading, but he gave me a "D" after I cut most of his classes.

7. A man's home is his castle; no City Commission is going to stop me from raising pigs in my front yard!

8. Is there any evidence to suggest that four more years under this President will not merely prolong for four more years the economic chaos under which this nation suffers?

9. A questionnaire distributed to professors of American law schools revealed that American legal education is far superior to that of other nations.

10. Writing for publication takes a lot of time. Therefore, since Professor Smith does not publish much, he must be a great teacher.

11. Dunebuggy riders pay taxes and therefore have as much right to ride their buggies in national parks as other people have to hike in the parks.

12. To prevent more people from becoming addicted to heroin, marijuana must remain illegal, for many heroin users report that they smoked marijuana before starting to use heroin.

13. Any man who can become the president of XYZ corporation at such an early age must know what he is talking about; welcome John Smith, who will speak tonight on nature conservancy.

14. You must decide whether to be a loyal democrat and accept the entire party platform or to renounce your party affiliation.

15. Since some religions oppose blood transfusions, all Red Cross blood banks should be closed.

16. James Smith, noted authority on the sex life of minnows, will speak today on the formula for a successful marriage.

Answers to Chapter Five, Section B
(Logical Fallacies)

1. *Argumentum ad Populum*
2. *Non Sequitur*
3. *Hasty Generalization*
4. *Dicto Simpliciter*
5. *Ad Hominem*
6. *Post hoc*
7. *Dicto Simpliciter*
8. Rhetorical question and *Ad Hominem*
9. Circular reasoning
10. Either/Or and *Non Sequitur*
11. *Tu quoque*
12. *Post hoc*
13. Misplaced Authority
14. Either/Or
15. *Non Sequitur*
16. Misplaced Authority

INDEX

†